No More Sad Refrains
THE LIFE AND TIMES OF SANDY DENNY

By Clinton Heylin

OMNIBUS PRESS

London / New York / Paris / Sydney / Copenhagen / Berlin / Madrid / Tokyo

Text © Clinton Heylin 2000
First published by Helter Skelter 2000
This edition copyright © 2011 Omnibus Press
(A Division of Music Sales Limited)

Cover designed by Fresh Lemon

ISBN: 978.1.84938.698.2
Order No: OP53856

Exclusive Distributors
Music Sales Limited,
14/15 Berners Street,
London, W1T 3LJ.

Music Sales Corporation,
257 Park Avenue South,
New York, NY 10010, USA.

Macmillan Distribution Services,
56 Parkwest Drive
Derrimut, Vic 3030,
Australia.

Every effort has been made to trace the copyright holders of the
photographs in this book but one or two were unreachable. We
would be grateful if the photographers concerned would contact
us.

Printed in the EU

A catalogue record for this book is available from the British
Library.

Visit Omnibus Press on the web at www.omnibuspress.com

No More Sad Refrains

THE LIFE AND TIMES OF SANDY DENNY

For Christine, who knows where the time goes.

Contents

Preface

It had been a fraught weekend. It had begun early, last Thursday evening, when Trevor, her best friend's husband, had phoned from a telephone box and informed her that he had left her best friend, Sandy, and that he had taken their nine month-old daughter, Georgia, with him. His last words to her had been, "You say you're her best friend. So prove it. You look after her." It was a surreal conversation, set against the background bustle of – Miranda instinctively knew – a railway station, or airport.

If Miranda had ever liked Trevor, she had certainly never trusted him, especially after the occasion, a few years earlier, when he had come on to her one evening over dinner, when Sandy was out on the road, singing 'Solo'. And, she knew, Trevor had always resented the influence she continued to exert over his wife of four and a half years.

Miranda well remembered that overcast September day, when Trevor and Sandy had tied the knot at Fulham Registry Office. If every relationship has its peaks and troughs, Sandy and Trevor had scaled most of their peaks in the five years they had already known each other, and both Miranda and Sandy's mother, Edna, viewed the marriage as a hasty, ill-conceived attempt on Sandy's part to regain higher ground. It was not to be, and when Sandy's final gambit, a child, failed to turn the relationship around, she began to spiral downward.

Trevor's attempts to catch the falling star had been tinged with a sense of futility for some time now. Ironically, it would appear it was his wife's bequest of a daughter that had finally convinced him to put Georgia's interests ahead of her mother's. Sandy had recently sustained a bad fall, at a time when Trevor had done one of his disappearing acts. Though Georgia was not apparently party to the fall, he seems to have realized that, next time around, she could be. That what if now pushed him to contemplate a return to his antipodean homeland, abandoning his wife to her friends and family.

Sandy, though, seemed quite unaware of Trevor's change of heart. Around five in the afternoon, four hours before the fateful phone call, she had phoned Miranda from her home in Byfield, an hour-plus swing up the M1 from Miranda's flat, two minutes south of Hammersmith Bridge in Barnes, to say that Trevor was in town, with Georgia, and that he might be stopping by on his way home so that Georgia could be fed. Feeling a tad guilty about not being in touch for a couple of weeks, Sandy promised to see Miranda real soon. Real soon.

Around eleven o'clock Sandy phoned again. This time there was an edge to her voice, though she remained outwardly calm. She had noticed a bunch of Trevor's clothes were missing and wondered if Miranda had heard from her husband. Miranda had little choice but to tell her the truth and, after threatening "such a bollocking" if Sandy did not "keep herself together," promised to drive to Byfield and bring her back to Barnes. Only one problem, Trevor had told Miranda that the keys to the car, which was parked in Washington Road, had been sent by registered post. Depending on when he had posted the envelope, they might not arrive until Saturday morning.

He'd lied. The keys were delivered through the door, around midnight, by a stranger who ran off when Miranda called after him. Miranda, with little traffic left on London's notorious arterial roads, made it to Byfield by quarter to two in the morning, to find Sandy dozing, and her two beloved Airedale hounds nowhere to be found. A frantic search managed to wake most of the sleepy little village but failed to yield a single Airedale. Finally, at five in the morning, Sandy recognized the futility of further forays and allowed Miranda to transport her back to Barnes.

It was now Monday morning. Trevor was nowhere to be found. A shroud of silence as to his whereabouts had descended, and would only lift when Sandy had sunk into silence herself. Signs of that flinty resolve that had been Sandy in her twenties had manifested themselves through the weekend, buffeted by the inevitable mood swings but, as morning dawned, Miranda was roused by Sandy, in dire need of pain killers. A severe headache, the worst of many she had been afflicted with in recent weeks, had awoken her around six. Miranda found the necessary pills and by the time she was ready for school – having crash-landed from her Sixties' job as *Hit Parader*'s English correspondent into the needs-must calling of school teacher – Sandy was asleep and it was all Miranda could do to write her a brief note, before heading off for work.

She would later write in her diary, "Somehow couldn't leave but did." The note she left Sandy was full of the combination of helpful practical advice and positive thinking that she hoped would get Sandy through the initial shock, enabling her to focus on a future that was already ebbing away. It read, in part:

"I spoke to [Sandy's brother] David. He thinks you should ring around. I have doubts – it's too like your usual possible panic. However – up to you. If you are going to ring around please hold horse until I've seen you...

Doctor['s appointment] at 4.00 pm – I'll be back as soon after 3.00 as I can...

Remember to eat!!

Fires off! Don't try lamps – too dodgy!

Toaster doesn't stop on its own! The smell will tell you if you forget!! Don't panic, just shut kitchen door!

Talk to cat but tell her I'm not starving her.

You'll win out! Chin up and all that blah!

Write a song – Two lost dogs chased by sheep and farmer and farmer's wife....

[Friend] Jon Cole [is at] 748 6693 – but he'll be at meeting all morning – will come in after that."

In fact, Cole would call in on his way to his meeting-cum-rehearsal, on a day still etched in the present twenty one years later:

"I am heading for a rehearsal in central London. It's a clear bright day. I leave my flat in Church Road and get into the car. It is a red Datsun Cherry. Past Olympic Studios, before the traffic lights, and then into Castelnau, left by MacArthur's the hamburger joint, and the Red Lion pub on the right. Castelnau is wide, flat, straight, some trees, mansions on each side. I slow down for the pedestrian crossing by Miranda's house. By the pedestrian crossing is a bus shelter. I hear, quite clearly on my left, a [single] word. Help. Who said this word? I know it's odd, but it sounded like it was from someone in the passenger seat. Now, I'm not unusually psychic ... Most likely, the word came from someone at the bus shelter. Just a coincidence. Wherever it came from, the word triggered a memory, that Miranda had asked me – if I was passing – to call into her house to see if Sandy was okay, if she wanted anything. No pressure. As I am not running late, I decide to pay the courtesy call. Into Miranda's drive under the tree, use the key she gave me a few days earlier, turn right, then dog-leg left, up the first flight of stairs. On the stairs I hear, somewhere, a cat. A mew. Rising up those few stairs to the first floor, Miranda's apartment, I already had a feeling which was not good; it was disquiet, and probably came from the cat.

"But then I saw Sandy. My eyes were at her level as I came up. She's lying on the floor, not quite on her back, just enough on one side to look like she is asleep, eyes closed, breathing regular. What the hell has happened to the ruddy woman? Her feet are by the bottom step of the stairs that lead up past a full-length window, steep, narrow stairs, with books piled up in the way, up to the top-floor room where I [presume] she's been staying. Behind her, a few inches away, the door of the loo is closed. It doesn't look to me like she's just come out, because she's fallen across the doorway, feet by the bottom step of the stairs, as if her last movement was from those stairs. She has obviously either passed out, or for some other reason fallen. I bend over her to check that her breathing is not obstructed. I smell no alcohol and see nothing untoward, no blood, no bruising. To me it looks like she just went to sleep on the floor and will be okay very soon.

"Something in me says that I should talk to her, which might help to bring her round. I straighten up and I say, 'Sandy, are you okay? Sandy, I'm going to call an ambulance, don't worry.' And I make for the telephone, Miranda's number two phone in the kitchen. The kitchen is directly opposite the loo on the landing where Sandy has fallen. It's a small kitchen, quite spicey-smelling, with a window over the front and the phone. I dial 999 and give the details. They say they'll be there in 10 minutes. I am now stuck uneasily in the kitchen. But there is a kettle ... I say, right out loud as if she was standing there, 'Sandy, I'm making a cup of tea, OK?' I mean, she did not look ill, not even pale; perhaps she was just a little concussed and would wake up any moment. And there I'd be with a cup of tea. I made the tea, two cups. I checked she was breathing. I waited. The ambulance arrived in good time. The ambulance men took her away. They were too casual. I can see them bumping down the stairs. I don't remember a stretcher. Perhaps their names were Burke and Hare. I must have found out where they were going. After that I made some telephone calls. But the rest of the day is a blur."

Sandy Denny, perhaps the finest singer of the modern folk milieu, died four days later, at 7.50 p.m. on Friday, April 21, 1978. She was barely thirty-one years old, and had been a mother less than nine months. By her side, when they switched the life support machine off, was her husband, Trevor Lucas. After much ringing around, a phone-call from the consultant at Saint Mary's to the Melbourne home of Lucas Senior had informed the errant husband that if he got on the next flight, he might just find his wife still alive. He had, and he did, but she would never know. Sandy never regained consciousness.

The verdict delivered at the inquest, the following week, was that the first lady of folk-rock had died as a result of a "traumatic mid-brain haemorrhage," as a result of a fall. The party line, which soon ossified into an incantation, was that she had fallen down a set of stairs at Miranda's flat. The traumas of the previous weeks – her original fall, her husband's desertion with Georgia, the splitting headaches, indeed all of Sandy's seemingly hellbent decline – were written out of history as the Fairport family closed ranks on a tragedy they had all seen coming, but had felt powerless to affect. The funeral, at Putney Vale cemetery, was a truly maudlin affair. The burden of guilt had descended on all too many well-meaning bystanders, though not as much as on an ashen Trevor. Genuinely mired in his own private pit of despair, Trevor found himself ostracised by Sandy's grieving, and unforgiving, parents, neither of whom had ever accepted him as their son-in-law in aught but name.

Others proved equally unforgiving. As Christine Pegg, wife of Fairport bassist Dave Pegg, put it, "There was a whole army of people who wouldn't answer the phone to him. We all felt incredibly guilty. Deep down we knew it had all been going wrong, we knew Trevor was thinking of going, but we'd got into the habit of keeping our heads down while the storm passed – and this time it didn't."

The tributes in the various papers were suitably elegaic, headed by those from perhaps the two journalists who had known her best: Karl Dallas, who had first come across her singing back in 1964, furnished *Melody Maker* with his thoughts; and Robin Denselow, husband of Sandy's good friend Bambi Ballard, penned some lines for *The Guardian*. But the folk-rock roster of Chris Blackwell's Island label had been all but swept away by the new wave of punksters then assailing the charts. The death of Sandy Denny was accorded nothing like the acreage of newsprint it might have warranted barely a couple of years earlier when – fronting another makeshift Fairport and selling out the Royal Albert Hall – she dedicated a brand new original, 'I Won't Be Singing Any More Sad Refrains', to her proud father Neil, from the stage of London's most prestigious venue. But her decline from that day in June 1975 had been precipitous. As it is, 'No More Sad Refrains' would end up closing out not only Sandy's next album, *Rendezvous*, but the considerable musical legacy she would leave in her name.

Clinton Heylin, March 2000

Part One
RISING WITH THE MOON

1

1947–65: THE TENDER YEARS

Sandy (left) with Edna's mother.

"I always feel, well maybe Sandy was delivered by a spaceship. Her parents were these two extremely thin, pinched people. And David was as straight as a die ... But she was just wild."

Linda Thompson

Alexandra Elene MacLean Denny barely knew her paternal grandmother, Mary Smith MacLean, the matriarch who – proud to be one of the MacLeans of Douart, from the Isle of Mull, seven miles west of Oban – insisted on her clan name being handed down through the generations. It was she who first dubbed her grand-daughter – born on January 6, 1947 at Nelson Hospital, Wimbledon, to her son, Neil, and his wife, Edna – just plain ol' Sandy. Neil and Edna had chosen the name Alexandra "because it was the only name we could agree on. My wife [always] used to insist that she be called Alexandra but my own mother called her Sandy, the Scottish dimunitive of that name, and within a week of going to school, everyone called her Sandy."

The young couple were temporarily dependent upon Neil's parents, who were letting them share their house on Worple Road in the months after they had been demobbed, and doubtless felt especially beholden to the household head, which was assuredly Mary Smith. According to singer Linda Thompson, the matriarchal hierarchy was destined to extend down through the Dennys, where Edna "wore the pants," to her only daughter, who, "being [from] such a matriarchal family, didn't [ever] think she was a little woman."

Mary Smith MacLean bequeathed an equally important legacy to her one and only granddaughter, one that must have been in the genes. Though Sandy apparently never heard her sing, unless it was in the cradle, Mary Smith MacLean had been something of a ballad singer in her nineteenth-century youth, being born in August 1879. A Highland lass, she spoke both Gaelic and English. According to her son, she could actually go to Gaelic-speaking parts of Ireland and be understood. She would also, in Neil's words, "dirge away at ... things like 'The Seal Woman's Croon'" (the song Neil remembers his mother singing may even have been the legendary 'Grey Selchie of Shool Skerry', a ballad only ever collected in the Orkneys and Shetlands). Mary Smith's repertoire was truly arcane, steeped in a balladry centuries old in conceit and conception. The Scottish ballad tradition, though, seemed to all but bypass the side of the family Sandy was born into.

Neil Denny: My brother and I could vamp, and we all had our little piece to do ... [when] the family in Scotland used to have these family music things ... [but] my wife wasn't particularly musical. My family was, but not our lot. My three cousins all played instruments. [CD]

The one song Neil remembered his mother singing, and which he hoped his daughter might learn to sing, was a Scottish Gaelic song called 'Fhir A Bhata', or 'The Boatman'. He recalled Sandy saying she would one day record it. He even went to the trouble of photostating the music book in which it lay, without ever hearing Sandy sing it. And yet Sandy was true to her word, singing the song at her first real session, a recording by Peter Kennedy at Cecil Sharp House for the BBC World Service 'Folk Song Cellar' series, on December 2, 1966, at the tender age of nineteen. Even here, on her earliest extant recording (save for half a dozen home demos), that voice soars and glides through this traditional tale of weal and woe with a real sense of its subject matter. Everything is in place, save the stamp of originality. For that, she could hardly turn to her now dead grandmother. It would have to come from somewhere within.

Karl Dallas: That was the incredible thing about [the young] Sandy – here was this silly little girl, dithering about onstage, tripping over the mike leads – who stood up onstage and told you the way life is. And I remember thinking, "But you don't know how life is, Sandy. How are you doing this? Where is it coming from?"

Growing up in the suburbs south of London in the Fifties, with rationing still in place, must have seemed like a life left permanently on hold. As it is, Sandy quickly learnt to keep any hidden depths to herself, until the opportunity arose for them to come out in song. The Denny/MacLean clan was as steeped in the auld Scottish austerity as in its traditional balladry. If the MacLeans came from the Isle of Mull, the Dennys were a more nomadic breed, as perhaps befits a family name derived from the Danes. Of similar Presbyterian stock, Sandy's great grandfather William Denny, born October 16, 1873, had made his living as a boiler maker, necessitating a fairly unsettled existence bound by the notoriously volatile ship-building industry. His seven children, David Skinner, William, James, Allison, Hannah, John and Elizabeth were all born in various locations throughout Scotland and the north of England.

Though David Skinner, Sandy's paternal grandfather, would be born in Dundee, he was destined to be brought up a Glaswegian, and it was in its infernal soul that he would meet and marry Mary Smith MacLean during the Indian summer of prosperity that coincided with Edward VII's brief reign. David Skinner Denny made the momentous move to London in 1923, with his wife and two sons, Neil and David Jr. He had been told that there were only two places to live in London, Hampstead or Wimbledon, and chose the latter. Neil was ten years old when the family moved south, and was obliged to start school, and doubtless soften his harsh Scots brogue, part way through a summer term at Queens Road in Wimbledon. His parents aspired to send both him and his elder brother to King's, a private boys school with a solid reputation, near Wimbledon Village, but the fees ran to nearly twelve pounds a term, a sum they couldn't afford, and Neil "was packed off to a new school in Surrey".

Despite having to scuff his way through the national school system, Neil's aspirational background and natural wit eventually secured him a scholarship to the London School of Economics, to read a BSc in Commerce, whence he graduated in 1934. When war broke out in 1939, Neil was working in the civil service, a reserved occupation that afforded him a get-out-of-service card. However, he preferred to volunteer and in 1941 he duly signed up for the Royal Air Force. The previous summer RAF pilots had successfully staved off an imminent German invasion, improbably winning that squabble in the skyways over southern England Winston Churchill duly dubbed The Battle of Britain.

Having signed up in the Long Room of Lord's, home of world cricket, located in the fashionable north London suburb of St. John's Wood, Neil found himself being billeted during initial training in one of the luxury flats on the perimeter of Regent's Park's Outer Circle, whilst the mess-hall was located at London Zoo. However, he soon found himself posted to Babbacombe, a couple of miles from Torquay, in south-east Devon, where he completed his training at the RAF's Number One Training Wing.

Neil learned to love south-west England, and the Dennys would later retain a holiday cottage in the picturesque region. Of course, this lifelong love may well have been bound up with the happy memories of his courtship of another lifelong love, a bonny lass from Liverpool, Sergeant Edna Jones. Edna may have originally joined the Women's Royal Air Force in Birmingham, but her family were 'Scousers', through and through. Her father, Thomas Jones, a seaman, had found regular appointment out of the Empire's busiest port. His father had been a blacksmith who had done well enough to own property on the North Wales coast. Edna herself grew to prefer coastal climes, and succeeded in posting herself from Gloucester to Babbacombe in the winter of 1942.

The uncertainties of war accelerated many a romance, and Neil and Edna's was no exception. Despite a misunderstanding leading to Neil 'standing up' Edna on their first date, by December 21, 1942, they were being married in an old church in Newton Abbot, honeymooning in North Devon, before returning to base for the New Year. In war, the wedding vow "till death do us part" had a certain built-in poignancy, especially as with his training complete Neil was now awaiting his first stationing.

Neil and Edna knew that, for the duration, theirs would be a lifestyle even more uncertain than his grandparents. Thankfully, with Edna in personnel, Neil's postings usually miraculously coincided with a posting in the same vicinity for Edna. Thus it was that when Neil was posted to Drem, a station north-east of Edinburgh, to guard the approach to the Firth of Forth, Edna found herself posted to St. Andrews. Likewise, when Neil was posted to a base in Lincolnshire, Edna followed along, with the happy news that she was pregnant.

David MacLean Denny was born on January 23, 1945, in Gainsborough, as his father awaited orders to support the successful invasion of Normandy. By the time David was joined by his sister, two years on, almost to the day, the Dennys were back in Wimbledon, whilst Europe, in the wake of Germany's capitulation, was being divied up into the great power blocs of East and West.

Before Sandy could grow from baby to toddler to infant, the family found itself temporarily uprooted. Relocated to Kent's rugged coastline, the Dennys found themselves housed on the outskirts of Broadstairs, while Neil found himself required to manage the Ramsgate office of the Ministry of National Insurance, a by-product of welfare reforms instigated by a new Labour government elected in a 1946 general election landslide on the promise of caring for its citizens from the cradle to the grave. Soon enough, though, the family returned to Worple Road, this time to their own home.

The two years separating Sandy from David proved no great barrier, as they became the best of friends, inseparable allies against the occasional paternal frown of disapproval. If David was the elder sibling, when it came to trouble Sandy was usually the instigator. Where David was neat and orderly, Sandy was impulsive, with an oft-displayed disregard for consequences. But it seems to have been a happy enough household, run by Edna during the day, when Neil would be carrying out his new duties as commissioner of the National Savings Committee, duties that took him the

Sandy (left) with David as children outside their Broadstairs house.

Sandy, David and dog.

length and breadth of London, and eventually as far afield as Birmingham and Newcastle, but always brought him back to Wimbledon Common, the expanse of common land where Sandy and David would often play.

Sandy's first school was Cottenham Park Infant School, in Raynes Park, a short bus-ride from Worple Road. Big brother David was already there, ensuring a playground companion and protector. If Sandy was not precocious in these early years, she displayed an early proclivity for attention-seeking. Her mother recalled one occasion when, having gone in search of her daughter, she found her hanging from the top of a lamppost, near the common, whilst her classmates gazed up admiringly.

Of her aspirational parents, Edna seems to have been the more generous-spirited, generally forgiving Sandy her many trespasses. Sandy's father was a more dour soul. Neil came of a generation, and a breed – the working-class Scottish male – who found it hard to express their emotions. Confronted with such a demanding daughter, he perhaps unconsciously felt compelled to maintain a disciplinarian guise that could all too easily mask the love he undoubtedly felt for his ebullient child.

In her later life, Sandy would bemoan the lack of warmth from her father, and contrast it with the physical affection of some of her friends' parents. Sandy once confided to one of her closest friends that "when she hit puberty, he actually stopped giving her hugs or cuddles." For someone who remained, all her life, "a very tactile person", her father's physical distance only exacerbated the neediness in her soul. Whether fairly or unfairly, Sandy would come to feel that, where her parents were concerned, her best was never quite good enough.

Though Sandy rarely talked about her parents, even to her closest confidants, Philippa Clare recalls "once ... when she was very drunk," it all came out: "They were very controlling, her parents. David was the one that was going to be educated, and Sandy was only a girl ... One minute [Edna]'d be very pushy with Sandy, and then she wouldn't be. Usually, she was, 'You're not good enough, you're not good enough', to Sandy. Instead of encouraging her, [she] was criticising her, but from the 'right' place ... which was why anybody paying [Sandy] a compliment, she would attack."

How early these feelings manifested themselves is not clear. Certainly Sandy's desire to 'please' her parents never went away, hence the occasional dedications in concert. Quite possibly her initial interest in the music of the day, fed into their household via the ubiquitous family wireless, was initially a sub-conscious attempt on her part to please her Dad, whose musical tastes seem to have been considerably more bourgeois than his mother's. Neil himself would later admit that he had "sung Gilbert & Sullivan at school – that was about the extent of my musical education ... [But] I did have a good interest in ordinary dance music, jazz, that sort of thing," and it would be this that, in Sandy's own words, "really started me off ... listening to the jazzy stuff, Fats Waller, the Inkspots, the stuff that my father and mother used to love to listen to."

On her third solo album, Sandy would elect to record two of her father's favourites. Though she thankfully managed to avoid Gilbert & Sullivan at school, her father in his later years would fondly recall a performance of 'Away In A Manger', at an infant school Christmas pageant, that reduced a number of fellow classmates' parents to tears. It may even have been this rendition that prompted a proud mother to "be very pushy with Sandy", seeking out an authoritative opinion of her daughter's talents.

Neil Denny: When she was very young, my wife took her to the Royal College of Music, and they said, "Yes, a very nice little voice and it could develop very well, but don't let her join the school choir or take part in amateur dramatics – let her sing naturally." [CD]

Despite this learned opinion, Sandy recalled that she "used to sing in the choir at primary school – solos – and everyone was quite impressed." Her musical gifts were less in evidence when she was required to apply them to the discipline of learning an instrument. With Neil and Edna encouraging both David and Sandy to learn the piano, Sandy started lessons around the age of nine, though she would give up the instrument before secondary school because, in her own words, "I didn't like the idea of this woman telling me to practice scales and arpeggios for an hour every night." Perhaps, in truth, she simply didn't like having her bluff called.

Neil Denny: She had a wonderful ear, and she would ask her teacher to play a piece and then she'd go away, and come back next week and she'd play it pretty well. Her teacher must have had some sort of suspicion because she [decided to] put a few mistakes in, and she found out Sandy wasn't reading it – she was doing it pretty well from ear. [CD]

Her extraordinary ear for music was already in evidence in other ways. Her Liverpudlian cousins recall a Sandy who was always singing around the house when she came to visit them in school holidays. Her Dad also recalled, with some pride, an occasion when "she electrified the school, much to the disgust of the music mistress, by playing a Fats Waller song, 'Ain't Misbehavin', in assembly. It didn't go down well with the music teacher who was strictly a classical woman." Sandy would later tip her hat to Waller by recording 'Until The Real Thing Comes Along' "as closely to the aforementioned recording by Fats as possible," for her 1974 album, *Like An Old Fashioned Waltz*.

Having passed the eleven-plus exam, designed to sort out the educational wheat from the chaff, Sandy expected to join her brother at the nearest grammar school, which was in nearby New Malden, only to find that David had secured a scholarship to King's, the school the exigencies of family finances had denied his father. Sandy displayed little scholastic ambition, missed her brother, and quickly came to dislike her new school. Even music, which had previously provided her with some solace, if not yet a purpose, had become a chore. She promptly locked horns with her new music-teacher, who failed to share the RCM's assessment. As Sandy herself later put it, "I just hung around waiting for my talents to be discovered by my music teacher. She didn't like me."

In later interviews, Sandy would be very critical of the way she was treated by the majority of teachers at Old Central. Her distaste for conventional learning would never leave her – even when, like many an auto-didact, she went on to become a voracious reader on any number of subjects. At the time, though, Sandy wouldn't conform to the school standards, wouldn't do her homework on time, and was generally ill-disciplined. As one of nature's natural conformists, Sandy's father was at a loss as to how to deal with his daughter's rebellious streak, failing to recognise a burgeoning contempt for all forms of authority, parental included.

Sandy Denny: I could never be one of those people who automatically say schooldays were the happiest days of their lives. I hated it, and I especially hated the attitude of most teachers. It really worries me that so many teachers have so little experience of life and yet they have to teach life to students. A student who wants to be a teacher goes to school at five, leaves at 18, then goes straight to university ... before returning to school as a teacher – and all without ever finding out what it's like to survive without school dinners ... At school I began to think that the hostile authority of the teachers was what happened to everyone when they became adult and I thought, "What a terrible drag it must be to grow up." [1970]

If Sandy felt she had been forced temporarily to abandon any formal musical training as a result of her music-teacher's antipathy, she continued to develop her love of language, first given air in verses like these, on the subject of clouds, the earliest her Dad chose to preserve:

"Clouds, higher than the trees,
Looking down on us from above.
Moving swiftly on the breeze,
More gracefully than a wingèd dove.

In their hundreds they rest on high,
On the sun they seem to lie,
Till twilight comes,
And dark is nigh."

Written shortly after she began secondary school, in her best spidery, girlish scrawl, these lines barely hint at a writer's search for an original voice.

However, the fact that they conclude with as Dennyesque an image as "and dark is nigh" suggests that Sandy's fear of (and fascination with) the dark night, came early and stayed late. It would remain well in evidence in the commonplace books she began to keep in college – in one of which she asked for "mercy on me when the darkness/ fills the room in which I stand/ [and] I feel alone, though someone holds my hand"; in the formative poems and songs she began to write in her teens, most of which she withheld from her workbooks; and in the few opportunities offered for creative writing in school.

At the age of 14, Sandy wrote an essay in her English class, called 'Empty Houses', in which she imagined seeing an empty house "down a dark and ill-lit lane, my first reaction be[ing] to break into a sprint until there was no trace of it in view." Imagining "strangers under the beds, dead bodies in the cupboards, snakes behind the door, and murderers crouched behind every chair and table," she finally admits that "there is no need to be frightened of empty houses ... they hold no vices except for that scurrying passer by with the vivid imagination. That's me."

Though the essay apparently warranted only a B+, Sandy at least recognized she was equipped with a "vivid imagination." The following summer, her cousin Hilary was exasperated when her childhood chum seemed less interested in playing than in locking herself in her room, where she insisted on peace and quiet as, "she said she was writing songs! ... I was never allowed in." It seems more likely that she was scribbling poems, though as her father Neil remarked to Colin Davies, one time, "She was very secretive – you never knew what was coming out." Even at this early stage, Sandy seems to have had a sense that she was gifted. It was a feeling that never left her, even though no obvious direction as yet suggested itself.

Sandy Denny: Deep down inside me I thought I would do something, but maybe every little girl has that. I thought I was going to be this great ballet dancer, and a sculptor, and Edith Cavell. I had an incredible amount of confidence in my ability. And how much you succeed depends exactly on how much confidence you've got in yourself. Because I don't look like the dolly-bird singer, I had to have confidence. [1972]

Confidence in her own ability was already offset by a singular lack of assurance when it came to her physical appearance, betrayed not only by that final sentence to Annie Nightingale, above, but by the many drawings Sandy made of the female form in her notebooks, invariably long, lithe, pencil-thin individuals.

Despite insecurities about her weight, Sandy was already beginning to take an interest in boys. A girl by the name of Winnie Whittaker, who attended the local convent school, was approached by a 15-year-old Sandy one day, and bluntly asked if she knew a Mary O'Keefe. When Winnie owned that she did, Sandy asked if said friend was 'going steady' with a certain Edward. When she responded, "Yes, she's in love with him," Sandy informed her that a friend of hers was also dating the same lad. A sceptical Winnie asked her the name of this girl and when Sandy replied, "Myrtle Snodgrass," it became more than a little obvious that Sandy and Myrtle were one and the same, and that Sandy was looking to put a dampner on the opposition.

Though the luckless Myrtle never seems to have dated the popular Edward, Sandy and Winnie became fast friends, for a time acting as each other's alter-egos. Since Winnie was a large, plain girl, she represented little threat to Sandy's fragile self-confidence when it came to the more competitive elements in such a friendship. As a friend of Sandy, Winnie was assured of a steadfast loyalty that would last all her days. She would also be assured of a riotous time in her company. In return for this, she was expected to participate in any pranks that sprang to mind. Even Sandy's headmaster, unimpressed as he was with her scholastic record, told her parents that, naughty as she was, she was also very loyal, and would shoulder the blame whenever there was trouble, never revealing the co-conspirators she had sucked into her latest cock at authority.

At the same time Sandy was renewing her interest in music, sharing in the mass hysteria British pop bands were inspiring, and revelling in the rebellious urges it fed. This was, after all, circa 63, the year of Beatlemania. She had taken the piano up again, having previously been "conned into playing violin for the school orchestra", and had even advanced to the stage where she was asked to play at a school concert, a scary but rewarding experience that betrayed early signs of stage fright.

Sandy Denny: My most terrifying experience was again at school when I had to play a solo piano piece at a special service. My fingers were shaking so much I wonder how I managed to find the notes. Afterwards this lovely teacher – the only one I really got on with – came up to me and said, "That was lovely, Alexandra," and I felt really good. [1970]

Sandy would never shake that initial rush of fear, though she later learnt to surpress it with alcohol. Initially, she was more addicted to the applause, and yearned to feel that good on a regular basis. Her problems at school, though, continued. According to her father, when she attempted to get a portfolio together in order to apply for a place at Kingston Art School, her teacher refused to help. When she still secured an interview, "this created a good deal of bad feeling."

According to Sandy, "my father [had] persuaded me to stay and take [two] A-Levels, but the more I hated it, the less I wanted to do it. I did take Art at school, but I had a bust-up with my musical mistress." Having originally signed up for Music and Art, she quickly dropped Music to concentrate on Art. She had always taken a keen interest in drawing, and her mother was now going to evening classes at the Wimbledon College of Art. By Sandy's own admission, "I was terrible at painting, [if] quite good at drawing." But her "real love was sculpture. I'm not sure what form it would have taken. I really just like shapes." Her interest in sculpture was real and enduring. Bambi Ballard remembers how, in the early 1970s, "Sandy and I used to talk about [how] we were gonna get somewhere in the country, where we'd have a big room where we could just sculpt.".

Sandy, though, continued to resent the school system and had probably already abandoned her studies when a letter from Kingston School of Art, dated February 11, 1965, arrived at Worple Road. In her own words, "I actually left school a term early because I really couldn't take any more." The letter, offering her a place in the one-year, Pre-Diploma Course, commencing September 20, did not require her to complete her Art A-Level. Unconditional as the offer was, though, it still required her parents' agreement. Sandy later admitted, "I was surprised when my father allowed me to take the art school place."

In all likelihood, Neil hoped he might persuade his daughter to continue with the vocational training she had recently begun, at Brompton Chest Hospital, as a state-enrolled nurse. If Sandy always considered nursing as something to tide her over until she began the art course, several friends have suggested that Neil dropped a number of hints implying he hoped she might continue nursing, even if Sandy told everyone at the hospital she was not a trainee nurse but a temporary nurse because she was going to college in September.

Almost everybody who encountered the slow uncoiling of Sandy in those days seems to recall seeing her in her nurse's uniform. And yet she was only ever a nurse in the months that separate her application to Kingston from the beginning of her pre-diploma course, a letter from the Ministry of Health, dated October 1966, regarding her superannuation contributions, confirming that she ceased her "employment with The Hospital for Diseases of the Chest on 24 August, 1965." With employment came a degree of independence, just as Sandy began to experience life, and death, firsthand.

Sandy Denny: I worked for that term at Brompton Chest Hospital, and lived in a flat in Kensington with some girl friends ... The hours were very long and I appreciated what nurses must go through. Some of the things I did there really shook me. [1970]

She would hate it when her father would drop her off at the hospital, and she would have to cut through the mortuary to get to her ward. She would go on to claim that her experiences at the hospital played their part in acquiring one unhealthy habit, "I needed to smoke to steady my nerves." Soon enough, she was working her way through a couple of packs a day. Her father later recalled how upset Sandy would get when one of her favourite patients died.

Neil Denny: She had some harrowing experiences. There was an American fellow, I think he was an artist – Sandy was particularly good at talking to him – and he gave her a pound to put on the Derby ... and he told her what horse to put it on, and it won. We went to fetch her coming off duty and she said hang on because I've got to go and see Mr So and So, and tell him about his winnings, and she was there when he died – they were holding hands at each side of the bed. Sandy said [to his brother], "I'm afraid he's gone." ... And he said, "You must be very used to this." – to a kid of seventeen. [CD]

However, her nursing career doesn't seem to have inured her to the gory side of healthcare. When she later escorted her friend Linda Peters to hospital, it was Sandy who ended up needing treatment.

Linda Thompson [née Peters]: I was having a mole removed from my back and she said, I'll come. I know all about this, being a nurse. So off we go, and they cut the mole off my back, Sandy's holding my hand. The next thing, she's on the deck, and everybody in the room, doctors included, are dealing with Sandy. [I thought,] Typical Sandy attention-getting thing, but she'd actually passed out. She'd seen the blood. I'm going, Hey, I'm the one with the mole, and they're all going [to Sandy], Are you okay?

Sandy preferred to keep her actual duties at the chest hospital to herself, though Winnie Whittaker believes "there was a lot of pretty mundane, clean-out-the-bedpans work." If the job held minimal appeal, above and beyond its subsistence wages, Sandy also found that she was required to put up with a degree of bitchiness and backbiting that even her experiences at Old Central had not prepared her for, something she later confided to her closest friend at Art School.

Gina Glazer: She was at nursing school first, and that wasn't for her. She told me how bitchy the other students were, thought they were hot shit. There were a lot of cliques. And [that was] part of her need to be famous – to get back at these people. I really believe that.

If nursing never gave Sandy a sense of vocation, and her fellow nurses only reinforced her sense of separateness, her time at the Chest Hospital was the first time she had lived away from home. Sharing a flat in Kensington, she seems to have quickly discovered not only the Troubadour folk club, on the Old Brompton Road, but also a place called Gobbles that Philippa Clare recalls was "this amazing restaurant where you'd go downstairs, musicians used to fall in there after gigs, and you'd get the most amazing jam sessions. It was a muso's restaurant." The experiences she gained, living and working in west London, seems to have been central to the dramatic transformation from austere schoolgirl to the Sandy her father says he "never saw – an effing, blinding, hard-drinking girl."

Trevor Lucas: To understand her, I think you have to consider she'd had a very restrictive childhood, until that time when she actually broke away from home. And when she did get out, and saw there was a good time to be had out there, she was determined to have it. She started working as a nurse at the Brompton Chest Hospital, and that was really the first time she'd had any freedom at all. And, like most people who've been confined in that way, she was only more eager to live life to the full. [1989]

2

1964–65: THE BLUES RUN THE GAME

One of Sandy's early sketches.

"Somehow in the back of my mind I knew I would sing eventually. When I was very small I used to sing a lot. And then when I went to my grammar school I never sang ... except in a choir, very innocuously in the background. [But] then when I left school, I went to art college, Kingston Art College, and just down the road there was a little barge on the river, The Barge Folk Club, and I thought, well I can sing as well as these [folksingers]". [1972]

Sandy Denny

In fact, by the time Sandy Denny went to art college, in September 1965, she was already singing in the folk-clubs of London Town. Her version, above, of how she came to be a folksinger not only suggests a large degree of happenstance, but places her entry into the folk nexus a year after the fact. Her first appearance at the Barge was as premeditated as her choice of art school, and her motives as fully realized. Genuine as her interest in art and sculpture was, she had gradually become aware that Kingston had a very active folk scene 'on campus'.

Sandy had begun to feel increasingly drawn to a form of music that – in the wake of Dylan's chart entry in May of 1964, with his second album, *Freewheelin'*, and a sell-out show at the Royal Festival Hall – had acquired an extraordinary resonance for the young beatniks of suburbia dream. Winnie shared Sandy's love of music, and was an early acolyte of the sandpapered chords of Robert Zimmerman a.k.a. Bob Dylan.

If Sandy's father betrayed an immediate and abiding distaste for that "horrible, grating voice", Sandy was entranced by Dylan and, like many a would-be 'folkie', was moved to pick up "an old guitar my mother had bought," not for Sandy but for brother David. She quickly acquired from her elder sibling the few rustic chords necessary to pass for an authentic balladeer. Her previous musical training and genetically-engineered ear ensured that she was a quick learner, and soon enough she was wheedling away at her father to buy her her very own guitar. Her ambitions already lay higher than her brother's mangy old soundbox.

Neil Denny: David was the one who egged her on to play the guitar. He played a little bit, he got the idea but then he threw it over to Sandy and said, "Here, you have a go." He [already] had a guitar and then Sandy wanted a guitar. There was a guitar for sale at Tattenham Corner, Epsom Downs, advertised as a Gibson guitar ... Sandy said, "That's a nice guitar, Daddy." So I said, "Let's go and have a look." She was very clever. We got to this house and he produced the guitar, and Sandy was very non-commital. I don't know if it was settled there and then but when we got out of the house, she said, "Daddy, what a wonderful guitar." [CD]

Her friend Winnie, who "was already starting to think that Dylan was a bit old hat because everybody else in the class was starting to like him," was soon extending her interest beyond Dylan's skewering of tradition, back to the music he later described as "the only true, valid death you can feel today." Initially, it would appear, Sandy's own tastes were less developed than her friend's and so, for the moment at least, she remained the pupil, and Winnie her guide. Sandy, though, would never abandon her love of Dylan. On her very first home demos, she would attempt 'It Ain't Me Babe' and, in 1971, told a journalist, "He's as near as I would get to worshipping anyone." It was presumably via Dylan that she arrived at the largely-traditional albums of his then-current paramour, Joan Baez.

Soon enough, Sandy found a haven all her own, where aspiring troubadors would gather to play guitar and sing, in the convivial surroundings of a local pub.

John Renbourn: I was [at Kingston Art School] in 1964 and that's when I used to see her. The main guys that were actually playing publicly in the clubs were people like Alex Campbell and Steve Benbow. Early on, Sandy was playing much the same repertoire as those guys ... A bunch of us from Kingston Art School used to meet at a pub in Wimbledon – the Prince of Wales Feathers – and play our guitars. Sandy used to come along – still in her nurse's outfit – and join in. She became the girlfriend of my musical buddy, Derek, so I got to see rather a lot of her, often having to do the talking for him when he stood her up. She had a nice husky voice and an easy going manner. I didn't realize then that she was kind of ambitious ... Most of us were on the skids, as it were, and it seemed rather entertaining that Sandy should have this nice family ... In fact, I think Sandy really got the idea she wanted to go to the Art School because there was such a good folk scene going on there. I don't think she did it 'cause she wanted to be an artist. In fact, I'm sure she didn't. It was like the hub for all that music.

Without any audible documentation, and with thirty-odd years of overloaded memory banks separating Sandy's contemporaries from total recall, establishing Sandy's early repertoire has proved a tad problematic. A couple of early friends remember her doing Dylan's 'Ballad of Hollis Brown', itself set to the tune of the traditional 'Pretty Polly', but little else. In general terms, they remember a lot of songs derived from the Dylan/Baez axis, and little from the tradition whence they came.

John Renbourn: I don't remember Sandy playing very much guitar at that early stage, I think she used to come down and sing mainly standard folk-club kinda fare but I remember that all of us had our sights set on going up to play in London, at some of the clubs there – the Ballads & Blues was one in Rathbone Place – and I think even at that stage she really wanted to stop nursing and be a singer.

Of course, barely eighteen years old, with only a few months of guitar self-tuition under her plastic belt, Sandy was still some way off playing the West

End clubs. But she placed herself quite readily on the self-same learning curve as her friend John Renbourn, attending each and every folk club, north and south of the river, wherever on the spectrum of tradition they might choose to lay, even the farther flung clubs like producer Bert Leader's El Torro, on the Finchley Road, which Gill Cooke recalls her attending when she was "claiming to be a nurse."

> **Sandy Denny:** I used to go to folk clubs when I was quite young ... listening to people singing there, and learning how they presented their stuff. It all rubs off on you. [1974]

Anthea Joseph, who ran the Troubadour on the Old Brompton Road, a gentle lob away from the chest hospital, also recalled Sandy the nurse attending most Tuesday nights, soaking the whole vibe up, even though in those days she was so self-conscious that she wouldn't even join in on the communal jam session at the end of the evening.

Singing at the Barge came easier. It was indeed a barge, docked at Richmond, and the folk club was run by one Theo Johnson. It was in this less intimidating atmosphere that Sandy first sang to a paying audience, albeit not an audience that had paid to see her – this was, after all, the era of floor singers and it was as a floor singer, between booked acts, that all fledgling folkies began their careers. As Heather Wood of the Young Tradition concisely put it, "the way you got into folk clubs was you learned a couple of songs and you sang from the floor, and that way you got into clubs for free." Despite the subdued level of expectation that greeted this young lass, stage fright showed its face again, until she opened her lungs and cast him to the wind.

> **Sandy Denny:** The first time ... I ever stood up on my own ... my mouth went all dry and I could hardly sing, but when I came off and they all applauded, I knew that although it was a great effort, I'd always want to do it. [1972]

Though no record exists of that unbilled performance, it evidently took place when Sandy had just begun nursing. Judith Pieppe, one of the mother hens of the folk revival in Britain, first caught Sandy at The Barge, singing a song that would have made her paternal grandmother proud.

Judith Pieppe: She had a lovely voice, and was a nice, bright girl. She was still doing nursing, but not for long. I first saw her at a club on a boat, and I thought she was [just] lovely ... The only song I remember her singing was about a bloke who accidentally shot a girl, it went something like "she'd her apron all about her/ and I took her for a swan."

'Polly Vaughan', or 'The Shooting of His Dear' as it is better known, remains one of a small number of ballads of metampsychosis, based upon an idea later appropriated by Richard Thompson for 'Crazy Man Michael' – that the girl in the song spent a partial existence as a bird, during which she was accidentally murdered by her lover. First published back in 1806, and assuredly Celtic in origin, it suggests that by the time Sandy began singing at the Barge, she had begun to incorporate purely traditional material into her repertoire.

In an era when folk-singing has reverted to a cyclical subtext to popular sounds it is hard to conceive of a time, just three decades ago, when, in Sandy's own words, "there was a folk club on virtually every corner ... like there was the Scots Hoos, the John Snow, there was Cousins ... You could go up there any night and you'd be sure of finding the little crowd like John Renbourn and Bert [Jansch] and Jackson Frank and Annie Briggs ... It used to be a fantastic little community."

As the young nurse immersed herself in this "fantastic little community" she witnessed the aftershocks of a number of fractious divisions. Bound as much by the socialist bent of its instigators as more musicological concerns, the English folk revival required any wouldbe folkie to declare their position on a spectrum capable of encompassing everything from unaccompanied, indigenous traditional singing, a la Mary MacLean, to the self-conscious songwriting of a whole host of New Dylans. Though Sandy later insisted, "I was never in the traditional clan – I was in the layabout section with Bert Jansch and John Renbourn," she did initially venture down to the Singers Club, run by Peggy Seeger and her husband, Ewan MacColl, a fiery Scottish bigot of the old school.

By the time Sandy, and indeed her fellow 'layabouts', Jansch and Renbourn, came on the scene, the Singers' halcyon days were behind it – thanks in part to Dylan's dismissive set at the club in December 1962, on his first trip to London. Though MacColl's 'exclusivist' policies may, in Jansch's words, have "seeped through to other clubs," its effect was never that strong. Jansch, like Sandy, wandered on down "to the Singers Club a couple of times but I didn't like the way it was presented – it was too academic for me."

The eighteen-year-old Sandy must have been mystified by the academic baggage that so many of her peers carried onto the stages of these dingy clubs. Though her father had on his shelves a copy of Marjorie Kennedy Fraser's book of highland music, a popular collection of Scottish song, he lacked any authentic ballad collections. Nor did his library extend to the six-volume *Johnson's Musical Museum*, co-edited by Robert Burns, which took pride of place in Mr. MacColl's library.

It was the songs, not the process by which they had endured through the centuries, that held an audible fascination for Sandy. Any sense that she came at the end of hundreds of years of oral processes, in which the songs themselves had metamorphosed multiple times, crafted from within a creative tradition, was lacking in our Sandy. And yet, she was already drawing from tradition for the likes of 'Polly Vaughan', 'I Once Loved a Lass', 'Green Grow The Laurels' & co., even if her apathy for the folk process led her to disregard one of the most sacred conventions of the folk revival, explaining the historical background of a song to an audience.

Karl Dallas: She'd stand up and she'd say, "I'm gonna sing so and so, and I don't know what it's about and I can't remember who wrote it," and made herself look a right idiot. I said, "Look, you can't do that. You must research your material. You must tell them, This is a song from Kentucky, tell the story." ... Well, I never even saw her try and do that. It just wasn't Sandy.

Having drifted away from Singers less than impressed, and given that she was living and working down the road in Kensington, the folk nights at the Troubadour held an obvious appeal, thanks to their 'open floor' policy and laissez-faire attitude to source material. It was there, one Tuesday, that Sandy met another singer destined to be a lifelong friend and occasional singing partner. Linda Peters was an equally young, inexperienced folksinger, who shared her penchant for a good time, a healthy disregard for cliques, and even the odd boyfriend. Her boyfriend at the time, Paul McNeill, had already been discarded by Sandy, affording an opportunity to compare notes.

Linda Thompson: We used to meet up at The Troubadour in Earl's Court. She used to sing there on Tuesday nights and so did I ... We had the same stage presence – rather like a stick of wood ... She was always tripping over things and I always stood there petrified – so we weren't electric performers

– but when Sandy started to sing it was a completely different matter ... There were audiences who would coil in horror at contemporary folk music, but Sandy never had any problem. She wasn't known as a traditional singer by any means, [but] was accepted as a contemporary singer.

Casting admiring glances at those already crafting their own templates from tradition, Sandy was soon mixing the songs of Alex Campbell, Tom Paxton and Dylan into her musical melting pot. Having barely made it as a floorsinger, it seemed she was already looking beyond the 'folk process'. It was undoubtedly the contrasting experiences of playing at the three main London clubs available to the young traditionalists between 1964 and the winter of 1966, first as a floorsinger and then, quite gradually, as a billed act in her own right, that forced Sandy to focus on the type of material to which she intended to apply that remarkable voice. When she first encountered Karl Dallas, sometime folk columnist for England's premier music weekly *Melody Maker*, he was of the firm opinion that she was working in the wrong field, and should concentrate on jazz.

Karl Dallas: I saw her first at Bruce Dunnet's Scots Hoose on Cambridge Circus ... What was later to become an engaging gaucheness was at that time sheer, wooden amateurism. But that voice, even then, before maturity had conferred the understanding that was to make her a superlative interpreter of her own and other people's lyrics, stood out in the crowd ... When I heard [her], I knew, I absolutely knew, that this was something else. And I thought she was in totally the wrong place – I thought this woman will never be a folk singer, she's greater than anything like that. I thought that she should be a jazz singer ... because I could hear the vocal control, she had a way with a melody even in her very earliest days that was unique in the folk-scene ... and I told her that. I said, "Listen to Billie Holliday, listen to Ella Fitzgerald. Listen to these people, 'cause you got the voice, what you need is the technique." She wanted material, because she was doing things like 'The 3.10 To Yuma', which were songs I didn't know and couldn't see the point in singing ... She was a very pretty little girl, [though] overweight, as she was all her life, real puppy fat. She was a nurse at that time, and [had] this incredible voice. I really wanted her not to get locked into the folk scene. So I sort of took Sandy under my wing. I gave her a lot of very bad advice.

If Dallas's initial interest in this "pretty little girl" was bound as much by amorous intentions as career guidance, he was quickly rebuffed by a Sandy already inured to older men, and their predatory inclinations. However, she was also shrewd enough to let him down gently, aware that he occupied a position of some importance on the scene, such as it was, being one of the few outlets to a wider-ranging media. Dallas continued, on occasions, to drive Sandy back to Wimbledon, when Sandy felt the need to return home.

The evening Dallas had caught Sandy at the Scots Hoose had almost certainly been the one night of the week when this steadfastly traditional club – under the gruff captaincy of another stereotypical Scot, Bruce Dunnett – allowed itself to metamorphose into The Young Tradition, in order for it to be invaded by heir apparents of the grand tradition.

Heather Wood: Basically Bruce had started a club called The Grand Tradition, with people like Joe Healy, Margaret Barry and Michael Gorman, but they kept not turning up. The only people that turned up were the young kids like Pete [Bellamy] and Royston [Wood] who came along to hear 'em. So Bruce, being something of an entrepreneur, said, "Well, we'll just call it the Young Tradition" ... It was one night a week at the Scots Hoose. The Young Tradition club didn't last too long, [as] Bruce was too mean to pay anything more than ten bob a night.

For Sandy – thirsty for experience, personal *and* musical – the weekly rounds of the Barge, the Troubadour and the Young Tradition helped to fuel her need for applause. Only later – when the Scots Hoose keeled over from the deadweight of Dunnet's penny-pinching ways, and the Barge lost its initial allure – did it seem like the opportunities for singers of a folk bent had visibly contracted, just at a time when a whole new generation wished "to strike another match, go start anew."

There was a brief residency at the Deane Arms in South Ruslip but little else, save nursing, to occupy Sandy's raging mind, or libido, that summer. Some welcome diversion came when a handful of regulars from the Young Tradition established their own quasi-commune on Somali Road in Hampstead, one of whom was her old friend John Renbourn. It was here that Sandy probably first spent any time with an American singer-songwriter, by the name of Jackson C. Frank, then just 'passing through'.

Heather Wood: All of us used to hang out together and visited each other's houses and sing in an assortment of combinations of groups ... We weren't very deep in those days. We were into making music and getting laid. [Sandy] was very much going between contemporary singer-songwriters and a few of the more popular traditional songs, trying to find what she wanted to sing ... The Young Tradition had an apartment with a guy called Dave, and upstairs was Bert Jansch and John Renbourn, and everybody came through. We had the key on a piece of string behind the letterbox, so you'd fish through the letterbox, pull the key out, open the door and walk in. And there were usually two or three odd bodies lying around the floor. All the visiting Americans came through, either upstairs or down ... Jackson came through, Roy Harper was a regular, Donovan used to drop in a lot.

Whilst it is not clear when (or if) Sandy gave up her flat in Kensington, the Somali Road commune certainly served as an occasional respite from the conformity that awaited her in Wimbledon. For a short while, Sandy even maintained her double life, as her parents continued to cling to the belief that this New Self was just a passing phase. Karl Dallas, as someone with a 'proper' job, was one of only a handful of her new friends Sandy deemed safe to introduce to her parents, though John Renbourn remembers one time when, "Alex Campbell played in the area, and Sandy took him home to meet the parents, to show [them] that it was possible for somebody to sing folk music and actually make a living at it!" Campbell evidently failed to convince Neil and Edna of the golden opportunities about to unfurl.

Karl Dallas: [Her parents] weren't into it at all ... [that] was my impression. They never [actually] said anything. She introduced me to them. They were quite hospitable and friendly, but I got a feeling, "She'll grow out of this rubbish soon. She's a nurse, that's what she is, that's a career."

Her father's state of denial would not come to an end with Sandy's departure from home. Even after her tragically premature death, still clutching at diminishing days that brought no rest, he would accuse Joe Boyd, who accurately portrayed the Soho Sandy as this "effing, blinding, drinking girl," of "blackening her character". Neil continued to insist, even after the fact, that he and his wife "never saw it." This set of blinkers, to which Neil and Edna took increasing recourse, would play a crucial part in their daughter's demise.

Not that Sandy didn't go out of her way to maintain the façade, at least in these years of financial dependence. One incident, sometime shortly after Sandy became her own wicked twin, illustrates the lengths to which she would sometimes go in order to present herself as the dutiful daughter, even as she passed beyond her parents' command, not to say their ken. A girl who one minute had been in suicidal despair, at a particularly painful breakup with a fellow folkie, upon realizing where she was bound, transformed herself in a matter of minutes into the respectful, self-composed daughter of Neil and Edna Denny.

Al Stewart: She seemed to be attempting to play dodge with the taxis in Cambridge Circus, obviously a bit the worse for wear, so I just basically grabbed her, and instead of letting her run in front of one, I waved it down and put her in it, and took her back to Wimbledon ... She [had been] saying she wanted to end it all ... [But] during the course of the drive back to Wimbledon she went from being totally manic to being totally self-possessed, and when we arrived at her parent's house in Wimbledon, she looked at me and said, "Do you realise how much this [is going] cost?"

The conflict, though, was bound to be an uneven one. The New Sandy was already discarding her adolescent chrysalis. Once she began to bounce between Somali Road, Judith Pieppe's house in the East End and an all-night club in a basement on Soho's Greek Street, the return trips to Wimbledon became more and more occasional, and the sight of a "totally self-possessed" Sandy decidedly rare.

3

1965–67: ALL HER OWN WORK

A poster for Swindon Folk Ballads and Blues Club from 1966.

"Everybody used to go down the Cousins when it was open all
night and everyone would be on – Martin [Carthy] and Swarb
and all kinds of people like Alexis Korner would do an overnight
thing, and Bert Jansch and John Renbourn would be there, and
the Watersons and Les Bridger. Davy Graham would do the all
nighters as well. Those were really good days. John Martyn used
to do it too, and Jackson Frank. There were so many visiting
American people. Paul Simon used to go down there, then there
was Mike Seeger, Tom Paxton." [1973]

Sandy Denny

The Cousins, as all but the uninitiated came to call the basement club at
49 Greek Street, smack in the heart of London's Soho, officially opened
its doors on April 16, 1965, and closed them in the winter of 1970 (fittingly,
Sandy was one of the last acts to play the club, making her unbilled post-
Fairport debut). In the interim, it would welcome every one from a Them-less

Van Morrison to an in-Experienced Jimi Hendrix. Its early habitues, though, were largely the detritus from Scots Hoose, and initially it served more as a place to share thoughts and contraband than the centre of London's fragmented folk domain.

> **Bert Jansch:** It was run by Andy Matthews, but he didn't do anything ... his parents, who ran the restaurant upstairs ... did most of the work. They were beautiful people. Every wayfaring folksinger would always get fed. That's why his business went down ... the food was superb but he used to feed any folkies that wandered in, which put all the ordinary customers off ... Cousins was much more of a meeting place. The Scots Hoose was my thing. It was just me and occasional friends, like Sandy Denny, who dropped by ... [and] you could play for three hours if you wanted to.

And yet it was Jansch who helped establish Cousins with a weekly Thursday night residency, starting in May 1965, at a time when the club was one of London's best-kept secrets. Al Stewart recalls catching one of Jansch's early sets, and estimates the attendance at no more than nine wandering souls. Of those, doubtless more than half were itinerant folkies awaiting a floor spot to sing, and/or a floor to sleep.

Val Berry, who was about to be ousted from her slot as the singer in The Young Tradition, recalls a period pre-Jansch, pre-Davy Graham, when the unnamed club was emptier still, "There was hardly anybody going down there. We used to just meet there. It was basically a couple of people we knew asking, 'Come and do a couple of songs, help us out, we're trying to get something going.' I don't know how we all drifted in there, but we did ... The Cousins didn't really get off until it got this all-night thing. [Initially] it was just yet another coffee-bar trying to become a folk club, not much different from Bunjies."

The policy by the time Al Stewart became M.C., in the summer of 1965, was simple, "They'd book one main guest, and they relied on people coming off the street to sing, and everybody could sing three songs." The result, in time, would be "people like Cat Stevens getting up and doing floor spots." Though it never secured a liquor license, only the hardy and the wasted frequented its portals in the early days, thus ensuring a fond if slightly miasmic hue to people's memories of those times.

Dave Swarbrick: We all used to hang out at ... the Cousins – I been carried out feet first a few times – it never started until you were incapable. Everybody seemed to go down there, all the late night bingers. [The owner's] father used to own the Greek restaurant, and his father indulged him by letting him have the cellars.

Sandy seems to have picked up this blip on the Soho radar very early on. Val Berry thinks that the first time she saw the young nurse down there, she was accompanied by one of her parents, possibly her mother in pushy stagemother guise. Berry would later be "amazed that she ended up singing all that traditional stuff with Fairport 'cause that [really] wasn't her [thing] at the time." At a time when "we were all influenced by the Joan Baez bit," Sandy seemed particularly prone to emulating the million-selling soprano with a top-end that could perforate a bat's eardrums.

The snobbery that had surrounded Singers played no part in this new, younger scene. Berry felt part of a new breed, "people like me and Jacqui [McShee], who were doing traditional stuff but loved the other stuff anyway ... the people that did their own singer-songwriter things, or other people's material, all the time." The Cousins would be the centre not of a new tradition, or even another folk revival, but of a bevy of singer-songwriters initially mollycoddled by the folk scene, now looking to add their voices to those coming from the other side of the pond – the spawn of Dylan. A number of these American souls – Arlo Guthrie, Danny Kalb, 'Spider' John Koerner, Derroll Adams among them – gave the Cousins the kind of once-over that helped it to achieve its own makeover. The Cousins also wrapped its tendrils more firmly around a couple of American singer-songwriters with no such reputations to consider.

Paul Simon and Jackson C. Frank may even have imagined they might turn the Cousins into London's answer to New York's Gerdes Folk City. Simon certainly seemed determined to remove himself from Dylan's shadow, geographically *and* psychologically, writing some of his finest songs in his 'English period'. Frank's decision to settle in London seemed far more casual, and his attitude to his 'art' equally lackadaisical. In the opening verse of his most famous song, 'Blues Run The Game', he concisely outlined his fatalistic approach to life and love:

"Catch a boat to England,

Maybe to Spain,
Wherever I have gone,
Wherever I've been and gone,
Wherever I have gone
The blues are all the same."

And yet it was Frank's songs, and not Simon's, that prompted the likes of Bert Jansch to attach the epithet "a genius ... an absolute genius." Jackson, though, was already damaged goods by the time he landed in Southampton in the early months of 1965. Born in Buffalo, New York in 1943, Jackson Carey Frank had been caught up in a serious school-fire at the age of eleven. Though he was not amongst the eighteen fatalities, the physical and psychological scars were permanent, and even if he would not be diagnosed with schizophrenia until the end of the 1960s, the signs of a fragmented personality were already on display, in person and in his songs (in a postcard he was to send to Sandy in 1972, he would sign himself "the may wind").

At the end of 1964, with a hundred thousand dollar insurance settlement available to him on his majority, he abandoned his job at the local evening newspaper, and did indeed "catch a boat to England." With a few weeks to kill, and a guitar to hand – so the legend goes – Frank began his songwriting career onboard, disembarking with his signature-tune already penned. As Bert Jansch later observed, "'Blues Run The Game' influenced just about everybody who heard it." Even Simon himself would record the song for the third Simon & Garfunkel album, though not before 'producing' Frank's own rendering, title-track of the one and only Jackson Frank album.

Though Frank had none of Simon's desire to 'succeed', which perhaps more than anything explains why they could remain such strong friends, the months in London seemed to push Frank out of himself and into his songs. Soon enough, he had ten songs all his own. Legend again has it that, at this point, Paul Simon "offered to produce Jackson's first album with his own money." In fact, since Simon was decidedly poor and Frank was rather rich, it was surely Frank who financed the single day of studio-time it took to record his entire repertoire.

In attendance at the session for that eponymous debut (renamed *Blues Run The Game* for its CD reissue in 1996) were 'tea-boy' Art Garfunkel, 'producer' Paul Simon, Al Stewart (whose solitary contribution was second guitar on 'Yellow Walls'), Frank's landlady Judith Pieppe and, according to Pieppe, a shy girl called Sandy Denny. Frank was of a chronically nervous disposition and the intimidating pressures of cutting an album in a single day had induced such a state that, in Al Stewart's words, "Jackson had to have screens put all around him, because he couldn't play if we could see him." However, even with these surround-a-screens, and a steady supply of tea and sandwiches from Art, it seemingly took Sandy to realise something more medicinal was required.

Judith Pieppe: Jackson got very uptight. Paul was there, and Jackson was too uptight to do anything, and Sandy went to get him something to drink, [thinking about Jackson's lines], "Send out for whisky, babe, send out for gin." She thought right. [The] whisky relaxed him enough that he was able to sing properly.

Jackson Frank, despite a couple of obligatory, Dylanesque rallying calls to Change, still comes across as an extraordinarily mature debut – a number of times extending beyond anything Simon had recorded himself. Aside from the plaintive songs of loss – 'Blues Run The Game', 'Milk and Honey' and 'You Never Wanted Me' – that Sandy later made her own, the writing on songs like 'My Name Is Carnival' and 'Dialogue' gave lessons in songwriting to all those British contemporaries with ears to hear. Frank's guitar-playing also had an assurance that belied his twenty-two years. To an eighteen-year-old nurse he must have seemed a walking, talking, shooting star. Certainly Frank remembered a slightly awed Sandy.

Jackson Frank: When I first met Sandy Denny she was a little insecure, and somewhat shy. We were both hanging out at a club in London called Bunjies ... Sandy was working as a nurse and she was just starting out on the folk scene. She was learning the ropes about performing in front of an audience and she was building up her songs. She slowly built up confidence, and expanded her material. She [also] became my girlfriend.

Nobody seems too sure when (or why) Sandy and Jackson became an item. Heather Wood's slightly romanticised version of events has it that Sandy and Jackson were over at Judith Pieppe's flat, "I guess they'd gone over to hang out and it was late," when Pieppe asked the pair, "Do you want to stay? ... and she thought they were a couple, so she gave them a double-bed." The version lodged in Frank's deconstructed psyche had it that Sandy confessed to him one evening that an older man wanted to set her up in an apartment, presumably as his mistress, and as a means of talking her out of accepting the sordid proposal Jackson suggested that she become *his* "old lady".

Frank also insisted, in an interview he gave shortly before his death in March 1999, that he "got her to quit the nursing profession and stick to music full time." As we know, though, Sandy was already committed to beginning college, enrolling at Kingston Art College in September 1965. Despite having commited herself to a year or more of study, though, Sandy's primary focus remained music. A fellow student in her class, David Laskey, recalls a "Sandy [that] wasn't really socially involved in the school. She seemed to have a lot of friends outside the school." He also remembers how she would, on occasions, give recitals to her fellow students.

David Laskey: There was a lecture room over the main entrance, where we had History of Art lectures, and she gave us some recitals there. They were during lecture time. We used to do a period of Complimentary Studies each week as part of the lectures and people would do anything – poetry – readings ... one chap even did a demonstration of bull-fighting passes ... [Sandy] played guitar and sang, and [already] had a wonderful voice. No-one played [along] with her. [CD]

Her course was set, and it was to extra-curricular musical lessons that she continued to devote most of her attention. John Renbourn recalls a Sandy that, by this stage, "not only was ... singing well – because she had a lovely voice to start with – [but] was playing very nice guitar, finger-picking, rather in the style of ... Jackson C. Frank. From him she probably learned even more finger-picking, and her repertoire [began to] include not just the folk songs from the club."

On October 27, 1965, Sandy shared her first bill with Jackson Frank (and Paul Simon) at the opening of a new folk club at 22 D'Arblay Street, also in Soho. Leduce chose to bill itself as "London's only contemporary folk club," which gave away its intended niche. However, she continued to doubt her own playing skills. With the examples of Frank, Renbourn and Jansch, all regulars at the Cousins, to remind her how much she still had to learn, signs of low self-esteem began to invade her private thoughts, evidenced in a self-deprecating rhyme in one of her early notebooks:

May I say?
        That you may!
That you play
Appallingly!?
Did you know?
        I did so!
That you grow
Inflated-O.

As late as January 1967, having warranted an interview in *Melody Maker*, Sandy was still asserting, "I mean to acquire technical competence, as well as quality and judgement," as if her work to date wholly lacked such virtues. Part of the problem was that, however good a musician and mentor Frank was, he did very little for Sandy's confidence. As Pieppe notes, "I don't think, with Jackson, she had a chance of growing up. They were too different. [And] Sandy was very young."

It would appear that Frank took very little account of the age and experience difference. He was probably too wrapped up in his own pain to see beneath Sandy's bluster, to the deep insecurities within. Linda Peters recalls Frank as "an absolute nutcase, and fairly abusive – to everybody, not just to Sandy," while Ralph McTell remembers him as "a strange and brooding character." One particular incident, early on in their relationship, indicates how Frank could cut away at Sandy's self-esteem; and hence how inevitable it was that she would transcend this second father-figure in her life, just as soon as she felt she'd learnt enough to begin defining her own rebel yell.

Al Stewart: It was at Judith Pieppe's place in Dellar Street, where I was living ... One day I met Sandy, who was a night nurse somewhere. She came around straight from duty. I remember [asking], "Who are you?" "I'm Jackson's girlfriend." ... The first thing I ever heard her play was 'Ballad of Hollis Brown'. I didn't know she could sing or play ... It transpired that Jackson wasn't that keen on his girlfriend playing the guitar. He basically thought that was his job ... She had this great voice right from the start, although she was a little bit introverted about it all. She was only nineteen ... I would see Sandy and I would see Jackson, and occasionally I would see them together, but it seemed like they were a separate thing even at that early stage, 'cause he had another couple of girlfriends.

Frank's casual polygamy, as Heather Wood has suggested, was the norm on the folk scene, and Sandy herself seems to have been no stranger to the practise. However, Jackson seems to have been the first of her boyfriends to get under her skin. When she came to add 'You Never Wanted Me' to her own repertoire, the heartrending way she sang it transcended everything else in her repertoire, turning its sentiments back upon their author. The example Frank's songwriting set undoubtedly had a profound effect on Sandy and, though they would see little of each other after he returned to the U.S. in the summer of '66, she would tell an interviewer in 1972, "I really loved the way [Frank] wrote, and he has probably had more effect on me than anyone. I can still hear his influences in my songwriting now." As she rhetorically asked in 1971's 'Next Time Around', "Who [first] wrote me a dialogue set to a tune?"

Ironically, just as his example was inspiring Sandy (and a number of other Cousins regulars) to pick up their pens and guitars, Frank found himself stonewalled by writer's block. Though he would eventually record a handful of songs in the early seventies, Frank's mental problems were such that even coalescing his fragmenting visions into three verses and a chorus soon proved beyond his powers. By the time Sandy came to record her own versions of Jackson's songs, he would be back in the U.S. for good. Though Frank remembered "Sandy trying out her new songs for me," it required both the example he set and the experience of him leaving to prompt her to give her own muse rein.

By which point she had given up college for good, with few in her year at Kingston having made any lasting impression. However, Sandy had established one lifelong friendship during the sculpture classes, albeit not a fellow student. The lady with whom she became fast friends was often her given subject, an American lady nearly ten years her senior named Gina Glazer, who modelled for the school. Glazer had moved to England in 1958 to make a go of folksinging in the clubs of London, after growing up in a household that had often served as a crashpad for the legends of American Folk Music.

Gina Glazer: My father was a writer for People's Songs, so I grew up knowing Woody Guthrie, Pete Seeger and Cisco Houston actually sleeping on the floor ... [In 1958] there was work waiting for all of us [in London] because it was skiffle, Jack Elliott was there, Derroll Adams ... there was a lot of work for the American folksingers then ... I got married there, and I had two kids. And as a day job I was a model at Kingston Art School, where

I met John [Renbourn] and Sandy and Eric Clapton, who used to babysit my kids ... I worked in different classes for these preliminary year students. I got to know Sandy better because she was in sculpture, and it's a more intimate setting, and that's when we became really close. John, I just met socially more. And then we started having a folk club. But I met them within the same few months. Even with our age difference, we hit it right off. She was hysterical, wonderful sense of humour. She enjoyed [Art], she was very good at it, [but] she already was leaning much more towards music.

Glazer insists that when she first befriended the young Sandy she never knew she sang folksongs. The subject only came up during one of Gina's ubiquitous parties. The same shy, self-conscious Sandy who had sung to Al Stewart only when Jackson was away seems to have elected to leave Gina equally in the dark.

Gina Glazer: We were friends for months. I just thought she was fun, and she'd confide in me ... She'd come to my house after work but it wasn't until later, at a party at my house, that she picked up a guitar and started singing. I nearly fainted. I had no idea. Right after Joan Baez, there were a lot of young women picking up a guitar, sort of plucking away and singing, and they weren't very good. [But] Sandy had a beautiful voice.

Though Gina played 'the circuit' at this time, she was deemed authentic folk, playing the Singers and other 'traditional' outlets, and it is perfectly possible that she and Sandy successfully bypassed each other's public performances through 1964 and most of 1965. And yet, Sandy must have known that Gina was a folksinger in her own right, if not from clues in her record collection, then from their mutual friend, John Renbourn.

Renbourn seems quite certain that Sandy attended a number of the song-swapping sessions at Gina's house, near to the college, where "guys like myself used to go and sit around in her garden, listening to her singing and playing." Indeed he is quite convinced that "Sandy learned an awful lot from Gina, and even later it was hard not to notice how similar she sounded in her vocal texture and phrasing. Gina actually taught her a lot of her early repertoire ... [Gina] knew Odetta, Dave Van Ronk and Paul Clayton. She had sung a fair amount in the States ... she had a lovely, fragile voice and played old-style finger-picking guitar and banjo." Even if Sandy shared Renbourn's assessment, Gina herself denies the debt, though she owns up to playing some part in Sandy's transition from Baez clone into traditional singer.

> **Gina Glazer:** There was a similarity in voice quality [but] she had it the first time I heard her sing. I know a lot of her choice of songs [came from me]. Because I used to tell her where to look for good ballads. ... John [Renbourn] and Sandy and I would spend time together. We'd sometimes go up to London and go to the Cecil Sharp House to look up songs, and John lived very near so he'd drop in. I don't think she was too thrilled at the research, but it was something to do ... She didn't get as excited as I did when I'd [find] a version and say isn't this incredible, this was sung in 1500 in the north of England and this was sung in 19something in Virginia, and she couldn't understand how I'd get so excited about that oral tradition [thing].

The wondrous workings of the creative folk tradition may have continued to bemuse Sandy but, with Gina encouraging her to peak beneath its top soil, she began to apply her keen mind to finding traditional material that she could connect with, and that suited her remarkable vocal range. When Peter Kennedy wrote to her in September 1966, asking her to attend a recording session for his *Folk Song Cellar* radio series, he asked her for a list of songs she might wish to sing. The four suggestions that came back were all good Celtic folksongs, 'I Once Loved A Lass' (which Sandy later recorded as 'The False Bride'), 'Jute Mill Song' (made popular by Ewan MacColl), 'She Moved Through The Fair' and the ballad of 'Geordie'. When it came time to record the session, she preferred two other examples of British tradition, 'Fhir A Bhata' and 'Green Grow The Laurels'.

Earlier that summer, Sandy had also met Bert Lloyd, then in the final stages of writing his masterful textbook, *Folk Song In England*, and had asked him for the lyrics to 'The Handsome Cabin Boy'. Lloyd, in replying, wrote that he had been "thinking about other songs, but I need to hear you a bit more before I know for sure what suits you." He would later send Sandy lyrics for 'Sovay' or 'The Female Highwayman', which he suggested was "best [sung] unaccompanied, or at least not guitar-accompanied, so that the rhythm can really ripple."

Sandy seemed to hit a rich vein of inspiration in the months after Frank's departure, possibly inspired as much by Gina's presence as Jackson's absence. According to the man who had known the part-time couple best, the change in Sandy was profound. No longer was she content to sit in the shadows.

Al Stewart: It seems as though she was there, as this ghostly figure, and then after Jackson went back to America, it was almost like somebody had put their foot on the accelerator, and all of a sudden she was everywhere. And she was a lot better. I think Sandy found another gear in the gearbox after Jackson went back to the States ... She became a lot more confident.

Crucially, Sandy had made the momentous decision that college was not where it was at – quite possibly a decision Frank *did* influence. In the version she told her father, the college "had a little talk with her and they said, 'Well, Sandy, you seem to be doing well at this musical thing, what are you going to do? ... if you want to try the music and see how you get on and if you decide it's no good, we'll always take you back.'" In all likelihood, Sandy simply made it clear that she was not taking up a place on the diploma course, preferring to follow other Kingstonians into the potentially lucrative business of making music. Reflecting her new found confidence, she soon acquired Sandy Glennon as her booking agent and manager, after spurning the business advances of the curmugeonedly Bruce Dunnett. She also began a weekly residence of her own, in the heart of Soho, at Leduce, where she felt assured enough to debut a couple of her own songs.

The singer-songwriter genre seems, with hindsight, like one of the more obvious consequences of the folk revival, but at the time few folkies were taking traditional templates, à la Dylan, and moulding them anew. Yet Linda Peters remembers when Sandy told her that she was going to write some songs, down the Troubadour one night, and her startled reply was, "What do you mean, write songs?" Just as a twenty-year-old Dylan, on dropping out of his state university in the spring of 1960, would often claim one of his own efforts was actually an old folk song, so on the London folk scene of the mid-Sixties it was, in Trevor Lucas's words, "far cooler ... to say you'd 'found' a song from a traditional source, than to actually write something. History lent virtually anything some kind of credibility. And Sandy, from the time she'd worked the clubs ... always copped a lot of flak for writing her own songs, not singing traditional things."

Just like the young Dylan, Sandy usually preferred to play covers when she was performing – even after she began to write her own songs (ditto Dylan, who was performing 'No More Auction Block' six months after he set 'Blowin' in the Wind' to its tune). Unlike Dylan, though, Sandy never seems to have set her lyrics to arrangements of traditional melodies, a process Dylan did not transcend until his fourth album. Even her first documented song, known either as 'In Memory' or 'The Tender Years', had its own elegaic tune to go with its bittersweet words, even if it very consciously borrowed the idea of lost youth (and lifted the final line of verse three verbatim) from 'Bob Dylan's Dream':

I hear the sighing of the wind / like a murmur of regret
And as I close my eyes / I see a face I will never forget.

I see you running with the dawn / but that was many years ago
When you had seen the tender years / the only years you were to know.

I knew a time when you and I / ran through trees of green and gold
And gazed at clouds of feather grey / I never dreamt we would ever grow old.

But time has passed, my mind will dim / the hands will turn away my days
But you remain a timeless smile / who'd just begun life's tangled ways.

Though the young songwriter cannot avoid slipping into clichés in that third verse, thematically and structurally 'The Tender Years' was both original and ambitious. The listener only realises that the lost youth in the song is dead with the final line of the second verse. The remainder of the song almost basks in the romanticism of an early death. It was evidently based on a real incident. According to her father, "she had an experience at school where a boy hurt his knee on the Friday, got blood poisoning and was dead on the Monday. She was a pal and she wrote this little song for him, a sad little song ... it was a memory that stayed with her."

Drawing on incidents from her past for inspiration became something of a pattern in Sandy's songwriting. She also regularly turned portraits of people into vignettes-in-song, all the while disguising the songs' autobiographical elements. At the same time as displaying a remarkable ability to draw upon prior experience, she found she was able to actually rewind emotionally. One close friend recalls several examples of this 'emotional recall'.

Miranda Ward: Sandy had ... 100% emotional recall. If something happened that upset her, and it comes up in conversation five years later, laughing about it, by the time you've finished talking [it] through Sandy's as upset as when it first happened ... One classic case, she flew into Heathrow, and Trevor [Lucas] wasn't there to meet her and she was in an absolute state. She got a cab to my place. She was a wreck, and felt totally betrayed by Trevor. The asshole had run out of petrol driving to the airport. But Sandy would talk about it a year and a half later and she'd be back in the same state. Which [also] made the strong emotive thing in her music when she was writing it. Sandy didn't have control [of it] but something would happen to her, and she would go back into that emotional state, and out of that would come the song. She wrote the songs with 100% emotion, even though the emotion was something that she'd remembered. She didn't write them in the depths of despair or the heights of elation.

This capacity to recall emotions, vividly and with immediacy, had a downside – an inability to consign such incidents to the past tense. The incident that prompted 'The Tender Years' Sandy revisited again three years later, at the time of *Unhalfbricking*, offering an unprecedented glimpse into the process, as it unravels on the page. Reaching for the inspiration that drew out the original song, one senses, reading it, that she was hoping to find a better way to express the same sentiments:

"When I lie awake and sometimes catch the sounds of the wind in the branches of a tree,
I am reminded of a song I wrote when I was young,
About a little boy I knew at school
About my friend
Who cut his knee ...
We used to run around the waste land
It was a sad song, it was meant to be that way
I never sang it
No-one heard it because I used to be quite shy
But I sang its tangled words just now and then for [myself and for] my friend
I cried sometimes because I felt remorse about
It was something which I kept to tell myself I really cared.
And now I want to sing it well for [line blank].
His name was David and he died when he was young,
and I cried for him a long time ago.
The hands will steal away your time before you know.
When I sing I look as though I'm crying...
The tangled words I wrote for him, they did not scan, they did not ryme [sic].
But now the time is late

They meant so much then
They mean as much again
But I did not realise, and tears came to my eyes
+ then I did not care, my thoughts were there."

'The Tender Years' is not the only one of Sandy's early efforts to recall a lost period of innocence. On the demo tapes she made on her parents' reel-to-reel recorder in 1966–67 is another song, called 'Boxful of Treasures'. Already the obtuseness that will make some of her work impenetrable has found a home in song, as the lyrics dance between images of childlike wonder and an unmentioned hurt, from which the narrator seeks to rescue the song's subject. As with 'The Tender Years', there is a delicate melancholia to the melody, and though Sandy would abandon the words in time, she would save the melody for one of her finest works, 'Fotheringay':

A boxful of treasures, and a golden comb
I was surely give to you when the moon is [young]
And Christmas is in June.

I will paint an evening of which there will be few
When the sky is water, and the sun is blue
And all this is just for you.

A handkerchief of silver to brush away your tear,
A sword of finest leather to match your paper spear
For when the day draws near.

When I will write these words in languages unknown
I'll be the one to tell you your heart is made of stone
And Christmas will never be in June.

It is difficult to know when Sandy wrote these two songs, or how many others she penned in her first year as a professional folksinger because, as she herself wrote in 1969, "I used to be quite shy, I [only] sang [such] tangled words just now and then for [myself]." Other originals were treated with a similar scant regard. One song certainly lost to us was a number she wrote with fellow folkie Wendy Hamilton, 'There's a Red Light In Your Eyes', which

Al Stewart thinks she played once or twice at Leducé.

In the face of such rectitude, one is entirely reliant on the various home tapes that predate Sandy's membership of Fairport to form a picture of her songwriting. Among the twenty-four songs on these tapes can be found half a dozen originals, of which only 'Who Knows Where The Time Goes' would feature among her pre-Fairport recordings. The likes of 'Nowhere You Can Go'(?), 'They Don't Seem To Know You'(?) and an early 'Carnival' (which shares a single line with its 1973 kin), show a songwriter hovering on the verge of an original voice. In the final verse of this 'Carnival' she allows natural forces to finally envelop her:

I can see all of the country from the mound on which I stand
The autumn leaves still driftin' to the bosom of the land
Wind is roaring wildly, and the fury of the wintry sky
Beats down upon me, and I have no need to cry.

'Carnival' appears – on one of two early demo tapes, totalling ten songs, the only audio documents of Sandy Denny prior to her *Folk Song Cellar* appearance at the end of 1966* – alongside two traditional English folksongs, 'I Love My True Love' and a song usually listed as 'Let No Man Steal Your Thyme' but more appositely entitled, in its original 1766 broadside incarnation, The Maid's Lament for the Loss of Her Maidenhead.

'Carnival' is probably the weakest of her early compositions, vocally and lyrically, but she handles the two traditional songs with a certain assurance. The other demo-tape – undoubtedly earlier – suggests a Sandy yet to transcend her more obvious influences, with two songs by Jackson Frank, one by Dylan, Bert Jansch's 'Soho' (presumably learnt first-hand); whilst the familiar Scottish ballad 'Geordie' and that American perennial 'East Virginia' suggest Gina Glazer's continuing input. Only 'The Tender Years' lends an original tone.

On these two sets of demos the listener catches only glimpses of the Sandy to come. The voice on these tapes is as innocent as 'The Tender Years', the 'lovely', 'pretty' voice that everyone remembers, but the edge that separates the technically accomplished from the genuinely original interpreter is soon come. Indeed, the home demo of 'Blues Run The Game' almost sounds like a guide-vocal when A-B'd alongside the version Sandy recorded for the BBC in March

---

*They can be found on volumes three and four of the Attix Tracks fan club-only cassettes.

1967. The suddenly acquired undertow to that voice came on in a matter of months when she was leaving both ends of her candles burning, prompting more than an occasional comment about this walking contradiction.

Philippa Clare: Sandy was extremely insecure about her singing ... I remember Luke Kelly from the Dubliners, one night when she was here on the floor, just kicking her and going, "You stupid bitch. You sing like a fucking angel. Now behave like one." She was heavily admired, and a lot of her insecure behaviour was tolerated because she was so good ... [But] I never saw Sandy comfortable in her own skin, she was always on edge, waiting for an attack ... [But then I had] my [own] insecurities in those days, I always thought I was the wrong shape, wrong colour, wrong accent.

Not that Sandy had been exactly holding back since first tasting freedom as an auxiliary nurse. Linda Thompson believes "she got used to the drink and drugs thing as a nurse ... 'cause I knew her when she was working in the hospitals, and she always used to have pills 'n' stuff around." Perhaps Jackson Frank had managed to keep her penchant for excess in check. If so, when he caught a boat to New York, and she began to work her way through a series of folk-musician boyfriends who were as game for a good time as their personal Bodicea, a hedonistic Sandy burst forth and, for the time being, she was the life of the party. Lady-like, though, she was not.

Al Stewart: The Troubadour was run by Martin Windsor and Red Sullivan, and Sandy came down [one time], and she was in full steam, and it was like a tide of people opening as she steamed through, pushing her way through a whole roomful of people. She'd obviously come down to sing; and I remember Martin Windsor yelling across this sea of heads, "Sandy Denny, you're a girl, not a tank!"

Many of her part-time paramours from this time remember the tank-girl fondly, tinged with a touch of nostalgia for the times themselves. Marc Ellington paints a portrait that accords with the person Al Stewart once transported back to Wimbledon in a cab, "She was a mixture of straight-laced schoolteacher and someone who made Janis Joplin look like Mother Theresa, completely out of control. Not within an hour, within the same sentence." Dave Swarbrick, with whom Sandy had a brief fling after meeting him at John

Martyn's place in Hampstead, remembers the teenage Sandy as "wonderfully scatter-brained and giggly. In those days we were [all] intent upon having a good time, and if she was feisty she was only feisty in short bursts. Rest of the time was given over to hilarity."

Danny Thompson, who would become Sandy's most serious boyfriend in the years that separate Jackson Frank from Trevor Lucas, concurs with Swarb, depicting Sandy in slightly rose-tinted terms, as a girl simply bent on good times.

Danny Thompson: She was learning piano. I was with Pentangle at the time and she came up to me and said would I help her with her music. I said, "I'm not a teacher." ... I met her at the Horseshoe in Tottenham Court Road. Pentangle had only been going five minutes. I fell for her immediately. She had an amazing chuckle, great sense of humour, just a great bird to be with ... [One time] we'd clear[ed] off to Scotland, we stayed at this Castle Hotel, we went to the Edinburgh Festival. Our room was in the corner of one of those conical towers. We were locked out. I had to get her up the fire escape – give her a bunk up. She never complained about anything like that. None of this "Oh, don't" or "You mustn't." She was [always] up for a laugh ... She wouldn't stand any pomposity, or let anyone put her on a pedestal ... [But, even then,] I would keep her off the brandy and feed her towards the gin and whiskey ... Brandy made her belicose. [JI]

Fellow member of Pentangle, Jacqui McShee, who witnessed 'Sandy on the brandy' on a number of occasions, remembers that "she [also] drank a fierce amount of whisky, and she could [really] drink! ... That became her character, 'Oh that's Sandy. Good ol' Sandy, drunk again.' They expected her to be like that. But everybody drank. It was part of being who you were and where you were. I don't think I knew anybody who didn't drink. Danny, John and Bert were legendary." In the company of such prodigious drinkers, it didn't take much to get Sandy in a party mood. However, her late husband Trevor Lucas noticed some warning signs, at their early assignations, which suggested that her relationship with alcohol might be an unhealthy one.

Trevor Lucas: Sandy drank, yes. She liked to drink. She liked the effect of alcohol, the feeling of being drunk – which is always dangerous. [But] she was one of those people whose bodies don't metabolise alcohol very well, so the first drink really had the [same] effect as the last one. [1989]

As a key participant in a serious drinking culture – the world of folk – Sandy wasn't looking to establish some illusory common bond with the drinking classes, it was simply the cheapest, most accessible way to get out of oneself and, in her case, to effect a necessary transformation. Underneath the bravado, the boys'r'us laddishness, and the sheer spunkiness of the young Sandy was someone deeply uncertain of herself in some fundamental, deep-rooted way. Bert Jansch, a man of few words, had known her from her early days at the Scots Hoose and seems to be the only one of her early boyfriends still prepared to allude to that darkness within.

> **Bert Jansch:** She certainly liked to enjoy herself [even then]. [But] I [always] got the impression that she was looking for something, and not getting it. She always seemed a very disturbed person to me.

Beneath the bubbly exterior lived someone absolutely convinced of her abilities, but wracked with self-doubt about her worth. Sandy's laddish behaviour, designed perhaps to compensate for such feelings, only served to divert attention away from her growing skills as a singer and interpreter. Dave Swarbrick insists, "she knew how good she was, she didn't just belt off songs. She certainly knew what caliber of singer she was." Jansch recalls someone who "just wanted *somebody* to actually take her seriously as a singer." Because of her route to this world, she was always uncertain of her place in the folk pantheon. Even in the early days, she chose not to confine herself to the same ol' three club circuit. Willing to ply her wares when and wherever she could, the results were sometimes hilarious.

> **John Renbourn:** I can still remember standing outside Cousins wondering where my next meal was coming from when Sandy came along [and] bought me a big plate of spaghetti, and then took me down to a place where she had a gig. It was a basement gay bar, and Sandy thought it was screamingly funny to be up on stage, singing and playing as the clientele smooched around in couples.

By the end of 1966, Sandy had some kind of agenda, but it seems to have been one she kept hid from most everyone, even the folk musicians who shared her bed and booze.

4

1967–68: BALLAD OF TIME

Acoss the distant sky, all the birds are leaving
But how can they know it's time for them to go
Before the winter stay fire, I will still be dreaming
I have no thought of time.
For, who knows where the time goes

Sad deserted shore – your fickle friends are leaving
Ah, but then you know, it's time for them to go
But I will still be here, I have no thought of time
of leaving.
I don't count the time.
For who knows where the time goes.

And I am not alone, while my love surrounds me
I know it shall be so until it's time to go
So come the storms of winter, and then the birds
in spring again.
I have no fear of time
For who knows how my love grows
Who knows where the time goes.

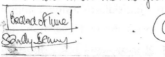

Ballad of Time
Sandy Denny

Original lyrics to 'Who Knows Where The Time Goes'

"When I was doing the folk clubs, I got the impression that it was a dying trade almost ... I'm probably putting it down ... [but] the actual incentive to become a folk singer has totally disappeared."[1977]

Sandy Denny

Sandy's first significant plaudits in the music press came at the beginning of 1967, when she was introduced by the obliging Karl Dallas to the readers of *Melody Maker*, as "a girl singer who scored a big success at a recent Vietnam concert in London," i.e. a concert by The Folksingers Committee For Peace in Vietnam at St Pancras Town Hall, held the week before Christmas 1966. She took the opportunity to bemoan the lack of professionalism on the circuit – "from the point of view of the folk scene, it would naturally suit the singers if things were arranged in a more businesslike way" – even as she had begun to put things on a sound business footing, taking on Sandy Glennon as her manager some time around September 1966.

Aside from expanding her circle of gigs beyond the home counties for the first time, the autumn of 1966 and winter of 1967 also saw Sandy make a number of appearances on radio and TV. The most significant of these would be her appearance on Peter Kennedy's *Folk Song Cellar* series for the BBC World Service. Allowed to sing her own selections, she acknowledged her family roots by performing her late grandmother's favourite, 'Fhir A Bhata'. The series of 37 programmes was an important landmark in folk broadcasting; and Sandy was recommended for the programme by two friends who were about to play their own key role in her story. Dave Cousins and Tony Hooper had been pounding the boards as a bluegrass duo/trio (with Ron Chesterman) for some time, under the as-yet-unabbreviated moniker of the Strawberry Hill Boys.

For the time being, Sandy was content to be a part-time constituent of another trio, puffed up to a quartet for BBC radio. It was as singer in The Johnny Silvo Folk Four that she would make her first entrees onto BBC radio, and into the world of the recording studio. With Roger Evans on lead guitar and David Moses on double-bass, Sandy and Johnny would swop songs (and identities, Sandy once being introduced as Johnny Silvo on the radio, when he had a dose of the flu). Though songs like 'This Train' and 'Make Me a Pallet on the Floor' were presumably imposed on her, and it was sometimes hard to appreciate her vocals over Silvo's fake skiffle accompaniment, the radio shows seem to have prompted one would-be entrepreneur to take a chance on the folk revival, giving the two stars of the 'Johnny Silvo Folk Four' their own album.

Karl Dallas: The man who ran Saga [Records], Marcel Rodd, was an entrepreneur. He saw there was a market for folk-music [and] that he could make lots of money if he hardly paid the artists anything, and sold the records very, very cheap. He was into classical music – he didn't understand folk music, wasn't interested in folk music ... He had these people just in, would pay them peanuts, probably no royalty deal. He did the same thing in other areas ... He was behind Trojan Records, so he recorded all the reggae ... That's why he recorded Sandy – y'know, pretty girl with nice knees.

In the space of a few months, in the summer of 1967, Rodd would release two budget-priced albums featuring the "pretty girl with nice knees." *Sandy and*

Johnny, recorded April 26, 1967, featured a good colour shot of the knees on the cover, and gave Sandy top billing. The sleeve-notes, pure sixties' kitsch, reported that: "Sandy Denny is twenty years old, very pretty and sings as beautifully as anyone we have heard for a very long time. She hates being compared with any other folk singer." And yet, save for powerful renderings of Frank's 'Milk and Honey' and Alex Campbell's anti-war anthem 'Been On The Road', Sandy does very little to distinguish herself from "any other folk singer[s]" brought up on a staple diet of 'Bobby and Baez'. Her takes on 'Make Me a Pallet On The Floor' and 'Pretty Polly' certainly forsake feeling for a hammy exuberance.

Sandy and Johnny, though, was not Sandy's only contribution to Mr. Rodd's money-making ventures. Recorded a month earlier, on March 22, and released a couple of months ahead of *Sandy and Johnny* was a hootenanny-style album, sold using the name of *Alex Campbell And Friends.* Designed to compliment a TV series, it afforded Sandy a greater opportunity to shine, even though she was allocated a mere three songs. Save for an embarrassingly hearty 'This Train', she succeeded in shaking the Silvo ensemble, proceedimg to lay down the best of her Jackson Frank covers, 'You Never Wanted Me', and another song possibly once sung by her grandmother, 'The False Bride' (a.k.a. 'I Once Loved A Lass'). Adopting authentic Scotch, as well as the persona of a heartbroken Scottish male, Sandy steps beyond the simple tale of infidelity, hinting at the depths alluded to in one of folk's most oblique codas:

> *"All men in yon forest they ask unto me*
> *How many strawberries grow in the salt sea*
> *And I answer them with a tear in my e'e*
> *How many ships sail in the forest?"*

For the first time, the voice glides effortlessly above the under-stated accompaniment, warranting a share of the hyperbole offered in the sleeve-notes, penned by Sandy's then-manager Sandy Glennon, which, needless to say, placed her at the forefront of some abstract revival, "reckoned by her fellow ' singers to be the girl of the year." Though Sandy wouldn't even get an arrangement credit for her songs (which went to Theo Johnson from the Barge, the main impetus behind the project), and was paid single session fees (of fifteen and fifty pounds, respectively) for her time, the albums must have increased her profile, especially in the provinces.*

Commission statements from Glennon confirm Sandy's expanding horizons, and earning power, in these months. In February, she ventured out to Norwich, Orpington and Manchester; March and April brought Brighton, Leicester, Great Yarmouth, Lowestoft, Norwich again, Coventry and even a four-day trip to the Lowlands of Scotland. Her monthly earnings also rose from forty-five pounds in January to a hundred and twenty in April (excluding session fees), as she began to command between twelve and fifteen pounds an appearance, compared with the five to seven pounds she had received just six months earlier. Not surprisingly, a single girl travelling late at night brought its own set of dangers, even if they were unlikely to faze "an effing, blinding, hard-drinking girl".

Neil Denny: She travelled considerable distances. I remember once she phoned up and said she was coming into King's Cross at two in the morning, and would I meet her. So I get out of bed and get the car up to King's Cross and she said it was always a rough passage, coming home sitting on her own in a train like that. She had a guitar case, of course, and there's always a rough type saying, "Give us a tune, love" and that nasty sort of thing. She must have had to adopt some sort of armour. [JI]

Sandy continued to frequent the clubs of Soho and West London, even playing the fabled Marquee club on three occasions – as well as regularly performing as the billed artist at the various folk clubs on London's outer perimeter, in Surbiton and Hounslow, Norbury and East Ham, Addlestone and Twickenham. However, she never took to the life of the road, nor the solitude of travelling solo. Talking about this period in 1970, shortly after quitting Fairport partially because of the rigours of their touring schedule, she revealed an early yearning for the joys of the hearth.

Sandy Denny: It's a very independent kind of life being a folk singer [but], although I felt I was more my own master, I always really wanted the comforts of home ... I also had a mews cottage in Kensington, where I lived with two very good friends, and I began to get very homesick for it whenever I was away for any length of time. [1970]

---

*Nine, and then ten, songs from these Saga sessions would be collected on, firstly, *It's Sandy Denny*, in 1970, and then *The Original Sandy Denny* in 1977, the latter subsequently being issued on CD, but only from a vinyl copy.

One option open to the lonely, long distance folkie was to join a band. Unfortunately, the economics of band-membership were rarely attractive unless they came with the prospect of a record and/or management deal. Though Sandy's brief association with Johnny Silvo's little set-up had hardly worked wonders for her music, when approached by Dave Cousins of the Strawberry Hill Boys one night at the Troubadour, she proved surprisingly receptive to the idea of making the Strawberry Hill Boys a unisex outfit.

Dave Cousins: It was downstairs at the Troubadour that I first heard Sandy Denny. She looked startlingly attractive in a white dress and hat, and she sang like an angel. I thought she was the best thing I'd ever seen and immediately after she'd finished her couple of songs, I asked her if she fancied joining a group. I was quite surprised when she said yes, although we did have a fair reputation on the folk scene by then. We cut some demo tapes with Sandy after rehearsing with her for a couple of weeks ... at Cecil Sharp House.

The Strawberry Hill Boys at this point comprised guitarists Dave Cousins and Tony Hooper, and Ron Chesterman on stand-up bass. Having been pounding the boards for a couple of years or more, they needed a focal point and, vocally, neither Cousins nor Hooper stood out from the crowd. Dating that night at the Troubadour, though, proves difficult. Sandy's association with the Strawbs had begun by October 1966, when Peter Kennedy wrote to 'Sandy and the Strawbs', at Sandy's parents, asking them to attend a recording for *Folk Song Cellar* on December 2, adding as an asterisk, "check that they [i.e. the Strawbs] can come on that day, to accompany please."

As it happens, both Sandy and the Strawbs did appear at the December session, though independently. However, they had probably already started playing the occasional gig, as photographer Ray Stevenson snapped them at the Troubadour around this time and, according to her agent, Sandy's only documented appearance at her old haunt between October 1966 and April 1967 was on December 20, 1966, when she was paid just five pounds, barely half her usual rate for a night's work.*

Not that Sandy was foolish enough to discontinue her solo status until such a time as she and the Strawbs had successfully gelled as a unit. Perhaps joining

---

*Possibly the equally-underpaid gigs at the Marquee were as part of the Strawbs.

the Strawbs was only ever meant as a metaphorical raised digit to some old friends who had recently formed their own folk combo, without even auditioning Sandy for the role of lead singer. Given that Pentangle included one ex-boyfriend, her current boyfriend and one of her oldest musician friends, in Bert Jansch, Danny Thompson and John Renbourn respectively, and that they had sprung from one of her favourite watering holes, the Horseshoe Tavern on Tottenham Court Road, she was entitled to be a bit hurt when not asked to be in the new band.

Gina Glazer: They felt it was too big a voice. They wanted somebody that blended in ... She knew she was a good singer, she had no doubts about her talent ... She had high hopes. I think, even then, she was not as devoted to traditional folk as I am. I already felt Sandy was a little bit bored with that. She wanted more recognition than just being in folk was going to give you. That was part of the appeal [of joining the Strawbs] ... that's when she learned to sing with a group. That's when she stopped doing straight 'Gina' stuff, and started experimented musically. And I think her singing became much more interesting from then [on].

In fact, Pentangle's manager, Jo Lustig, at some point in 1967 came to the conclusion that Pentangle's chosen female vocalist, Jacqui McShee, "wasn't commercial enough," and in the months before Sandy joined Fairport was angling for her to join Pentangle. According to McShee, what finally convinced Lustig to let the matter drop, aside from Renbourn threatening to quit, was when "he found out [just] how much Sandy drank." By this point, Sandy and Danny Thompson had ceased to be an item (though they remained close). However, the ructions in their relationship had enabled all the other members of the band to observe first-hand what a handful Ms. Denny could be, and the idea of a Sandy-led Pentangle was allowed to die a natural death.

Jacqui McShee: Sandy used to come along quite a lot on the Sunday evenings and do floor spots [at the Horseshoe]. It was basically a rehearsal place for us, we'd rehearse in the afternoon, and do the gig in the evening ... A lot of people came under Danny's spell, 'cause he was always the loudest and the jokiest. People used to come along, pre-gig, then everyone would start drinking, and Danny would be sitting there holding court, if you like. And Sandy was there a lot. But Sandy and I would sit aside and moan about men in general. She seemed to me quite a lonely person. She always said she had a rotten taste in men ... She used to come to gigs with us sometimes in the van, and there would be rows [with Danny]. It was quite volatile at times. She would often cry on my shoulder about it ... She was quite hard to handle, even then ... She had a lot of self-doubts. She used to unburden herself on me. Maybe she thought I'd be telling Danny the way she felt.

Whilst the Pentangle 'experiment' went from strength to strength that winter, thanks to the unique opportunity afforded by the weekly Horseshoe residency, there were few such avenues open for Sandy and the Strawbs. Just when the association seemed destined to fritter away to naught, they were invited to record some songs for the BBC World Service at a session on February 21. The five songs recorded that day comprised three from Cousins' pen and two from Sandy's repertoire, Frank's familiar 'Blues Run The Game' and the ubiquitous 'Pretty Polly', a song Sandy had already sung with the Johnny Silvo Folk Four(!). As a result of this BBC session, the foursome suddenly found themselves being asked to fly over to Denmark to make some recordings for a small-time operation in Copenhagen.

Dave Cousins: At that time Tom Browne, who is now a BBC DJ, was doing folk programmes on Danish radio, and he took the tapes over to Copenhagen, in order to fix us up with a couple of weeks' work at Tivoli. He also played the tapes to Karl Knudsen at Sonet Records, who said he'd like to record us and, since no one in England wanted to, we agreed.

Nobody seems too clear what exactly the deal with Knudsen involved, but it was evidently little better than the one previously offered to Sandy by Marcel Rodd. The carrot was the prospect of some record-label interest, or so the effusive Knudsen assured them.

Ascertaining when exactly Sandy and the boys travelled to Tivoli, for the two-week residency and recording sessions – problematic enough in itself – is not helped by the claim on the rear-sleeve of the 1973 album of these sessions that they were recorded in August 1968, three months after Sandy had joined Fairport Convention. Joe Boyd insists that he heard an acetate of these recordings the third week in May 1967, shortly before the release of *Sgt. Pepper*. Perhaps the sessions occupied the first two weeks in May, when Sandy's sole commitment was a booking at the Horseshoe. By the time Sandy was in

Glasgow, in August, being recorded by Alex Campbell at his home in Rupert Street, Saga's *Sandy & Johnny* was already in the shops, complete with notes referring to Sandy playing Tivoli Gardens "on behalf of British Folk Week."

The songs they planned to record in Denmark were hardly the kind of fare with which Sandy had made her reputation. Rather than performing singer-songwriter material interspersed with traditional fare, the Strawbs preferred to rely upon Dave Cousins' lightweight confections for what was intended as a pop album. Not that Knudsen was exactly pulling out all the stops, production-wise, the recording studio being in fact the soundstage of a cinema. Cousins later painted a picture to *ZigZag* of just how primitive the set-up was, "There was no masking for sound, it was just straight down onto tape. I realised at that time we really needed a drummer – on that album we used a Danish drummer ... the mastering machine was three-track and sprocket-driven."

Though singing duties largely devolved to Sandy, she was content to utilise that 'pretty voice' with which she had first mounted a stage – save for a single performance where she sang, solo, words of her own making, ensuring that an album of anodyne pop ditties would warrant at least a footnote in the history of popular song.

If the 'clean' copy in one of her early notebooks represents an early draft, 'Who Knows Where The Time Goes' originally had a more apposite title, 'Ballad of Time'. Where exactly it was written, no-one seems too sure. Neil Denny thought it was written when Sandy "was living in a flat in Kensington with a Canadian girl, whose father was a professor of art at the Tate." Gina Glazer insists that Sandy, "unhappy in a love affair – it was Danny – had come and stayed the night at my house, and she had started it, and she asked me what I thought." Sandy herself insisted that she finished the song in Denmark, where she self-consciously unveiled it to Cousins and Hooper. They agreed to include it alongside their own songs, from which it stood out like a diamond in a coal mine. That wistful quality Sandy had been reaching for on 'The Tender Years' and 'Boxful of Treasures' was effortlessly realised in that first verse:

"Across the distant sky, all the birds are leaving,
But how can they know it's time for them to go?
Before the winter fire, I will still be dreaming,
I have no thought of time.
For who knows where the time goes."

As the lyrics are buffeted by that minor-key melody, the narrator turns to face the future with a new assurance – "So come the storms of winter, and then the birds in spring again/ I have no fear of time," at least "while my love surrounds me." That enveloping love, though modified in performance to "while my love is near," would continue to demand nourishment. The performance that day in Denmark – best heard on the 1973 vinyl original (the CD reissue has a mawkish fiddle warbling away in one's woofers) – has a sense of stillness even the Fairport rerecording couldn't rekindle. As Australian journalist Shane Danielson recognized, in a posthumous tribute in *RAM*, there is something almost otherworldly about this recording:

"Her voice is pure, effortless, perfect; she will never again possess quite this quality of tone. The tremelo will deepen, the range narrow ever so slightly. It will become the voice of a mortal rather than a goddess – yet all the more gorgeous for that."

Sandy's ballad of time would come to haunt the songwriter – when asked about the song by a journalist six years later, she would snap, "I just wish people would listen to some of the other ones" – but at the time she knew it represented some kind of breakthrough. When she played the song for Alex Campbell at his Glasgow house in August, her pride in it was audible. The rest of the album she was not so sure about. It might have been some kind of statement for the Strawberry Hill boys, but not for the Wimbledon Green girl. And yet, she did play Joe Boyd an acetate of the album as originally configured, he believes the third weekend in May.

Joe Boyd: One Friday evening in May 1967, when I was running the UFO Club, I'd stopped in at Cousins and Sandy was there, and we just got to talking, a few drinks, and I invited her to come over to UFO. And we spent the whole weekend hanging out and talking about music ... That's the first time I ever heard Sgt. Pepper – we went to her house and her brother had taped the record off of Radio Luxembourg, who'd gotten hold of a copy and played it a week before its release. We had to keep the volume down so it wouldn't wake her parents – it was like 5 am.

Having come over to London to run Elektra's UK division in the summer of 1966, Boyd had managed in a single year to become quite the entrepreneur. The Incredible String Band had been an early discovery, and he had quickly taken upon himself both production and management duties. Setting up the UFO Club, he was the first man to take The Pink Floyd into the studio, and was responsible for producing their groundbreaking debut 45, 'Arnold Layne/ Candy & A Currant Bun'. When he first met Sandy, he was therefore an alluring example of commercial and critical success, as well as tall, attractive, opinionated and twentysomething. Sandy was something else, and Boyd was not quite sure what that else was.

Joe Boyd: She was incredibly funny, with a very quick mind, jumping from one subject to another, dropping in comments obliquely, interrupting herself with footnotes – a chaotic intelligence just poured out. [JI]

Smitten by this earthy, exuberant, pretty young thing, Boyd forced himself to push aside his own set of attendant prejudices.

Joe Boyd: At that time, I had an aversion to American style singer-songwriters ... the Jackson Franks. I'd come to England to get away from that sort of thing ... I think I'd seen her at Cousins and had rather grudgingly acknowledged that she was pretty good, even though I didn't really approve [that] she was singing something like 'Blues Run The Game' ... I hadn't really heard her that much on stage, and usually in those very short sets at Cousins, where you got up and sang three songs. [But] she was pretty pig-headed about what she wanted to do. I think there was definitely a frustration in her against the folk scene as such, and she had a certain contempt for a lot of the prejudices and schisms that pertained within it.

Sometime shortly after their weekend rendezvous, Boyd was obliged to return to the States for a few weeks, to attend the annual Newport Folk Festival. Meanwhile, Dave Cousins continued to shop the 'finished' *Sandy & the Strawbs* album around a number of UK labels. Polydor had expressed an interest, but when they heard an actual test pressing, they decided its crude production values were no longer acceptable. Cousins believes, "they wanted us to re-record it, and Sandy said, 'Oh no'." If the prospect of rerecording the album was unpalatable, so was Cousins' alternative, a return to the world of budget, corner-cutting labels. Sandy passed again.*

---

*Ironically, when the album was eventually released in 1973, under the title *All Our Own Work*, it would be on a budget label, Hallmark, for whom it apparently sold some 60,000 copies.

Dave Cousins: In the end I ended up at Major Minor, 'cause they had the hits with the Dubliners and so on, and Major Minor said, "This is wonderful, we want to sign it," and Sandy said "Over my dead body! I really can't stand the idea of that lot." Somehow she'd heard they weren't quite what she wanted to be with. I was bitterly hurt at the time.

Quite possibly, Sandy's sights had been set somewhat higher by her brief taste of the world of Joe Boyd. It seems likely that a series of conversations they had upon Boyd's return from Newport had a direct bearing on her decision to nix the release of *Sandy & The Strawbs*, electing to return to the boards solo.

Joe Boyd: [Later] in that summer she handed me this white label pressing, which was different from the eventual release, the whole running order, but it was the memory of the test-pressing that led to me reconfiguring Sandy & The Strawbs [on CD] ... During that summer of '67 I got to know Sandy, and heard her record, and we discussed at some length her questions about what she was gonna do with herself. She felt that she'd gotten as far as she could go doing the circuit of folk clubs, and she liked the idea of being in a group, but she wasn't sure that the Strawbs were the right outfit for her. My surmise was that she was more ambitious than that. Dave thought she was great, but she was dubious. We talked about maybe I managing her, my producing a record with her. I think she asked me if I would like to produce a record of her, and I said, "Well, what's gonna happen with this record with the Strawbs. I don't wanna come out with a Sandy Denny record and have another Sandy Denny & the Strawbs record coming out competing. You gotta decide what you're gonna do."

The Danish sessions may have been consigned to the vaults, but a tape of Sandy's solo recording of 'Who Knows Where The Time Goes' found its way across the Atlantic, reaching American songstress Judy Collins, who proceeded to not only record the song for her own forthcoming album, but to make it the title track, generating a whole new level of interest in Sandy Denny the songwriter. By the time Collins' album was released, though, in November 1968, Sandy had found the ideal setting for her song/s.

Sandy would later insist that she longed to join a group simply because, "I wanted to do something more with my voice. Although I can play guitar adequately, I was feeling limited by it ... I always had it in my mind to join a group. [When] I joined the Strawbs ... I wasn't really ready for it." When interviewed for a feature in *Melody Maker* in September 1967, she was already talking about finding songs for the solo album she had discussed with Boyd, having seemingly taken one of Karl Dallas's earlier suggestions to heart.

Sandy Denny: I want songs that mean something to me. If they are folk songs, well okay. A lot of them are. But there are other songs that have something I want to say in them. I'm collecting material together now for my first solo album. I want it to really represent what I'm trying to do ... Of course, what I really want to sing is jazz. [1967]

There is precious little evidence in her home demos of someone who had made such a musical passage. If anything, Sandy was reimmersing herself in traditional song, recording British and Irish folk songs like 'Seven Virgins', 'She Moves Through The Fair', 'Come All Ye Fair & Tender Ladies' and 'The Quiet Land of Erin'. The only vestige of her previous exposure to Frank's contemporaries was a fine cover of Fred Neil's 'Little Bit of Rain'.

Perhaps Boyd's prejudices had already wormed their way into her psyche! If so, her sounder instincts remained unimpaired. As her fellow folkie, Val Berry, notes, "She had confidence in where she wanted to go. I always got the impression she knew what she wanted to do, and where she wanted to go with it." Those who only knew the ultra-confident young Sandy find that person hard to reconcile with the thirty-year-old Sandy, drained of all that assurance, and terrified of performing onstage. That person, though, was someway off. The twenty-year-old Sandy was prepared to learn what she could about 'making it' from any would-be scene-shaker, and so much the better if she could have a good time doing it.

John Renbourn: I used to see her around Soho occasionally, hanging out with various music business types – visiting different afterhours haunts. She seemed to be trying to get her career up a few rungs of the ladder ... Lot of those guys used to hang around the drinking clubs round in Soho, and there was a whole clique of them, all to do with music publishing and deals ... Sandy used to [like to] hobknob with that crowd.

In all likelihood, her interest in Boyd contained a measure of career-opportunism. Boyd himself admits as much, "She was [probably] initially intrigued to meet me because she'd probably heard about me." On the other hand, as Boyd soon realized, Sandy the opportunist would never have been able to countermand her more pointed self and, "she was very, very sharp. She had such little tolerance for boredom and for fools [that] if she had thought to herself it would be a good career move for me to bond with so and so, and they were tedious and boring, that determination would have lasted about five minutes." Linda Thompson concurs, "She *was* very ambitious, but she [really] didn't have any kind of methodical plan."

And yet, Sandy the folksinger seems to have found the whole apparatus of fame just as beguiling as any teenybopper. Part of the appeal was simply, as Maddy Prior observes, that "she liked hanging out. It was better champagne with the rock [fraternity] – and she *did* like the champagne!" When she enjoyed a midnight tryst with Frank Zappa, over with his Mothers of Invention to film a *Colour Me Pop* TV special, she breathlessly telegrammed Gina Glazer.

Gina Glazer: I had no phone, and the night she met Frank Zappa I got a telegram the next day from Sandy saying, "I'm in love, I'm in love." But she prefaced everything I'm in love, I wasn't supposed to take it seriously. It just meant she'd met someone, and especially since he was famous. [That] was her love-affair with Frank Zappa – about twelve hours.

Zappa was not alone. Her many liaisons, partially indicative of the times (and Sandy's age), suggested deeper insecurities. Given that it was those circling around the periphery of the music Biz that Sandy began to attach herself to (and detach herself from) with a certain regularity, she was bound to occasionally find herself catching her own reflection. One night, out on the town with Miranda Ward, pop correspondent and party animal, warranted an observation in her diary about "these American blokes [Miranda] dragged down with her to hear me ... [who] laughed a lot at my jokes, which made me suss them out pretty quick, for someone who's not much cop as a 'susser'." Still under 21, and alive to each and every new experience, her inner fears rarely bubbled to the surface.

Joe Boyd: [Though] she looked for reassurance about her female attractiveness constantly, which led to her having brief, romantic encounters with a lot of different people ... that was [also] part of her exploration of the whole music scene, having encounters. She was incredibly curious, and she wanted to know about everything.

That curiosity only further stoked a burning desire to make a first-hand contribution to the seismic shifts rippling through popular music. After almost nine months back on the circuit, playing further and further afield without finding a dent in folk's copper kettle, one simple twist of fate made all those dues worthwhile.

Karl Dallas has, over the years, been happy to take credit for 'introducing' Sandy Denny to Fairport Convention, one of Joe Boyd's small Witchseason roster. As he remembers it, "I had seen Fairport at the Middle Earth but I was quite remote from them … [and] I got this phone-call … and it said 'Hi, this is Fairport Convention … and we're looking for a girlsinger.' And I said, 'Only one name … comes immediately to mind – that's Sandy Denny.' And the person said, 'That's interesting. Because other people have made the same suggestion.'" Val Berry remembers it slightly differently. According to Berry, "Karl Dallas phoned me and said, "Val, they're auditioning for Fairport. Go." And I didn't." When it came to Sandy's audition, Sandy gave the credit for this precious chance to her friend Heather Wood, the Young Tradition's female singer.

> **Sandy Denny:** Heather Wood … said to me, "There's this great group and they're looking for a girl singer." It was just something to do at the time. I phoned up the bloke who was in charge of them, and he said why don't you come along and do an audition … They played to me and I played to them … They played me some of their tunes – blasting out all this electric music all over the place! But then they expected me to do something. [1972]

Heather Wood had no real connection with Witchseason, save that Ted Lloyd, Boyd's financial backer, was someone to whom she "was at one point married … and when Judy Dyble left, Steve Sparks came to me and said, 'Are you interested in singing with Fairport?' And I said, 'Well, I like the group but I'm singing with the Young Tradition. Why don't you ask Sandy Denny?'" Strangely enough, none of the members of Fairport Convention, even bandleader Ashley 'Tyger' Hutchings seems to have encountered a singing Sandy at this point, though Richard Thompson believes, "we'd … read about her in the *Melody Maker*." All parties, though, are agreed that Sandy's audition was as much of an audition for Fairport as for the brash female folksinger.

> **Ashley Hutchings:** I never saw Sandy once, till she walked into the pub where we were gonna have the so-called audition – which she ran. I'm pretty sure no-one had seen Sandy before – we were aware of her. It was [not] a conventional audition. Sandy's was just for Sandy, just to try [her] out. And she breezed in like only Sandy did, probably tripped over something, the whole place came alive with this big smile and this big personality, and the first thing she wanted to do was for us to play for her. So we played her a few things, and she liked them, and then we asked her to play something and she started to sing.

Fairport had been getting by for a year or so with a will o' the wisp female vocalist in the form of Judy Dyble. Though the addition of a male lead, in the guise of Ian Matthews, had already added some much needed substance, the difference between Denny and Dyble was night and day.

Sandy elected to sing 'You Never Wanted Me', one of her stronger songs, at the audition, and as Ashley puts it, "that was it. We didn't have to go into a huddle, we didn't even look at each other. There was a kind of a uniform understanding. I'm sure we didn't ask her to go out the room."

Guitarist Richard Thompson was so impressed that, when he found out "that night or the next, she [had] a gig at the Fiesta [on] Fulham Road," he "went down to hear her. She still sounded great."

5

1968: SANDY & THE MUSWELL HILLBILLIES

Angel woman – drawing by Sandy Denny.

"The music suddenly leapt up 100%. She was such a classy singer, it made the rest of us sound [so] much better." [PH]

Richard Thompson

Sandy Denny's membership established at least one pattern Fairport Convention would return to with a certain reckless regularity – the knack of ensuring that the line-up who recorded an album no longer existed when said album was released. Three of the first four albums bearing the Fairport name would be released by line-ups that existed only in the past tense. Their debut album was a particularly dubious concoction – not only was there very little on the self-titled effort to suit Sandy the Singer, even less warranted the effort.

Many a band has issued their debut album on the downturn from their early peak. Few have been offered the opportunity whilst still scrabbling up the hill backwards, unaware of their true strengths. Fairport, as in so many ways, proved just such an exception, essentially because they had been witnessed by the ever entrepreneurial Joe Boyd, whose enthusiasm for their potential, and need for a production roster, ensured a premature recording debut. It is worth remembering that Fairport had made their named debut less than a year before Sandy joined and, in the interim, had made an album and two singles, whilst passing through at least two line-up changes subsequent to its evolution out of an earlier quasi-skiffle combo, the Ethnic Shuffle Orchestra.

Ashley Hutchings: The Ethnic Shuffle Orchestra was a bunch of cronies from London, not necessarily Muswell Hill, and Simon Nicol was one of the [original] members. He had a 12-string at that time. It was just a fun group. There was a kazoo, acoustic guitar, washboard, upright bass. The Ethnic Shuffle Orchestra was kinda rag-time things and bluesy things. We seemed to practice more than anything else, in the front room of my house. Through that group, another group, which pulled in Richard [Thompson] and Judy Dyble, did a few gigs. We didn't really have a name. We did one or two gigs under stupid names ... There was probably an Exploding Something as a name. That was a bit more melodic – and folky. Changing into this group, it was more song-oriented. It was a little bit of Bob Dylan, some of the singer-songwriters, as well as folk songs, traditional folksongs – probably traditional American – [We'd do] the occasional pub gig or folk club floor spot but nothing more than that ... We got a drummer, Sean Frater, who did one or two gigs with us. The St. Michael's Hall Golders Green [gig on May 28, 1967] was the first gig we did under the name Fairport Convention, and Martin Lamble was in the very small audience. He was very precocious, and came up at the end and said, "I think I'm better than your drummer," and we actually took him at his word and gave him an audition. I felt we had a good group – it was now obviously rockier, and we were now doing quite strong Dylan numbers, and maybe even at that stage we might have been doing [Paul Butterfield's] 'East/West'. At that point I gave up my job, specifically to help push the band. For a time it was very tough. We were getting the odd third support at The Speakeasy, going on at three in the morning. And then Joe Boyd 'discovered' us. I think he heard a band that was away from the norm. Most people were doing extended, wanky kinda things. With one or two exceptions, we were performing short, very musical, densely lyrical songs, with proper solos and good singing.

Soon enough, Fairport acquired the tag of England's answer to Jefferson

Airplane. And in some senses they were – resembling the pre-Grace Slick band that recorded a patchy but impressive debut album, *Takes Off*, rather than the more famous *Surrealistic Pillows* line-up. Like that early Airplane, the early Convention lacked two things – a really strong singer and apposite material.

Initially, they were doing mostly covers of American singer-songwriters like Joni Mitchell, whose early demos Joe Boyd had acquired through his publishing contacts, Eric Andersen, Phil Ochs, Richard Farina &c. Drawing from the collections of two early friends of Fairport, Kingsley Abbott and Richard Lewis, bassist Ashley Hutchings recalls that, "we built up a repertoire which was pretty unique in that psychedelic period." And these were interesting times. In the days when imports were hard to come by, songwriters were often known by those who covered their songs rather than by their own interpretations. Such was the climate in which Fairport established an underground following.

Richard Lewis: There was a shop called One Stop in South Molton Street, and that got the new imports in. So I would get the new Phil Ochs or the new Eric Andersen from there. In fact, [with] the first Band LP, they only imported two copies and I bought one of those first two copies. I would have thought that the first place [Fairport] would have heard it would have been my copy. Ashley and Simon would come to my house in East Side Avenue and listen to my records, and I'd take my records round there and play them at Fairport.

Taken under Boyd's Witchseason wing, Fairport were immediately pushed into becoming "stronger and heavier." In the summer of 1967, Richard Lewis went to the States for a six-week period. On returning, with a whole chest of new albums from which to cull songs, he found that "they were already starting to transform themselves. They were already becoming much more polished."

If his memory serves him well, Boyd had an agenda from the off: to badger and cajole guitarist Richard Thompson into accepting more of the limelight; to bolster the band vocally; and to encourage them to rely more on their own resources. Despite the recruitment of Ian Matthews, from a rapidly imploding Trapeze, on vocals, and a number of earnest, early efforts from the pens of Richard and Ashley, the amalgam of styles made for a very disjointed debut album. And vocalist Judy Dyble remained an intractable problem.

The band may have visually benefited from a pretty, fey female but musically Dyble was way out of her depth and by April 1968, when Fairport flew to Europe to play a festival in Italy and perform three songs for French TV's *Bouton Rouge*, the cracks in the band's shopwindow had become all too apparent. Dyble's singing was sucking the air out of songs, no matter how much Thompson and co. pumped into them. On their return, the male members made their feelings known.

The fact that Fairport Convention went ahead and recruited a replacement singer whilst Boyd, their ostensible manager, producer and financier, had gone on one of his ubiquitous trips to the States may not have unduly fazed him. That it was a "pig-headed, chaotically intelligent" folksinger by the name of Sandy Denny, however, set alarm bells ringing.

> **Joe Boyd:** I felt she was temperamentally very, very different from them ... Sandy was a very loud, rather raucous person, with a broad and rather bawdy wit, sometimes a foul tongue, not known to be a cautious drinker. And Fairport at that time were very meek, polite, suburban youths and somehow I kept trying to picture Sandy with them. I was afraid that she was going to chew them up and spit them out for breakfast. [PH]

Even Sandy seems to have considered the possibility that this would not work out, initially keeping her options open by doing the occasional solo gig. Barely two months on from her recruitment, though, she was informing *Melody Maker* readers of the joys of being in a band, "Once you know what can be done with six people, and like the result, the simplicity and naiveness of one voice and a guitar is rather insipid ... [And there's] no more standing alone with your thoughts on draughty railway stations. In the group van there's always someone to talk to – or at – even if they are asleep." Sandy was prepared to admit that she was "the one who tends to get uptight. They watch me as an element on my own. They let me blow up, then cool down." Ashley Hutchings suggests that their approach was mostly borne of ignorance as to how to cope with a volatile, 'emotionally unstable' member of the opposite sex, rather than any great understanding on their part.

> **Ashley Hutchings:** We were a pretty young bunch, and pretty inexperienced in the big wide world. It was also a time when it was hip not

to communicate – to wear dark glasses and mumble on about philosophy – and I know that affected our band. [We could all be] willfully difficult. And she just came in, like a twister, and blew us away – and probably opened us out as a band ... One of the many things she did was blow away some of this intensity, knock us off our pedestals a bit ... She had a temper, we didn't have tempers ... Had we been more worldly we might have been able to handle better her difficult moments. We didn't know how to handle it, we just had to let this hurricane blow out, and then just carried on. [But] there was nothing horrific about her.

Those close to Sandy often learnt the hard way just how intimidating this petite but feisty female powerhouse could be. Her late husband Trevor Lucas, a week before his own death, remembered Sandy as "in many ways an extreme person, who inevitably tended to get her own way most of the time. And she had an ability to put the shits into most people when they first encountered her. Most people realised almost as soon as they met Sandy that you ... [must] be precise: don't bullshit her around. She didn't tolerate fools easily."

Linda Thompson concurs, whilst pointing out the historical context, "This was before it became the norm to have women in bands, so [Sandy] was unusual. If you asked the drummer to play a little faster, they'd look at you as if to say, 'What do you know?'" Not with Sandy they didn't. An entry in her diary, from the winter of 1969, hints at some underlying tensions, "I felt quite pleased to be pleased [sic] to finish singing. For one thing that night I'd had a ghastly row with [Fairport roadie] Harvey about the monitor which wasn't there, and we both threw moodies all evening, but it was alright later."

Initially, though, her input into the Fairport set-up was undoubtedly positive. She sounded like she'd been in the band from its very first ethnic shuffle – and in less time than it took a worried Boyd to conclude his business in America, and catch a plane back to London.

Joe Boyd: I got back [from America] and went to a rehearsal and it was obvious that it had all worked incredibly well ... She may have just joined the group because she wanted a bigger vehicle for her songs, and just to learn about being in rock, and getting out of the folk world but ... I definitely felt a tremendous release of energy in both Sandy and Richard. It was musical love at first sight. I think that they had an incredibly stimulating effect on each other, and the group was all involved and caught up in that process. She said to me at one point, very early on, [something] to the effect of, "Jesus Christ, what a fucking genius." ... [But] she would have grabbed him by the scruff of the neck and shaken him and said, C'mon, I want more, more, more ... She was like a bomb. She wouldn't have been prepared to settle for anything [less than his best] ... [Richard] and Sandy were completely opposite personalities, and yet I think they both had huge respect, one for the other. Sandy was finally a real foil [for him].

Having auditioned for the vocalist slot the second week in May 1968, Sandy was playing her first gig with Fairport, at their home away from home, the Middle Earth, on the 20th and, a week later, was in the BBC's radio studios at Maida Vale recording her first *Top Gear* session with her new musical bedfellows. Of course, a BBC session was nothing new to Sandy, who was already booked for a solo session a month later on *My Kind of Folk* (at which she sang 'The Quiet Land of Erin' and Alex Campbell's 'Been On The Road').

Fairport Convention had also already made appearances on John Peel's legendary *Top Gear* radio show, as well as Radio One's *David Symonds Show*. Peel had even felt compelled to give their debut single, the pop oddity 'If I Had A Ribbon Bow', a few airings. In an era when bands were expected to supplement the Musician Union's permitted rote of 'needle-time' with live sessions, BBC sessions were an opportunity to try out ideas and explore new directions.

For most bands, a new singer might have been deemed enough of an innovation for a *Top Gear* radio session. Not so, Fairport. The five songs they recorded the afternoon of May 28, at Maida Vale, included just one song, Joni Mitchell's 'I Don't Know Where I Stand', from the already redundant debut album Polydor planned to issue in another month's time. It also offered a preview of what the music papers reported was to be Fairport's next single, the Everly Brothers' 'Some Sweet Day'. However, it was two songs suggested by Sandy that showed the immediacy of the lady's impact – her 'audition' song, Jackson Frank's 'You Never Wanted Me', which had been cleverly rearranged to accomodate Sandy and Ian Matthews, both vocalists still learning when to ease themselves back into the musical flow; and one of the most mysterious of those traditional ritual songs, the truly murky 'Nottamun Town':

"In Nottamun Town not a soul would look up,

Not a soul would look up, not a soul would look down,
Not a soul would look up, not a soul would look down,
To show me the way to fair Nottamun Town.

Met the king and queen, and a company more,
Come walking behind, and riding before,
Come a stark naked drummer a-beating his drum,
With his hands on his bosom, come marching along.
Sat down on a hard, cold frozen stone
Ten thousand stood 'round me, yet I was alone.
Took my hat in my hands for to keep my head warm
Ten thousand got drownded that never was born."

Quite. 'Nottamun Town' must have startled many a Fairport fan listening to its inaugural broadcast, the weekend of June 2. Firstly, it was the first time the band had recorded a traditional song. Secondly, it was a song whose meaning was almost entirely impenetrable. And, thirdly, the arrangement was startlingly ambitious, as if Thompson was raising the stakes on his two true rivals in folk's guitar-God stakes, Bert Jansch and Davy Graham – both of whom he had caught at "all-nighters at Les Cousins" – by making the song almost raga-rock. Both had already tackled 'Nottamun Town' on memorable indeed groundbreaking albums, Davy Graham back in 1964 when, along with Shirley Collins, he had attempted a grand alliance of folk tunes and middle-eastern tunings on *Folk Roots, New Routes*, and Jansch on his equally innovative 1966 collection, *Jack Orion*. Both performances were known to the Fairport collective, as was Dylan's 'Masters of War', also based on the same original template, Jean Ritchie's original Fifties recording. Ashley Hutchings is sure that he and Simon Nicol already knew Ritchie's original.

Indeed, Ashley and co. knew many of the songs Sandy now introduced to the band, "We weren't novices when it came to any of these music forms. In many cases, we knew authentic versions from our youth." Richard Thompson vividly recalls, at the end of the session at Maida Vale, Ashley turning to him and saying, "At last that's something that we can be proud of." Thompson, too, felt that "we had actually waxed something that was worthwhile – even though it was only BBC mono. It just had some real quality to it." Ashley still remembers the feeling.

Ashley Hutchings: I felt up until that stage we were a local group who were trying to break out, be bigger than our boots. But when Sandy came we had that stamp of authority, and I felt we could achieve anything.

Karl Dallas, who may well have caught the first show of the new line-up, also immediately recognised how easily Sandy now slipped into her long-awaited niche.

Karl Dallas: The first concert where I saw her and Ian Matthews, they stood on opposite sides of the stage – and Ashley Hutchings was wearing his 'gaters – and it just blew me away ... I realized that I'd been right and wrong – right that singing solo in a folk club was not where [Sandy] was destined for, but wrong in thinking that it would be as a jazz singer.

Boyd, too, began to get excited about a band that had previously seemed almost a token addition to the Witchseason roster. Having signed a band destined to make pleasant records, "but [was] not actually going anywhere," he found "Richard writing new songs, in a way probably stimulated and challenged by Sandy, [as well as] the first steps in various directions ... real interesting steps, rather than just lack of direction." Fairport's reinvention also presented Boyd with a conundrum. He simply did not have the time to handle the daily travails of this newly-energized unit. Turning to another old friend from the Troubadour days, he asked her to hold some hands.

David Sandison: Anthea [Joseph] was working for EMI in Dublin and Joe called her and said, "Look, I need help at Witchseason. I've taken on Fairport Convention, and I need some help." So he flew her over from Dublin and when she arrived, she discovered that Sandy was the lead singer and nearly backed out ... because Sandy, when she'd last seen her, was fairly lightweight, artistically anyway, and she said, "Oh God, this is not going to work." She'd seen early Fairport with Judy Dyble ... [But] they were a revelation, and Sandy was a revelation. In the [period] since she'd last seen her, Sandy had just become Sandy – she wasn't trying to be anybody else, she wasn't trying to copy anyone else, she was just doing what she wanted, her way. I think [Anthea] saw them at the UFO Club, and at the end of it, she said to Joe, "Right, I'm on."

Hutchings' assessment, that Sandy "probably opened us out as a band," qualifies as something of an understatement. Thompson, in particular, now found himself ushered into the limelight. In the early days, journalist Colin Irwin recalls, "He'd be standing right at the back, in the shadows, and often would even be playing into the side. This amazing guitar solo would come in, [and it'd be] who's doing that? You'd suddenly see this shadowy figure at the back." Sandy also dispensed with the self-conscious introductions that had been Simon Nicol's sorry task. Richard Lewis, who had seen all the band's sea-changes first hand, noticed immediately that, "on stage they were much more confident ... When Sandy came along, here was someone who not only was happy to introduce, but would crack jokes as well, or collapse laughing in the middle of an introduction. When everybody saw that this was okay, and you could do this, everyone became [much] more relaxed."

Just a single four-song set at the Festival Hall in September, and a five-song performance on Dutch TV from the same month, provide audio documentation of the six-piece Fairport in full flight. On both, though, there is an edge lacking from the early *Top Gear* shows and first album. Fairport's extraordinary rearrangement of Leonard Cohen's 'Suzanne', ebbing and flowing right upto the moment Lamble's stacatto drumming turns the tide, was first performed for the BBC that August, but the song really came into its own at the Festival Hall, as did a nine-minute 'Reno Nevada'. On the same bill was Joni Mitchell, on her first trip to the UK. If Fairport wisely refrained from interpreting any of Joni's songs that night, the contrast between Joni's stage persona and Sandy's could not have been starker.

Joe Boyd: [Sandy] was a real handful, [but] her manner on stage was a fumbling with her guitar strings, and tripping over wires and laughing at her own clumsiness, and making off-hand, off the cuff, very funny one-liners, and making mistakes but laughing about them [while] maintaining a dialogue with the audience. She certainly wasn't somebody who got up there on stage [with] her long hair hanging over her face, and didn't look at the audience. That just wasn't Sandy at all.

Having such a big personality fronting the band, though, was bound to have its downside, and even in the early days it occasionally manifested itself in performance. As Hutchings suggests, "She *was* the drinker in the band and that occasionally led to erratic performances. If she was under the weather, [the voice] would suffer." Bernard Doherty remembers one show at the Roundhouse, with bottles of brandy visible on the piano, when she was clearly the worse for wear.

Sandy admits to another occasion in her diary, when her desire to emulate one of her heroes went a little far, "I was feeling a bit strained ... probably on account of the mixture of gin and Southern Comfort which I'd decided to experiment with to see if I too could produce the shattered effects which Janis Joplin seems to acquire as a result of drinking it. No, I really must say I didn't like it. I thought it tasted like apricot brandy, and I had only about three or so, just to make sure I didn't like it, but I did have a few gins and a couple of glasses of wine." This was prodigious consumption by anyone's standards, least of all a physically slight, twenty-one-year-old gal. In the early days, though, Fairport had someone on hand who knew exactly how to handle the high-strung singer.

David Sandison: Anthea had to pour black coffee down her throat on more than one occasion ... Anthea was the only person who ever told her she was being a complete prick and a selfish brat, and Sandy knew that. So Sandy would be chastened and would straighten herself out for a couple of days, and then get naughty again. She adored Anthea.

Anthea was the subject of one of Sandy's earliest efforts for Fairport. The song in question evolved out of some scribblings about someone (Anthea's name has been visibly scratched out) whose "smile is beautiful" and whose "tears will make me cry as well." The narrator "dreamed she met a wonderful man called Neddy, although I know his name is Pat and he lives in Ireland." Soon enough, she had penned three verses that, in spirit and style, would lead on to the more realized 'Pond and the Stream' (also sketched out in the same notebook):

"How does she bear to have no phone
To dig the garden all stone
And smile, although she's on her own
I know she loves someone who lives in Ireland.

When she smiles she's beautiful
And when she cries, I cry as well
To see her sad is so unusual
I know she thinks of one who lives in Ireland.

She lives within the city boundaries
And walks for miles alone among the trees
I often wonder what she sees
Perhaps the quiet land of Ireland."

In its original draft, Sandy ponders why, "She works so often and so hard/ I wonder that she never tires/ and also how she finds the patience/ to deal with a motley bunch of scruffs like us." The dreadful insecurities that were to increasingly plague Sandy were often held in check by Anthea Joseph, whose size and demeanour was usually enough to cowe Ms. Denny.

Being a good girl did not always come easily. As Linda Thompson confirms, Sandy would never allow her sex to make her into a lesser citizen, "She wouldn't let the boys dominate her. She could be difficult herself. She could really take over. Then the next minute she'd display a total lack of self-confidence." That sudden pressure drop in confidence has been commented on by many, and may already suggest the rapid mood swings alcohol was wont to engender. It was usually only after the exhilaration of performing that the crash came, but when it came, her mood-swing would be visible to all.

Richard Lewis: However she was feeling, you could tell [immediately]. When she was happy, she was happy. When she wasn't happy, she let you know it, and everyone else know it, so you knew when to be there. Or not. If I ever went backstage to Middle Earth, and you could see that Sandy wasn't happy, it wasn't a good place to be. But when she was happy, everything was fantastic. She was such an exuberant personality. When you heard her laugh, you really knew here was somebody laughing ... Sometimes she was sure that she could do everything, but sometimes she didn't believe in herself [at all].

Ensuring that the times when Sandy was "sure that she could do everything" outnumbered the times when "she didn't believe in herself" was Anthea's role on the road, and Joe Boyd's in the studio. But everybody in the Witchseason 'family' played their part in keeping the ship on course. In joining Fairport, Sandy was the most obvious beneficiary of a 'hands-on' management team. It was a unique set-up, and though it may have ultimately proved financially disastrous, it was the perfect artistic environment for a set of young, naive musicians looking to conquer the world by stealth.

Ashley Hutchings: I don't think we asked [Joe] a single question about money in the first year or two we worked together, which later in life was a cause of great disruption and bad feeling. [But] we didn't care. We were young and we were making the music we wanted, and as long as we got our ten pound a week we were quite happy. So we did put a lot of trust in Joe. And he looked after us. He took care of all that, and let us get on with the music ... Though we were making it up as we went along, that is the way to do it. Joe took all that off our hands. He would offer opinions, in the studio in particular, but he didn't interfere, even as producer of the records. His style of production was just to create the right atmosphere in the studio and very, very occasionally gently suggest [something], here and there. And then [to use] very simple, natural sounds, make sure the vocals were nice and clear ... We needed a little bit of time to find our own way. We didn't take long.

Anthea Joseph's description of the Witchseason office, to Patrick Humphries, shortly before her death – "It was one of those Georgian houses, you went up a rickety staircase, you came to our floor. Joe had an office ... I had an office, then we had a sort of open-space bit which people congregated in ... there was very little furniture, and everything came off the back of a lorry ... People spent a great deal of time sitting on the floor" – reflected the slightly ramshackle nature of Witchseason itself, which had grown from a production company into a production/publishing company into a management company, almost by default. Indeed, rather against it's instigator's intentions.

Joe Boyd: I just wanted to be a record producer. And then I found myself continually in the trap – I recorded [the Incredible String Band] for Elektra, and it became clear that there was no-one in Britain who saw their potential ... When I left Elektra, the first thing I was gonna do was [the] UFO [club], which was gonna give me some cashflow. And then the ISB asked me to manage them. The same thing happened with Fairport. In the end, Witchseason took over the management, and I hired Anthea Joseph ... Management, my deal was I took 25% of profit[s only], which there never was much, but on recordings the original deal was that we split 50-50 the recording income. And the publishing was the same, which by todays standards is hard cheese on the artists. The fundamental problem was that the records didn't sell. Taking Fairport, and Sandy, everybody got a weekly salary, and all the money came into a pot, and when the pot had more money in it, we'd increase the weekly salary, and then when windfalls came in, there would be bonuses, and that system worked fine for a while. As long as the group was full of nice, well brought up, middle-class people, there was never really any problem with it.

The precarious juggling act of a set-up at Witchseason was doubtless a factor in Fairport being quite so many records in these years. Post-*Pepper*, many bands had begun to baulk at the two-albums-a-year demands of record labels. How could Artists be expected to work under such constraints! For Fairport, and Witchseason, however, each album continued to be made relatively cheaply and, because the band's contract was with Witchseason Productions, not Polydor (for the first album) or Island (for subsequent albums), each album generated its own advance from the record company, as well as having the potential to crack the charts.

The fundamental problem, as Boyd points out, is that the records didn't sell. This would only become a problem in the fullness of time, when the Island record company began to refuse albums, or delay their release. As of the late sixties, Chris Blackwell's fledgling label was more than happy to put out all that Witchseason had to offer, particularly as Boyd had cross-collateralized the artists on his roster so that the losses of the Fairports and Nick Drakes were effectively subsidized by the success of the Incredible String Band.

Having been left to "get on with the music", Fairport's direction was increasingly propelled by a duel force. Sandy's inclinations had quickly moved into alignment with guitar-prodigy Richard Thompson's. The result was a whole set of songs from Thompson's pen that seemed tailored to Sandy's demands. Ashley 'Tyger' Hutchings, the ostensible leader and founder of Fairport was initially delighted by the new energy, and still remembers "the turnover of material at that period, 1968. [It] was incredible. I mean, we would learn new songs and perform them on stage almost weekly. I have never been in a band since that has done that."

Subtly, but surely, Sandy's folk bias was warping the band's heretofore American leanings, the singer-songwritery aspects of their sets gradually being superceded by original songs and/or material culled from these fayre isles. Aside from 'Nottamun Town', the band quickly worked up an arrangement of 'She Moved Through The Fair', a quasi-traditional song (the words being penned by Padraic Colum) that had been a perennial in Sandy's solo repertoire, having probably been acquired via her father from the famous Irish tenor John McCormack, who had made the song popular in the Forties. In the November 1968 issue of *Beat Instrumental*, Richard Thompson was keen to distance the band from any previous tag:

> **Richard Thompson:** There are similarities [between Fairport & West Coast bands] ... but there's one big and basic difference. They all seem to be doing a sort of cross between rock and soul – look at Big Brother, Country Joe and Jefferson Airplane – it's not all that far from the sock-it-to-me thing, and very American. We think of ourselves as a folk-based band. This is even more pronounced now that Sandy Denny is with us ... She really knows what the folk tradition is all about.

The force was now with Sandy, as she pushed the band in a more "folk-based" direction. Aside from Thompson, whose musical tastes remained admirably eclectic, Simon Nicol, by his own admission, "used to go up to the Saturday night folk evenings at Cecil Sharp House and see people like Alex Campbell, Shirley Collins, Ewan MacColl, real stalwarts ... before – even in the most vague terms – I was thinking of myself as a musician, just soaking up live music." Hutchings, too, had doused himself in the same pool, venturing down to the Cousins "one memorable night [when] there was Paul Simon, Phil Ochs, Danny Kalb, Bert Jansch all getting up one after another." Just as willing to immerse himself in the real thing, having been for a time a regular at Ewan MacColl's Singers Club, Ashley insists that, even though "people think we discovered traditional folk music [in 1969], it wasn't true, we went *back* to it."

The passing of Fairport into the folk camp clearly appalled some of those for whom Dylan's 1966 electric tour had not been a necessary apotheosis. One unregenerate 'Tradie' wrote a bitter letter to *Melody Maker* complaining at the addition of Fairport to a 'folk concert' bill in July, sharing the bill with Julie Felix:

> *"I would like to express my horror of the Folk Concert put on at the Central Hall, Westminster by the commitee of Human Rights Year. We were subjected to a neo-pop group called Fairport Convention. In the second half there were people walking out, and a group [that] gave us twenty minutes of just noise." – R.E. Browne,* MM *3/8/68.*

Also sharing the bill that night was Al Stewart, who remembers coming off after his own set and going "into the dressing-room, [where] they were all sitting around, physically working out a new song that they'd (sic) just written, which it turned out was 'Fotheringay'." Sandy's first contribution to the pool of original songs, 'Fotheringay', was one of a number of songs she had previously penned for a possible solo album. However, it had taken her a couple of months to muster the nerve to throw one of her own hoops into the ring, and compete with the songs of Richard and, at the time, Ashley. 'Fotheringay' itself is a masterful reworking of her earlier 'Boxful of Treasures', centering upon the imprisonment of Mary, Queen of Scots. However, knowledge of its historical setting and/or subject-matter is hardly required to respond to this song of permanent exile, from its oppressive opening:

"How often she has gazed from castle walls o'er,
And watched the daylight passing, within her captive wall,
With no-one to heed her call."

to that evocative final verse:

"Tomorrow at this hour she will be far away,
Much farther than these islands,
Or the lonely Fotheringay."

And yet, despite the originality of her themes and the musicality of her melodies, Sandy proved a reluctant contributor to the repertoire. Never one to pen her own throwaway street puzzle, Sandy worked long and hard on the songs she wrote and, as Dave Swarbrick recalls, "she did many, many rewrites before she'd let it out."

Ashley Hutchings: Sandy wrote very few songs in the time that we were working together and when she did write a song, she would lock herself away for a day or two, not answer the phone, not doing anything. I remember Anthea saying, "Oh, you can't get her at the moment, she's in the throes of the muse." Which meant you couldn't ring her up for the next two days. But she probably found it very painful to write.

By the time Sandy had overcome an innate self-consciousness about presenting herself as a songwriter, the sessions for her debut platter with Fairport were all but over. Though 'Fotheringay' would announce the album on its release, she would have to wait until the next album to bring more hidden pearls to the surface.

The album Fairport were recording that summer was quite different from the shows and radio sessions they had been performing, for which Joe Boyd says he is prepared "to take part of the blame." As he confessed, in his own notes to the official release of Hutchings' *Heyday* compilation of BBC tapes, "I felt the Fairport should use their considerable talents in developing their own material and becoming as, well, English as possible. Thus I discouraged committing most of [these] songs to vinyl back in ... 1968." Ashley has a different take on why so many staples from their live/radio repertoire failed to be recorded in the studio.

> **Ashley Hutchings:** We did a lot of radio sessions and we didn't want to repeat ourselves, so we'd just go in and do different songs, maybe songs we'd just do for radio and never do 'em again – it doesn't happen nowdays. I ... put together the Heyday tape because I was proud of the stuff.

From their endlessly evolving live set, Fairport would use just two non-originals on *What We Did On Our Holidays*: a quietly understated cover of Dylan's 'I'll Keep It With Mine', that showed the twin towers of Denny and Thompson at their interpretative bests, retaining none of Nico's discordancy; and another of Joni's word-schemes, 'Eastern Rain'. Superceding the likes of 'Reno Nevada', 'Bird On The Wire' and 'Morning Glory' were some five Thompson originals – including Fairport's come-all-ye anthem 'Meet On The Ledge', which was issued as a single, as well as being featured on Island various artists sampler, *You Can All Join In*. Along with the remorselessly bitter 'Tale In Hard Time' and three more examples of Thompson's die-cut doom & gloom, Ashley's stomping 'Mr Lacey', Sandy's one example of penmanship, and the two samples of 'tradition', they had a beguilingly different take on the direction Rock might take from other members of Island's soft centre of excellence.

Though engineer John Wood remembers "the atmosphere at the beginning of the record [being] a little easier than it was at the end," and that, "it was very much the band in transition," *What We Did On Our Holidays* was an audacious advance on *Fairport Convention.* Boyd remembers a sense of quiet camaraderie, "We were all in it together, and everybody had their say. A very egalitarian atmosphere." The album, finished in mid-October, would not be released until the new year, by which time the band would have undergone another change in line-up. Meanwhile, it gave enough hints as to their potential on a number of fronts – notably Thompson's richly detailed songwriting and Sandy's seemingly effortless singing.

And yet, such was the pace with which Fairport were developing that the album version of 'Mr Lacey' sounds like little more than a demo when contrasted with the blistering roustabout of a performance on a December 1968 BBC session (later included on the Richard Thompson double-album anthology, *Guitar/Vocal*). The few flaws in *What We Did On Our Holidays* may well stem from that "egalitarian atmosphere," and could be what Wood is alluding to when he hints at problems towards the end of the sessions. The weaker songs, the weaker arrangements were being made to rest on Ian Matthews, not because he was a weak singer, as Dyble had been, but because the songs that suited him vocally reflected a Fairport Convention the remainder of the band no longer seemed intent on preserving ('The Book Song', Matthews' one co-credit on the album, being a case in point). With Sandy's growth as a singer and personality, Matthews' role was accordingly reduced. He was also the one personality in the band less than enamored by the passage into a "folk-based band." All but sidelined, he was about to be sidestepped.

6

1969: COME ALL YE ROVING MINSTRELS

Lucas lookalike in long grass – drawing by Sandy Denny.

"There was a feeling in the industry in general, and in Britain in particular, in the rock group world, that long, extended tracks were kind of an indulgence and that they disqualified you from getting played on the radio. The Pink Floyd used to do a version of 'Arnold Layne' that went on for ten minutes, but when we recorded it, we did a three minute version. Most songs were like that ... There was definitely a feeling at the time that recordings were supposed to be compact. That if you'd heard a track with Richard playing five choruses as a solo, you would then go into the studio and record him compressing the best ideas from those five choruses into one ... [Part of] the artistic success of Unhalfbricking is that it started to occupy the space on record that the group occupied live."

Joe Boyd

However much *What We Did On Our Holidays* advanced on *Fairport Convention*, it remained as unrepresentative of the band's live performances as *Piper at the Gates of Dawn*. The difference was that Floyd had at least attempted to place their key extemporisation, 'Interstellar Overdrive', in studio captivity, signalling an increasingly beguiling direction. How much the ideas behind a song like 'Interstellar Overdrive' inspired the rookies from Muswell Hill, who shared many a '67 bill at the UFO with the now commercially consolidated Floyd, has never been documented. The Floyd's audible evolution from a simple blues band to psychedelia's cutting-edge, bound up with that one song, surely affected the fledgling Fairporters, even if Thompson says, "What Floyd did was beyond us."

Ashley may have defined early Fairport sets as comprising "short, very musical, densely lyrical songs, with proper solos and good singing," but at the UFO they were also prone to working their way through their own take on Paul Butterfield's epic 'East/West', until it evolved into something called 'Ghetto'. Fairport also had, in its backpocket, an increasingly outlandish ten-minute take on Richard Farina's 'Reno Nevada' that survived the Sandy transition, flowering in the hot-room of Thompson's burgeoning self-confidence. So it was to prove with another song Sandy brought to the welcome table, early in the new year of '69. 'A Sailor's Life', though, was a folk song, and folk songs were surely not instruments of change, but of stasis.

Ashley Hutchings: Sandy sang folksongs in dressing rooms, and that's specifically how 'Sailor's Life' came about. She would sing songs and we might just come pick up our instruments and join in. A good example is 'She Moves Through The Fair'. Exactly the same as how we ended up doing 'A Sailor's Life' – except 'Sailor's Life' developed more. It came like a bolt out of the blue for most people but if you logically trace it, it can be traced to those [earlier improvised] things. It was surprisingly easy for us to fall into. It sounded right. Otherwise we wouldn't have gone onstage and done it ...[ ] ... We were at Southampton University waiting to go on stage and Sandy was playing around in the dressing room and picked up the guitar, and ... sang 'A Sailor's Life' ... we picked up our instruments and joined in. We had a little tuner amp in the dressing room and we busked along and then, when it came time to go on stage, we made an instant decision [to play it]. [CH/PH]

'A Sailor's Life' entered modern consciousness with its inclusion – from an 1899 East Sussex transcription – in the original 1959 edition of the hugely successful *Penguin Book of English Folk Songs*, certainly one of the gospels of the

English folk revival, if not its very Bible. An offshoot of the ubiquitous 'Died For Love', it had already been memorably captured by Martin Carthy on his second Topic album, and it was presumably this template that Sandy sang that night in Southampton. Unlike the likes of 'Nottamun Town' and 'She Moves Through The Fair', though, 'Sailor's Life' lent itself to a more brooding, elastic arrangement. Even in the university dressing room the tragic tale began to take on grander proportions.

As Sandy herself later observed, "the actual story, the sea, and the turbulence of both were perfect for that medium. You can't do that with everything ... It begins to pall after a while." What Fairport came up with that night, and refined over the ensuing weeks, was an approach unique in folk circles, that gave a musical momentum to the inevitable balladic fate of the two lovers, something not previously attempted within folk *or* rock. The results convinced five-sixths of the band that this could be their new direction home, and one member that it was time to ride.

Ian Matthews: The first time we did 'A Sailor's Life' onstage, I remember they worked it up in the dressing-room, and I had never worked up in the dressing room in my life, it had always been done at rehearsal. That was my first foray into it, and it didn't appeal to me at all. I think it became increasingly clear that there was really no place for me in a band playing that type of music. [PH]

The remainder of Fairport clearly recognised the import of what they had unveiled, evidenced by the fact that they uncharacteristically summoned their manager-cum-producer to a gig in Bristol to hear the results.

Joe Boyd: Before my trip down to Bristol, they told me that there was a new tune that they wanted me to hear. I drove down with Beverly Martyn and I sat in the balcony and they did 'A Sailor's Life'. I went back to the dressing room afterwards and told them I thought it was fantastic, let's record it. And then at some point ... they came to me and said, "We'd like to try it with a violin, something like a Dave Swarbrick." I said, "[Fine,] I'll call him up."

On the basis of a recently discovered acetate, it would appear that Sandy, Richard, Simon, Ashley and Martin made their first attempt to record 'A

Sailor's Life' without either the mighty Swarb or a disgruntled Ian Matthews. Doubtless it was this first draft of 'A Sailor's Life' that Matthews was alluding to when he says he "went along with ... do[ing] traditional things ... until it came to a point where they arranged a session to do a traditional thing, and didn't tell me, which was going a bit far." Though Matthews would not have to be formally asked to leave the band, jumping before he was pushed, it was, in Ashley's words, "just resoundingly obvious that once we tackled material like that, that Ian wouldn't fit in ... Ian came from a pop background. Once we started 'Sailor's Life', his days were numbered. We didn't need to discuss it ... You couldn't go back to singing Eric Andersen songs after that."

This first version of 'A Sailor's Life' features an unfettered Thompson for the first time in the studio, pummelling his guitar all the way back to Reno, Nevada. None of the chief participants, though, seem to recall the session in question and, were it not for its inclusion on the 1993 Richard Thompson boxed-set *Watching The Dark*, might continue to insist it never occured. The *Unhalfbricking* version, recorded at a later session – an equally remarkable performance – with Dave Swarbrick sawing away in tandem with a refettered Richard, seems to have obliterated all previous attempts from the collective consciousness of bandleader, producer *and* engineer.

Ashley Hutchings: The memory I have of 'Sailor's Life' is Olympic Studios, Dave Swarbrick, everyone sitting round, live, Sandy with a cold, one take, silence, Wow! That's it. I really don't know what [the other take] is. I haven't listened to it carefully ... it could possibly be a warm-up that Swarbrick sat and listened to. Maybe we played it for him, and they put the machines on.

Joe Boyd: The 'Sailor's Life' that's on the record is first take with Swarbrick – the first take that day. What we found on this acetate, which I have absolutely no memory of ever making, is clearly an attempt to record it without Swarbrick, and where we did it and when and why, I have no idea ... All I remember is that day at Olympic with Swarbrick where we did 'Si Tu Dois Partir' and 'Sailor's Life'.

John Wood: 'Sailor's Life' was extraordinary. Richard and Sandy came in and said, "We really think we can only do this once." They'd already got Dave Swarbrick in to play on it ... It was done in the old Olympic One, a big room. We put Sandy in a vocal booth and everybody else in a big semi-circle. When you want to cut that sort of track, it's not easy for people to work if it's all sectioned off, so it was very open and that was it, one take, done. No overdubs ... [One] afternoon, early evening. [JI]

Swarb's presence proved to be no hindrance. Indeed, his drafting in for this single session, has, with hindsight, become seen as indicative of a general push towards the folk nexus. And the impetus for the temporary recruitment of Swarb certainly came from within the band, presumably from Sandy, though they were slightly taken aback when Ashley asked him, "Do you like playing electric music?" and Swarb said, "No." What the partially deaf Swarb had thought he'd said was, "Do you mind playing electric music?" In fact, Swarbrick was as bowled over by the experience as the rest of the musicians: "I thought ['A Sailor's Life'] was magnificent. I didn't need persuading that this was a way to go. I'd been looking for something like this for a long time, sub-consciously." His time would come. According to Thompson, "Ashley ... was talking about a whole album of trad. material as early as *Unhalfbricking* – once Swarb came in, and he saw the possibilities."

For the moment, though, the remainder of the album Fairport were recording was given over to new songs from Sandy and Richard and a slew of old Dylan ditties, a not so radical departure from the just released *What We Did On Our Holidays*, even as Sandy and Richard raised their songwriting to a new pitch that augured well for an all original Fairport album somewhere down the line. One of Thompson's two contributions, 'Genesis Hall', suggested that he was already looking to apply traditional resonances to modern life, its opening couplet suggesting something a tad more timeless than the eviction of a bunch of squatters: "My father he rides with your sherrifs/And I know he would never mean harm." But it was Sandy the songwriter who conveyed the album's two strongest cuts to the sidemen.

Her fellow Fairporters seem not to have known about 'Who Knows Where The Time Goes' until the news filtered down that it was about to become the title-track on Judy Collins' latest platter. Richard Thompson says, "Sandy played me [the song] up at her flat on the top floor in Gloucester Road. I'd never heard the Strawbs version. This must be 1968." Absent from all the many radio sessions in 1968, it is only with the *Top Gear* debut of the five-piece Fairport on February 4, 1969, that the song received a documented outing. Duly convinced of its merits, the boys temporarily tethered Sandy's mock worldliness to its most appropriate arrangement, courtesy of Thompson's intercession between singer and song.

Legend also allows RT credit for transposing Sandy's 'Autopsy' from 4/4 to 5/4 time. In fact, Sandy herself had made a habit of transposing songs into 5/4 time (as she had for Alex Campbell's 'Been On The Road So Long' for a BBC session). The acoustic demo she recorded of 'Autopsy', as a guide for the band, also finds itself outside common-time, on what is a startlingly original piece of penmanship, dissecting a relationship whilst its cadaver remains warm, even as the song lurches into a contradistinct signature:

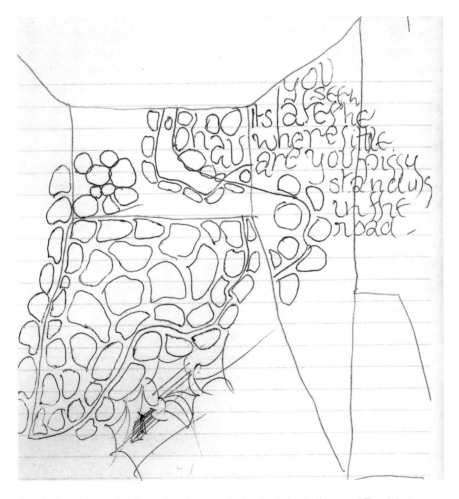

Doodle found in Sandy's journal on the page facing the lyrics to 'Now and Then' that may contain a coded message in the top right-hand corner.

"When you look at me
Don't think you're owning what you see,
For remember that you're free
And that's what you want to be.
So just lend your time to me."

Sandy's demo, on first hearing, smacks into one's ears. The whole vocal has a bite lacking on *Unhalfbricking*. Showing a side rarely heard, 'Autopsy' illustrated a woman capable of great bitterness. The song's subject remains a mystery, though her father said it was "about a girl that was always telling her troubles." It stands in marked contrast to the other demo Sandy recorded for the band's consideration on the penultimate day of 1968. Her search in her personal life for something solid enough to consign previous liasons, and the insecurities they unlocked, to the memory banks now came out in the form of 'Now and Then'.

As it appears originally in her notebook, it seems clear that 'Now and Then' was intended to be some kind of 'Parting Glass'/'Restless Farewell'. Though the song begins and ends by looking at how past affairs impinge on her current feelings, the bridge ended up being significantly reworked. In the rewriting process, the portrait of the man Now in her life, "smiling as no lips can do," has been carefully refined, and some old doubts – "let me know when it is that you must go" – coaxed into the first-person:

[draft lyrics]	*[final version of bridge]*
"They've past me by – many years,	
And I did stand well away,	
To give and lose love,	
And still no word had I to say,	
Not to anyone....	
And I see	*Now I see*
Now I could hold you to me	*How I could speak honestly*
But when you're gone	*But when you're gone*
Perhaps you long to be free.	*Perhaps you'll long to be free.*
Let me know when it is that you must go.	*I do know when it is that I must go*
For you can think of love	*For you can think of love*
Smiling as no lips can do	*Wandering far from you*
And of my warm heart	*Or of my warm heart*

Wishing well, always loving you.　　　　　　　*Wishing well and loving you.*

I do believe I'm learning how to live.
For I have loved many, as you have too,
All with the strength of the young,
But they serve as memories –
They are the words which I've sung."

Chronology – and the character of the man in the song, one who has "loved many ... with the strength of the young" – suggests a quite personal plea to the new love of Sandy's life, Trevor Lucas. However traumatic had been the experiences of Jackson Frank returning to America, and Danny Thompson returning to his then-wife (having knowingly entered an affair with a married man, Sandy ignored her mother's barely concealed approbation), these affairs had evidently failed to dissuade Sandy from falling for another ladies' man, and the draft lyrics to 'Now and Then' show that she knew it.

A large, cocksure Australian, all six foot-two of Trevor Lucas had arrived from Australia with his first wife, Cheryl, back in 1964. Almost immediately upon landing in London, he had transferred his affections to the first of his UK conquests, a girl on the London folk scene. By the end of their relationship, having learnt his way around town and made some useful contacts, Trevor was now free to introduce himself to as many women of London Town as the times allowed. A man known to enjoy a good time, and with a wild rover for an eye, Lucas is remembered affectionately by most fellow folkies. Dave Swarbrick's endearing image of Trevor is of someone who revelled in opportunities to pull legs and rattle chains.

Dave Swarbrick: I saw [Trevor] the first week he was here, and we took to each other. Physically he was huge, one of the funniest men I've known, but he had a lot more finesse than most [Australians]. Fine food, fine wine. Great lust for life. The best *mein host* you could come across ... But he was a gentleman. He was brought up to look after women, open the door for them, take care of them ... [ ] ... For a time, Trevor had this house up in Hampstead and he once brought a hearse to go around in. He'd bought it for about thirty quid and for another ten bob the undertaker had thrown in a coffin. The starter on this hearse was duff and I used to have to push this thing to get it going in the mornings – it was quite a sight! We just used to drive around London in it and have fun. One of our most successful missions was when we drove it up to Cecil Sharp House. We took the coffin out and took it upstairs to the shop, where we put it on the counter and told the poor girl at the desk that it was a two-man dulcimer they'd ordered. [CH/JI]

In many ways, it is surprising that Sandy and Trevor had not gone for each other in her pre-Fairport years. Trevor had shared a bill with Sandy as far back as 1966; was a regular at 'the Cousins'; shared many a mutual acquaintance; and had even lent a percussive hand (literally, on the back of a guitar-case) when she was cutting demos at Cecil Sharp House with the Strawbs. So their paths had crossed often enough. And yet only as 1968 turned to 1969 did Sandy and Trevor seem to become synonymous.

At the same time, Sandy seemed to sense that this new affair was something different. Gina Glazer remembers that it was an endless incantation from an ecstatic Sandy, "I'm in love, I'm in love. This is it." Gina very quickly began to see a lot of them together, and recalls a Trevor who, "was very devoted to her. From what I could see, he adored Sandy." Sandy seems to have felt positively redeemed by the love she now felt for Trevor. In a series of drawings, in the same notebook as her drafts for 'Now and Then' and 'Autopsy', an idealised Trevor is pictured naked in the grass, smelling the flowers, whilst a slimmed-down, Sandy-like figure has acquired the wings of an angel.

Work on Sandy's second album with Fairport was also proceeding apace, now that Ian Matthews had taken the hint (after a single duet on Dylan's 'Percy's Song'). If the band felt it "couldn't go back to singing Eric Andersen songs after" 'A Sailor's Life', a smattering of Dylan songs remained de rigeur and they proceeded to record a Cajun rendition of 'If You Gotta Go, Go Now', an equally rambunctious 'Million Dollar Bash', and a non-arrangement of 'Dear Landlord'. None came close to their compelling take on 'Percy's Song', though Sandy gave her all on 'Dear Landlord' (for which she painstakingly transcribed the words in one of her notebooks). Passing over the last of these, Boyd still felt that Fairport had an album with the jump on its predecessor, and that mixing and sequencing should begin – just as soon as they came up with an album cover and title.

The title came easily enough, a non-word Sandy came up with during a word-game called Super Ghosts, usually attributed to the famous Algonquin circle of wits, played to wile away another journey home from a gig. If

Unhalfbricking was an odd title, the cover was positively otherworldy. In the foreground stand an unsmiling, uncomfortably formal couple, guardians of a gate that leads into a quintessentially English world of church spires, spacious gardens and afternoon teas. Through the lattice the five-piece Fairport can just be made out, sipping from china cups. The cover evidently so disturbed their American label that they replaced the image with one of trampolining elephants, presumably in the process of unhalfbricking.

That couple gracing the English cover was none other than Neil and Edna Denny, it having been Sandy who suggested to photographer Eric Hayes that they go round to her parents' home in search of a photo 'op'. If the eventual cover was adopted because it was something out of the ordinary – and therefore in keeping with the inclinations of the photographer, the Island art department, and the band – Sandy later confessed to a friend a more disturbing agenda of her own.

> **Bambi Ballard:** I never met [her parents] but I knew about them ... [She talked about them] all the time – in a kind of jokey way, "Oh, my mother wouldn't approve of this." I remember seeing that [Unhalfbricking] cover, and I said, "God, what a lovely thought, to do that." She said, "No, I did it to placate them." And I said, "Well, what about." And she said, "Just because. I couldn't have gone on if I'd not done that." Almost saying, I threw a piece of meat to the lion so I could walk past while it's chewing it.

However safe Sandy and the boys felt inside that garden, the rough and tumble of their hurly- burly schedule was about to catch up with them, in a quite shattering way. With an album's worth of songs in the can, and the front-cover now captured, Fairport were booked to play at Mothers in Birmingham, on May 11, 1969.

Regulars at the club, which was a favourite haunt for most bands on 'the circuit', Sandy was particularly happy to be back, sharing another bill with Eclection. Founded by Trevor Lucas, Kerrilee Male, Mike Rosen, and Georg Hultgren back in 1967, Eclection had issued a single album on Elektra which, in Trevor's words, "never reflected what the group did musically." Further line-up changes, designed to add something original, had only served to unsettle the sound. But they were friendly, Sandy could keep an eye on Trevor, and in Doris Henderson they now had a female singer as ebullient and hard-drinking as Fairport's own.

After the show, Sandy was offered a lift by Trevor in one of those less-than-reliable Daimlers he had a habit of acquiring on loan from one particular nefarious connection, and elected to take it. Perhaps, at the back of a troubled mind, she had become a little scared about driving long distances in the group was Fairport roadie Harvey Bramham, whom Richard Thompson recalls, "made her learn about the workings of the internal combustion engine, so that normal sounds wouldn't terrify her," had appeared in one of Sandy's dreams back in February, the details of which she had written into her diary (taking up eight pages in the process). It began:

> *"I was in the group van, and we were driving along hazardous roads, it seems that it had been snowing, much the same as it has been at this present time. Harvey was fixing some kind of amplifier so that we could have some kind of sounds in the van while we were traveling. I was driving down a very steep hill and I was rather scared of what the consequences might be, as we were going very fast, so I handed the wheel to Harvey. Soon we came to a clear stretch of road, still dangerously icy. On the right hand side of the road was the sea and we were driving along the edge. The sea was black and choppy. The sky was stormy grey..."*

Harvey Bramham was again assigned driving duties when the other Fairporters, along with Thompson's new American girlfriend, Jeannie Franklyn (known to one and all as Jeannie the Taylor), travelled back to London after the Mothers' gig, in the band's 35 cwt transit van. Bramham was not feeling so good. Less than ten miles from the end of the M1, he fell asleep at the wheel and, as the van careered towards the central reservation, a now wide-awake Thompson grabbed the steering-wheel, only to over-correct, sending the van cartwheeling over the verge.

Simon Nicol: [Harvey] wasn't well. Although he did stop at Watford Gap for a cup of tea, [he] proceeded to London in a really rough state ... I remember waking up while the van was actually somersaulting, just by Scratchwood Services ... When I woke up I was the only one in the vehicle. Everyone else had gone through windows and doors ... I flagged down a truck, and the driver sprinted across to the services to get help ... I could see Martin was not moving; Harvey went through the windscreen and ended up ninety-one feet away, lying in the dark, moaning, both legs broken ... Richard and Hutch were wandering about. Hutch couldn't see, 'cause he had so much blood on his face. [PH]

Jeannie Franklyn had been killed, instantly. The survivors were rushed to the Royal Orthopaedic Hospital in Stanmore, where the staff wrestled unsuccessfully to save Martin Lamble's life. As for the others, Ashley was smashed up pretty badly, but was not on the critical list. Simon and Richard had survived relatively unscathed, at least physically. The psychological effect on the survivors, especially Richard, whose songs of the period are shot through with an all-consuming guilt, can only be imagined. Nearly three decades later, talking to his biographer, Patrick Humphries, Thompson still found it hard to articulate the long-term impact of the crash, "I felt in a state of shock for a couple of years – it was very hard to put stuff into perspective. It broke my perspective for a while – I couldn't get an overall picture of something, it was like being on a drug – seeing the world piecemeal, instead of as a whole thing."

The events of 'Percy's Song', Dylan's depiction of a man unjustly imprisoned for killing his passengers in a road accident – "four people lying dead/and he was at the wheel" – were now played out in real life. Harvey Braham was charged with causing death by dangerous driving and made to serve a six-month sentence (at least it wasn't the "ninety-nine years" the mythical Percy had been given). Sandy did not find out about the calamity until the following morning, when she was called by Anthea Joseph, who had been phoned from the hospital by Simon Nicol with the details of this living nightmare.

Anthea also endeavoured to track down Joe Boyd, who had travelled to New York, to arrange Fairport's US debut at the prestigious Newport Folk Festival and to mix and sequence *Unhalfbricking*. John Wood, who accompanied Boyd to New York, recalls that they, "used to use a studio in New York on 23rd Street, one down from the Chelsea Hotel. It belonged to Vanguard, and it really worked for us, we liked the sound of the echo plates."

Ashley seems to think that "we were just recording tracks at that stage, then we had the crash ... and while we were in hospital Joe said the tracks are great – I'm going to get them put out on a record," which would explain the unfinished nature of 'Dear Landlord', the couple of unnecessary novelty songs, and the fact that the album took until August to reach the shops. Boyd believes he played the sequenced version of *Unhalfbricking* to Jim Rooney, who was on the board of the Newport Folk Festival, and that the album was the finished article.

Rather than returning to the UK to lend some moral support to the shell-shocked survivors, Boyd suggested that Sandy – who was just as neurasthenic as those who had clambered from the van – Simon and Richard come join him on the West Coast, where delicate negotiations with their US label, A&M, were afoot. Ashley continued to be confined to hospital.

Sandy's legendary fear of flying was about to be sorely tested. As she noted in her diary, when she went down to Westminster Central to get her health card stamped, "I was hoping it would be closed, but it wasn't and there was nothing to stop me now from going to America." With Richard holding her hand throughout the flight, even after she emptied a drink in his lap an hour out from Heathrow, it was a relieved Sandy that finally landed at Los Angeles International Airport ten hours later. Though the week holiday provided some welcome therapy, Sandy was missing Trevor badly, and her diary of the trip is shot through with references to the unprecedented pain this physical separation was causing:

"[Wed.] I was upset to leave Trevor, and my fear of flying did not comfort me ... We went to Phil Ochs' house. I was amazed at the beautiful view, to see the whole of Los Angeles lit up like nothing else I've ever seen. He had a monkey and a cat and a beautiful house. It must be wonderful to have houses like that ... Eventually I got through to Trevor, it was great to hear his lovely voice, but [on] the other side of the world, it seemed so strange ... [Thurs.] Went to A&M ... What a change it is to see studios with some imagination applied to design and cosiness. Lighting dim, and lovely colours and lovely people too ... How I wish somebody could design and erect a studio like that in London. Mind you, know nothing of its recording qualities ... I talked to Trevor while I was at Michael [Ethridge?]'s. He was in Plymouth, it was a bad line and eventually we got cut off. Still, I feel very lonely without Trevor ... [Fri.] Flew to San Francisco, arrived about 8 p.m. ... Eventually got to the Fillmore where the Steve Miller Band were playing, and was too tired to stay, so went back to the hotel. Feeling a bit depressed. Wrote a letter to Trev. and phoned him. I miss him awfully..."

Even before she experienced separation at this transatlantic distance, Sandy had penned lines that expressed an ambivalent attitude to life on the road. As Fairport's reputation as a live band grew, along with the sheer need to maintain Witchseason's financial equilibrium, she scribbled in one of her notebooks these lines: "I travel away from the faces I know/the place that I love/And leave behind love/Goodbye, my love, till I come home again," before deleting each line in turn. The next verse suggested that the loneliness of long distance gigging exacerbated her drinking, "I often smile and drink wine till the morning/ in some foreign land where I think about," and then again the pencil cuts through the second line, before Sandy abandons her line of thinking, reverting to the kind of stock image that would become a trademark, "Along the shore I did wander and dance/I sang to the full moon."

Romantic as their relationship would remain, for some time yet, part of the pangs Sandy experienced in America were borne of a suspicion turned to fear, that Trevor, in the original words of 'Now and Then', "long[ed] to be free." However much Sandy wanted to believe in Trevor's love, she knew his reputation as a womanizer even before putting her hands to the flame. As Joe Boyd concisely put it, "She knew Trevor. I think that was the fundamental problem all along." Again, she reserved her inner doubts for her notebook. One abandoned lyric from the period certainly reads like an unposted letter from America:

> *"Do you love me now I'm gone*
> *Does it matter that I'm far away*
> *I did not leave you very long ago*
> *Although I know it was not yesterday...*
> *There are many who would love you too*
> *And they wait until I am not there*
> *But the love you have for me is true*
> *I like to think ."*

Even with all of her concerns, Sandy had become firmly entrenched in her relationship with Trevor. Their need to be together had even been allowed to come between her and her oldest friend, 'Wimbledon' Winnie. At some point, Trevor had become a permanent fixture at the flat in Stanhope Gardens that Sandy shared with Winnie. Shortly afterwards, Trevor became the blunt Australian long enough to suggest to Winnie, "There's one too many people in this flat, and it's you." Winnie took the hint and, though she bore Trevor no malice, she and Sandy were never as close again.

In fact, the lease on Stanhope Gardens was about to expire and upon Sandy's return from the US she and Trevor began searching for a new home. Word of mouth was probably all it took for them to arrive at 92 Chipstead Street, the home of Linda Fitzgerald-Moore. Having worked behind the bar at the Troubadour, and dated Tony Hooper of the Strawbs for a period of time, Linda knew both Sandy and Trevor well enough. As such, when the upstairs flat in her house came vacant with the departure of Stefan Grossman and his wife, the couple were able to move in without delay. The informal arrangement reached on the spacious flat suited all parties, and Sandy and Trevor would spend their happiest years together in the flat in Parson's Green, residing there until the early months of 1974.

Unfortunately for Sandy, Linda was one of a number of women whose morality remained firmly rooted in the 'free love' ethos of the Sixties. Though she remains convinced that Sandy never knew of the sexual favours she occasionally dispensed to her other tenant, Linda was assuredly one of those "who would love you too/And ... wait until I am not there."

Linda Fitzgerald-Moore: My recollection of Trevor is of an easy-going guy, a slut ... I mean, I slept with Trevor. But I'd slept with him before. It was just like a fun fuck. It was like, What the hell? Sometimes if Sandy was away, he'd come down and say, Go on. It wasn't hurting anybody ... It wasn't like he was really being unfaithful. In those days it wasn't a big deal ... it never came up between her and me.

It was at Chipstead Street that the Fairport foursome convened, shortly after their return from the States, to decide on their future path. As Ashley puts it, "things were happening, but we didn't really have a working band ... We had a meeting at Trevor's flat ... [and] we made a decision that we were going to reform." Among the things now happening was a surprise appearance in the singles chart with the curio 45 'Si Tu Dois Partir', their French language pastiche of 'If You Gotta Go, Go Now'. Given that it had already been a big hit for Manfred Mann, back in 1965; that the one thing the song had going for it was some mildly ribald lyrics, now lost to the French language; and that Dylan had never deemed it worthy of release, the song did not have Hit obviously stamped across it, having been issued primarily as promotional fodder for the forthcoming album.

The unexpected nature of its success seems to have caused a degree of embarrassment. Here, after all, was a band John Wood remembers as "artistically arrogant ... there were lots of thing they wouldn't do, they were very fussy ... they did go out of their way to be a bit precious." Nevertheless, a barely reconstituted Fairport was now cajoled into appearing on the decidedly mainstream *Top of the Pops*, the BBC's sole weekly concession to Pop on national

TV. Though no video remains of their one and only *TOTP* appearance, on August 14, 1969, the extant photographic stills beam self-consciousness. It seems unlikely that the majority of the TV audience realised the berets and stripey t-shirts, stand-up bass, accordion and fiddle were meant to parody the song's Cajun schtick, or that neither drummer Dave Mattacks or fiddle-player Dave Swarbrick had been a part of the band that had recorded the single.

Determined to remain precious, Fairport's *TOTP* appearance coincided with a long news story in that week's *NME*, in which these silly French-type people proclaimed that "the next album is going to be completely different; it will be based around traditional British folk music," erecting a gulf between their natural audience of progressive music fans and the mass audience this innocuous single had reached that would never be breached again. As if to further emphasize a band content to return to their side of the great divide, Sandy told the *NME* reporter, "We're not making it pop ... In fact, it will be almost straight [folk]; only electric. What [will] it sound like? Heavy traditional folk music."

The decision to make an album of "heavy traditional folk music" had prompted Fairport to send an emissary to convince Dave Swarbrick to become a full-time member. Like Sandy before him, Swarbrick had been earning quite a chunk of change playing the folk circuit, and the economics of a rock band came as quite a shock to him, "I was in the top [folk] outfit in the country at the time. Martin [Carthy] and I worked seven nights a week. I dropped to twenty pounds a week to join Fairport. I was earning at least twenty pounds a night, a lot of money for those years. And I'd got a wife and kid." Joe Boyd promised the usual untold riches further down the line but in truth Swarbrick, like Sandy, had tired of folk's false conformity, and was willing to embrace the direction laid out by 'A Sailor's Life', having, in his own words, "a fair idea [of] where it was gonna go to next."

During subsequent ructions, it would be claimed that Fairport's future direction had been decided at the single meeting at Trevor's, and that the band's reinvention of itself as pioneers of English folk-rock was absolute. However Swarbrick believes that originally, "they had the idea of doing a concept album of English traditional stuff, and they got me in to do [just that]." This corresponds with what Simon Nicol told *NME* in August, that this album of "heavy traditional folk music" was "a conscious project. We'll just explore it for a while ... It's another form that hasn't been explored, in the same way as the Americans have with their music recently ... We want to concentrate on an album of English material ... [But] we'll be making another LP of the sort of things we've done in the past, [though] it will be impressed by the other, and probably come out more English." What Richard Thompson proceeded to tell *Rolling Stone* suggested that Fairport were attempting to reverse what they saw as a trend towards the 'Americanization' of popular music:

> **Richard Thompson:** We feel as if we have a commitment to English music, that we have to follow the direction we're taking, to carry it over to people. Practically nobody here who listens to music is aware of their British heritage.

Between the producer and engineer of *Liege and Lief*, the impression has been given that the influence of one Ametican band, The Band, overarched all of Fairport's attempts at an original statement. Boyd puts much of the credit on the Band's first album, *Music From Big Pink*, which in his words, "kinda said, 'Forget it, you're not American, you're never even gonna come close to understanding this music.'" Presumably, he had forgotten that everyone in The Band, save drummer Levon Helm, was Canadian! In his *History of Fairport Convention* notes, John Wood proceeds to credit "the harder, heavier sound [on *Liege & Lief*], particularly about Richard's playing," to the second Band album, an album released *after* the *Liege & Lief* material had been debuted. Thompson himself attributes an influence, but as much for what they didn't do as what they did, "We admired The Band for their rootsiness, at a time of heavy drug-induced noodling. They had short haircuts, knew how to swing, blended styles from various traditions, and generally flew in the face of marketing common sense."

If any example provided by The Band informed the making of *Liege & Lief*, it was the informal set-up at Big Pink, the garish house in Woodstock where they lived and recorded that had resulted not only in their debut album but in the legendary 'basement tapes' they recorded with Dylan, a copy of which Boyd had acquired back in 1968, and from which Fairport continued to cherry-pick songs. 'Down in the Flood' and 'Open the Door Homer' were two basement tape ditties they would work up as part of their "commitment to English music". Dogma still played no part in the Fairport folk-rock process.

Just as Dylan had hunkered down in Woodstock with his backing Band after his own lil' two-wheeled accident, paying the rent on Big Pink and retaining the then-Hawks' services in order to make some music in quiet isolation, so Witchseason found the funds to rent the reconstituted six-piece Fairport a delightful country retreat just outside Winchester, where the process of their recuperation could coincide with some music-making. In much the same way as Dylan had tapped into the vaults of Americana to heal his psychic wounds, Sandy and the boys now steeped themselves in an essentially British sensibility, from the centuries.

Ashley Hutchings: We had a big house in Hampshire. Farley Chamberlayne – that's the name of the village – about eleven miles outside Winchester. Joe got the place for us to recuperate and rehearse. That was a very happy period for me – a very exciting period ... There was a lot of heart-searching going on. It was hard work to actually put these things into the rock format but it was exhilarating and magical in the most profound sense ... [ ] ... [It was] two months maybe. Certainly wasn't very long. Not for such amazing material. There's a whole sequence of photos [which] just tell the story. There's the room, big room, us sitting around playing, working on this material, Sandy holding a mike. Everything was set up, and in the morning we'd go down. Also there're photos of me and Swarbrick's dog, a couple of the guys playing football in the garden. You don't need captions. We played a bit, intensely, then we went out in the garden and we came back refreshed, and did it again. Incredibly exciting to be doing something that you know no-one has done before. [PH/CH]

Not only were Fairport "doing something that ... no-one ha[d] done before," using an entirely original fusion of sound, but they were doing it with two new recruits. If Swarbrick had been an obvious enough candidate, the replacement for Martin Lamble required a whole series of auditions, until they chanced upon Dave Mattacks, a.k.a. 'DM'. Mattacks had played all kinds of music in his five years as a professional, though never folk. And yet he found himself invited down to Farley after a single audition. After a further twenty-four hours, Ashley asked him if he would like to join the band. Mattacks' response was not the most conventional way of saying yes please.

Dave Mattacks: I said, "Yes, but I must tell you I haven't a fucking clue of what you're on about. I don't know anything about the music, I don't understand it ... I can't tell one tune from another, they all sound the same ... But if you really want me to join the group, fine, because ... I'm enjoying myself musically."

Initially, it would appear, Fairport intended to strike the same balance of original material to covers as on previous outings. Simon Nicol even claimed to the press that, "Tyger is writing some interesting stuff in the style of English ballads but without the dialect or language problem, and without the archaic imagery which makes them unsingable in an electric context. And Sandy's still writing, better than ever, and so is Richard." In fact, Ashley had become so immersed in the folk process that he all but forgot to apply the brush of originality. As he freely admits, "I [was] the academic in the band, so what was natural to me was to go to Cecil Sharp House and pour over the books and listen to the old recordings ... In some cases it wasn't needed because Sandy and Swarb – particularly Swarb – [already] had a repertoire in their head."

For Sandy, it was a question of reimmersing herself in the type of songs she had previously reserved for the dressing-room or van, or the occasional 'solo appearance'. An indication of what she had in mind for Farley came, late on the second day of August, when she played an unbilled set at her old haunt, Les Cousins. Interestingly, it was an almost exclusively English vision of folk she adopted that night. 'Nottamun Town', 'Green Grow The Laurels', 'Bruton Town', 'Newlyn Town' and 'Come All Ye Fair and Tender Ladies' suggested the enduring influence of figures like Bert Jansch, Bert Lloyd, Martin Carthy and Gina Glazer. Sandy also debuted a song from her own pen, the gorgeous 'The Pond and the Stream', a pastoral tribute to the eccentric Anne Briggs, that lived up to Nicol's billing, "in the style of English ballads, but without the dialect or language problem, and without the archaic imagery."

However, none of Sandy's selections that night would make *Liege & Lief*, even her own carefully wrought attempt to match the band's brief.* When she arrived at Farley, she found the remainder of the band all too willing to defer to Dave Swarbrick's vision of electric folk. Despite Ashley's claims to academic input, and Sandy's wide-ranging knowledge of the genre, it was the band's newest recruit that had the largest input when it came to song selection.

Dave Swarbrick: You could say I was the most aware of the material. Most of the songs came from me. 'Matty Groves', 'Tam Lin', 'The Deserter', all that stuff came from my background, and were songs I introduced to them.

---

*Ashley does recall Fairport playing 'The Pond and the Stream' at selected shows that autumn.

The bending was being done the other way ... [But] Sandy knew a lot of it, and had a big input on it. 'Matty Groves', Sandy and I put the words together from Child. We put it to an American tune, and I supplied the instrumental tune ['Famous Flower of the Serving Man'] at the end. 'Tam Lin' I wrote the tune for, based on a slip jig. I just took out all the beats till I got sevenths. 'Reynardine', I'd done with Bert. 'The Deserter', I'd done with Luke Kelly.

Fairport had seemingly abandoned their professed intent, to place traditional verites in a folk-rock context, and were now setting about grafting a folk-rock sound to traditional songs, largely composed to be sung acapella. Joe Boyd recalls Sandy being both amused and a little bemused, "at Ashley's fanaticism, which he came to very late in life. He was discovering things with the zeal of a new convert that she had been familiar with ... for years. She had been singing songs that he would come back from Cecil Sharp House with and say, 'I have just discovered this magnificent song.' And she would say, 'Well, I was singing that when I was 17!'"

It is probably no coincidence that Sandy reserves her best performances on the ensuing album for her own composition, 'Come All Ye' (Ashley Hutchings notes, "I get the joint credit because I wrote a couple of verses but she [already] had the music, the first verse and the chorus"), the two Thompson 'originals', and the one traditional song with which Swarbrick credits her direct input ('Matty Groves').

'Crazy Man Michael' and 'Farewell Farewell', the two Thompson lyrics, the former set to a Swarbrick tune, the latter set to the hundredth Child ballad, 'Willie o' Winsbury', bookend the sides of *Liege & Lief* with notes from a melancholic well that Sandy's voice alone could plummet. Whether the others realised it or not – and it would take Thompson a while to admit it himself – Sandy had been pushing for something like this for some time, songs that drew their water from such traditional wellsprings, but added their own original flavour. As it is, neither Sandy's interpretative skills nor Thompson's lyrical distillation of weal and woe would ever be bettered:

"Within the fire and not upon the sea, Crazy Man Michael was walking
He met a raven with eyes as black as coal, and shortly they were a-talking ...
Michael he whistles the simplest of tunes, and asks of the four winds their pardon,
For his true love has flown into ever flower grown,

And he must be keeper of the garden."

That both songs had clearly been forged in the furnace of Thompson's grief, to be interpreted by someone who understood each and every nuance, only made them doubly poignant (Thompson himself has never sung either song. As late as 1992, when 'Farewell Farewell' came up at a New York 'request show', he elected to sing 'Willie o' Winsbury' instead). This authentic highland melody was not alone in giving *Liege & Lief*, an album that promised "to concentrate on ... English material," a distinctly Northern flavour, each side being dominated by an epic Scottish ballad, 'Tam Lin' and 'Matty Groves' a.k.a. 'Little Musgrave and Lady Barnard'.* The bias would have been even more pronounced if the studio version of 'Sir Patrick Spens' had found a place on the album – preferably at the expense of the 'Medley', the first of a number of interminable instrumental jigs destined to pepper future Fairport albums.

Four days before they were due to publicly debut their 'new' material at the Royal Festival Hall, the band staged the equivalent of a dress rehearsal at Van Dyke's in Plymouth, on September 20, 1969. Richard Lewis, who drove down to Plymouth with friends, recalls it being very hot, pretty crowded and fairly cramped, even on the stage, but that, despite such hardships, "Sandy would sometimes just step back and watch, sometimes she'd almost go off the stage and look [at the band], 'cause she was obviously enjoying it so much." Sandy even turned the stage over to Richard for his two Dylan ditties, and to Swarb for 'Have You Had A Talk With Jesus' (on which Sandy played violin, while Swarb sang). The band came off elated, after an all-new 14-song set.

On September 24 they debuted the same show, minus the two Thompson vocals, at the Royal Festival Hall, to a sell-out audience that included what Swarb dubbed "the intelligentsia of the folk establishment," whose attendance had been requested to give (hopefully) the venture their blessing. Richard remembers "a real intensity to the playing ... it was a night when everything worked, except Swarb's fiddle, which died at the end of the show."

Richard Lewis: The Festival Hall has always been a nice place for concerts, and that was wonderful, really wonderful. When the band came on, it was a lovely big stage, and they'd obviously been rehearsing. They'd got the

---

*Though the latter exists as a seventeenth-century English broadside, a Scottish ms. predates its printed form.

sound right. It all came together. It was a good reaction, a really good reaction. I don't think most people had heard anything like this, and quite a few of the important people from the folk world were there. Bert Lloyd was there certainly, and you could see that he was enjoying it. So that gave an endorsement that other people could enjoy it as well. They weren't sure whether they were meant to or not.

After a month and a half of rehearsals and a handful of shows, the album itself came easily enough, being recorded in seven days of sessions in the last three weeks of October. The surfeit of material worked up at Farley probably warranted a double-album but the band's decision to record just eleven songs and release just eight left *Liege & Lief* a slightly skewered portrait of a highly creative period. Though the single album on display remains a landmark release, its impact undiminished by three decades, the inclusion of the likes of Richard Farina's 'Quiet Joys of Brotherhood', Dylan's 'Open The Door Homer' and 'Down in the Flood', Roger McGuinn's 'Ballad of Easy Rider' and Sandy's own 'The Pond and The Stream' might have made for a less alienating experience for fans of the earlier incarnations. As it is, there were those in the press who longed for the Fairport of old, a sentiment voiced most lucidly by John Mendlesohn, reviewing the delayed *Unhalfbricking* (favourably) and *Liege & Lief* (unfavourably) in *Rolling Stone*, and asking of the latter:

"Where is the group's folk-flavored rock and roll, where are the exhilirating harmonies, the sense of fun and feeling of harnessed electricity that made their first two albums together such treats? Where, essentially, is something to excite those of us who find artiness worthy enough of quiet admiration but a little boring?"

Only in live performance did the Trad. Arr. version of Fairport have the opportunity to present a more rounded new persona, and with three months of gigs separating the live debut of Fairport Mk.4 from the release of *Liege & Lief*, they had ample opportunity to attune their audience to the change in direction. Though the new six-piece would play barely a dozen more gigs before shedding yet more personnel, the shows they played that autumn have acquired a mythical hue. In part, this was because, through all the line-up changes, the o'erhanging spectre of tragedy, and their quiet determination to move ever forward, Fairport had acquired, in the words of rock critic Dave Laing, a "unique position and influence in British rock ... comparable only to the role of the Byrds in America." On a number of levels, *Liege & Lief* was as radical a departure as the Byrds' country-rock foray, *Sweetheart of the Rodeo*, going on to influence bands as diverse as Led Zeppelin (*III* reeks of continual replays of *Liege & Lief*), Traffic (ditto *John Barleycorn*) and avant-garage originators, Pere Ubu.

As another critic, Patrick Amory, observed, in a lengthy essay on the early history of Fairport for American fanzine *Too Fun Too Huge*, "*Liege and Lief* was the opposite of popular music at the time: gloomy, academic, precise." Unfortunately, just like the Parsons-era Byrds, the confluence of forces at work was as volatile as it was powerful, the *Liege & Lief* Fairport having at least two strong personalities too many for one band. Before they could reap the critical plaudits for going against the progressive grain in Rock, Fairport found themselves minus two survivors from the May cataclysm.

On November 2, 1969, less than six months on from the crash, Fairport returned to Mothers in Birmingham, to play a quite different set to the one they played that fateful evening (in the audience was bassist Dave Pegg, who remembers being mightily impressed by the Fairport rhythm section, unaware that he was about to be Ashley's replacement). After the show, the entire band elected to return to London. During that journey Simon Nicol found himself required to console an especially emotional Sandy, "who spent most of the journey in tears, [talking] about how she loved the band, and how she loved Trevor so much, how she didn't want to go to America, how she didn't even want to go to Denmark for a week."

The imminent prospect of an American tour, to promote the A&M release of *Liege & Lief*, had convinced Sandy that she did not want to put herself through a separation from Trevor even more prolonged than the one she had suffered that summer. Nor was her outburst an idle remonstration. When the car arrived, a few days later, to take her to the airport for a scheduled appearance on Danish television, she was nowhere to be found, and the band ended up flying to Copenhagen without her.

Ashley Hutchings: During the trip over to Denmark, we talked about the future as well as that current situation we had to tackle, and it threw up quite a lot of things about the future; which way the band might go, about whether this behaviour could be tolerated ... and I think I had made up my mind that it was going to go a certain way ... that we would get a traditional singer in and push it further [that] way ... [ ] ... Then we got there, and whipped up a sense of cameraderie, "It's gonna be alright, you can sing that bit, I can sing that bit," and we're actually onstage at the theatre, some kind of rehearsal, and Anthea rang to say she'd tracked Sandy down, and she was gonna be on the next plane. And suddenly I felt, "This isn't how it should be." It was like a letdown that she would be on the next plane. [PH/CH]

However much Sandy's no-show rankled with Fairport, the rest of the band remained thoroughly out of sync with Ashley's suggestion "that we ... get a traditional singer in." Simon Nicol believes that, somewhere between Chipstead Road and Heathrow, Ashley actually proposed Bert Lloyd should join the band, "a concept I couldn't cope with, and I think the others found hard to cope with." Like everyone in the band, he knew Sandy could be difficult. But a Fairport without Sandy at this stage seemed quite unimaginable. Meantime, as Island publicist David Sandison confirms, Anthea Joseph had done "a bit of detective work and finally tracked Sandy down, very drunk and belligerent, sobered her up and frogmarched her onto the next flight. Of course, as soon as she got on the plane Sandy clicked her fingers and ordered more booze. When they arrived, Sandy was completely drunk again."

Ever nervous of flying, Sandy became convinced, on the flight over, that this was not for her and, though her three vocals on the Danish TV broadcast suggest no dip in commitment to the *Liege & Lief* material, she had decided to plough her own furrow. Unbeknownst to her, Ashley had arrived at a similar juncture, aided as much by the rigours of the return flight as Sandy had been by the outward. Just as word of mouth was suggesting that the new album would be Fairport's long-awaited commercial breakthrough – made on their own terms – these two critical components were reaching for their parachutes.

Ashley Hutchings: We did the gig, we flew back, and it was the worst flight I've ever had. It was a thunderstorm, and internally I was freaking out. I promised myself that if I got down again a) I wouldn't ever go up in an aeroplane again, and I didn't for another ten years, and b) that there was going to have to be a change. And very shortly after flying back I just said, I'm gonna leave, guys. I didn't know what I was doing. I hadn't planned anything. I just had a vague idea that I wanted to play traditional music.

7

1969–70: A NEW LEAF

Fotheringay programme cover

"There was no reason why, with hindsight, we couldn't have carried on for years, incorporating all the needs of all the members. But what was at work at that time was the after-effects of the crash – a delayed reaction. Sandy and I were unsettled in our outlook. We were still coming to grips with the tragedy. We bounced back so quickly we didn't have time to grieve. Joe wasn't the kind of father-figure who would say, Listen guys ... I think I would have stayed, and Sandy would have stayed, had we not been wrestling with something else which made us behave a bit irrationally ... If we hadn't had such liberal management, if there's someone reading the riot act, "C'mon pull yourself together. You wanna talk about the material, we'll have a meeting." [Joe's] liberality allowed the whole thing to fall apart."

Ashley Hutchings

Ashley's assessment makes a lot of sense, not only applied to the seemingly irrational departures of Sandy and Ashley, but also Richard Thompson's a year later. All three were making decisions from a broken perspective, still living the aftershocks of the accident. At the time it must have seemed, to Sandy in particular, that the pressures just kept piling up until something, or somebody, was bound to blow. Joe Boyd has no doubts about the primary motive for Sandy bailing out.

Joe Boyd: I believe what it was about was Trevor. Here she was living with this guy, who she adored, who was the first sort of sensible domestic relationship she'd probably ever had. Although he was a rather mediocre musician, he had a big enough ego that he could handle being Mr. Sandy Denny, being the male half of this partnership with this incredibly talented, dynamic, ever-more-famous person. But part of that sense of self and ego, which enabled him to balance Sandy, came from his being a womanizer! He was a handsome, debonair guy that women liked. And so Sandy felt, either out of paranoia or out of reality, that every time she left town he would be shagging whatever he met at the folk club. Which probably wasn't far wrong. [PW]

The domestic situation with Trevor had certainly became a factor in band politics by the time of the Danish debacle, even if conflicts were inevitable with a frontsperson as insecure as Sandy. Never in her writing, though, is there a sense that she would forsake *all* in pursuit of her muse. In that sense her choice of Trevor as a lifetime companion remains a baffling one. In fact, if one of her closest friends has a correct take on the relationship, then no matter how much Sandy idealised (or demonised) their love in song, Trevor-as-the- specific-object-of-her-love did not provide the essence of her deepest cravings.

Linda Thompson: I thought [Trevor] was a nice guy, and he was very overawed by her talent, there was an element of that in their relationship. [But] I think he did pretty well by her … [If] neither of them were particularly faithful to each other – this was the Sixties or Seventies. She loved Trevor, but the people that she really adored were people where the relationship was never consummated. She adored Richard, and whatever he told her to do, she'd do. She didn't have tremendous respect for many people because she was in a different stratosphere. Trevor was like her anchor. I don't think she was head over heels in love with him. She loved him, but it wasn't the fierce thing even that she had for Danny.

Whether Sandy would have admitted as much to herself is another question. As Simon Nicol notes, "Sandy was a person who needed a lot of affection and attention. [But] she could [also] see the band getting bigger, and we were talking about going to the States for the first time." Nicol is quite right to connect the two, Sandy's need for "a lot of affection and attention" and the possibility (some would say likelihood) of "the band getting bigger." It would be unwise to underestimate the part Sandy's very real fear of success played in her act of commercial hari-kari.

Ever-ambivalent about fame, she would later talk about what she called "a success neurosis," qualifying it by insisting that what she was "terrified of [is] what happens to people when they become really famous." As early as the week of her appearance on *Top of the Pops*, Sandy assured a journalist that she was "quite happy just ambling along towards the big success, but when the big success is suddenly there at the other end of the street and getting closer, it is a bit frightening." She was not alone in desiring a certain kind of fame, fame on her own terms, that could be switched off at will. The most honest appraisal she ever gave of the spectre of success came in an interview with Karl Dallas, whilst working on her first solo album, when the prospect of fame was once again rapping at her door:

Sandy Denny: I do appreciate being slightly well-known, because I've got a bit of an ego. But I never want to reach the top. It's such a long way down. I'd rather hover about near the top, and never actually reach the height. [1971]

Sandy would never come to terms with her status, would never recognize how respected by fellow musicians she was. A mass of contradictions, if ever, she loved the hobknobbing aspects of being Somebody, but her fragile sense of identity was such that self-deprecation was never too far away in her mode of conversation. Though she had found someone who treated her as someone special, she would never be entirely convinced.

Part of the conflict now raging in her cranium was a by-product of being a woman in an avowedly man's world. Joe Boyd, able to observe this effect first hand on a number of occasions, believes that "there was a lot of conflict about being a woman in that role then, and the more successful you become, the more you leave people behind, so the more you run the risk of being on your own. Sandy was afraid of being a big success. A lot of female performers from that generation had that fear."

Sandy was also probably already an undiagnosed alcoholic. One of the corrosive by-products of a serious drinking habit is the way it eats away at your self-esteem, one-sixth of a gill at a time. The fact that a previous dislike of travelling had solidified into something akin to a phobia should have set some alarm bells ringing. Boyd now admits it was at this time that he "first started noticing her becoming more depressed, and more down, and more worried, and more concerned, in a somewhat self-destructive way. She became *very* afraid of flying and travelling."

At the same time, it was only when it became apparent that *Liege & Lief* was unlikely to be a one-off project that Sandy began to plan her escape from the Fairport democracy. Ashley's more academic, one may even say dogmatic, vision of Folk held no appeal for her and though her own songwriting, along with Richard's, gradually undermined Ashley's position in Fairport, he had always been, in Thompon's words, "the moving force behind the direction and the policy, all the way into folk-rock and into the traditional revival." That there had been murmurs since the halcyon days of Farley Chamberlayne, Ashley admits, though he continues to see the hand of Trevor in the subsequent ructions.

Ashley Hutchings: I think everyone was totally committed to *Liege & Lief*, doing it. I don't remember any dissension. Once we'd done it, that's when problems arose. Then there was mumblings of well, maybe we should get more of Sandy's songs, or maybe we should do some country songs ... I think it came a bit later and whether it came purely from Sandy, I have my doubts. I have a feeling Trevor may have made a few suggestions about her own material, and exerting her own authority. Certainly I don't remember at any point Sandy voicing any reservations.

In fact, the rest of Fairport felt just as compelled as Ashley to explore an English sensibility, they just had in mind a more original style, one related if not rooted in Rock. If Thompson asserts that, "once we started we obviously had to keep going, there was no going back," he also admits that, "there was a running argument between Ashley in one camp and Sandy and myself in the other – Ashley wanting to do more traditional material, Sandy and I wanting to do more trad-based contemporary songs." Sandy may have come to feel that *Liege & Lief* was a mistake, that she was in danger of ending up back where she started. As Joe Boyd told Patrick Humphries, "She had been involved with the traditional [scene] for a long time, but always rather ambivalently. She sang traditional songs as well as her own compositions, and she had [unclear] feelings about it."

As it is, the other members of Fairport may have been genuinely unaware how much Sandy had been working at her songwriting in the months since the accident (though Ashley's reference to "mumblings of ... maybe we should get more of Sandy's songs" suggests a dissatisfaction at least voiced). Despite the likes of 'Fotheringay', 'Who Knows..." and 'Autopsy", others may have considered Sandy to be first and foremost a singer; that Richard supplied the Robbie Robertson role in Fairport well enough – given that he would always be the more prolific writer. Sandy's reluctance to share ideas for songs with her fellow musicians would also endure long after Fairport. The drummer in her next ensemble well remembers just how tough an initial unveiling could be.

Gerry Conway: Sandy was always quite shy about bringing a new song out. She would always be a little reluctant to play it 'publicly' for the first time – first times were quite nerve-wracking, just to hear the song and start working on it. It was almost like she didn't know what she had ... Deep down, Sandy wasn't really that confident – she sought approval on things when she didn't need to. Everybody thought she was the greatest thing since sliced bread – but there would always be that, "Is it any good?"

Because of such bashfulness, it is all but impossible to discern how many of Sandy's contributions to the first album with Fotheringay had already been written by the time she left Fairport. 'The Pond and the Stream' certainly dates from that summer. In the same notebook are also the lyrics to 'The Sea', a curiously apocalyptic vision of a London where the "sea flows under your doors ... and all your defences are all broken down."

Trevor Lucas: It's about how London has lived on the point of flood all the time and ... [Sandy envisaged a] London [that] was really coming down and falling around itself because of the sea.

'Nothing More', the opening track on Sandy's next band's eponymous debut album *Fotheringay*, may also have been penned that autumn, though

Richard Thompson says she never played it to him, even though he spent many a weekend at Chipstead Street at the time, perhaps because its subject-matter was someone known to the narrator knows who has "suffered, although you are still young." It was one in a long line of portraits of those Sandy loved best, albeit in code. When asked about the focus for her songs, in 1972, Sandy initially sidestepped the question, "I can't tell you about my songs. They're so strange," but then allowed herself to confess, "They're about people. I don't know why they are – they just come out like that." As her father fondly recalled, "She had a most remarkable facility for working people out. ... [There would be] somebody 20 yards away in a room, and she'd say, 'That girl has just told that fellow to get lost'." In the case of 'Nothing More', perhaps no-one has summarised Thompson better, in any number of pages, than Sandy in these three lines:

"For you are like the others, he said,
I never can be sure
That you wish to see the pearls and nothing more."

If there was anyone aware of how much writing Sandy was now doing, it was Trevor Lucas. His recollection, twenty years later, was of someone openly telling him that she, "didn't want to sing Farmer Jones songs for the rest of her life. She had a huge amount of her own material, was writing very prolifically, and she could see that the band had less and less place for that." As her cheerleader and taskmaster rolled into one, Trevor doubtless voiced an opinion as to the direction the band was heading in. As it is, she would come to believe that "it was only when I left [Fairport] that I realized I could [write more]." Others believe it was inevitable that Sandy and Trevor would end up working together.

Richard Thompson: We were backstage at I think Newcastle University, and Sandy was in Eclection's dressing room next door. We could hear Sandy singing 'A Sailor's Life' through the wall, and Trevor was adding a terrific bass part to it, and we looked at each other, as if to say, that sounds a bit too good. ... One way or another, I think we expected Sandy and Trevor to be in a band together at some point ... It was hard for them to be working on the road separately ... she needed to be with Trevor.

Forming a band with Trevor was also a way for Sandy to be simultaneously self-effacing and artistically assertive. Initially, she doesn't seem to have realised what a hot property she had become as a solo artist. Joe Boyd promptly set her straight, perhaps exacerbating those fears of fame. As he prepared to fly to America to negotiate a solo contract from Sandy's American label, A&M, he was stunned to find that Sandy was talking about assembling another band to hide behind, within which would be her "would-be dream love of a lifetime," and his Eclection sidekick, Gerry Conway.

Joe Boyd: [When] Sandy had failed to make the flight [to Copenhagen], I ended up going round to her house and having a long chat with her ... Sandy was nervous that if she did leave the group she wouldn't get a recording deal. I said, you must be joking ... I think during that conversation she also expressed her reservations about doing a solo record, and said she might form a group ... [ ] ... [But] A&M loved Sandy. They signed Fairport because they wanted Sandy. They would have preferred to have Sandy without Fairport. And I knew that. She was always worried about money, she never had much, and I said, I can go and get you a big advance – Chris Blackwell agreed that we would pass the whole advance through the system ... and we would work it out down the line. I told her all of this. I was also aware of a political situation at the time, which I knew I could exploit. Abe Summer, this [American] lawyer ... was negotiating with Capitol to launch the Island label [in the U.S.] through Capitol, which would by default have had any Island artist not placed with other American labels. [He] was also representing A&M. He knew that if we didn't do a deal quickly for Sandy with A&M, that A&M would lose her to the Island label, and that his conflict of interest would be cruelly exposed. She had talked to me about forming a group with Trevor, and I said, Please, don't ... Trevor liked the trappings, he liked the good life. Fairport were down to earth, get a decent place to rehearse, get a van that'll get you from A to B, and think about the music. They weren't interested in hanging out at the Scotch of St. James. ... What Sandy and Trevor had in mind was [professional musician] guys who were not going to join a collective, and wait and see what came in the door. They were gonna need salaries. I said, "Sandy, listen you can put together a great band to go on the road after we make a solo record. We'll pay them to go on the road with you, we'll pay them to do the

recording with you, but don't put them on salary. It's a false collective."
[PH/CH]

The band idea, according to drummer Gerry Conway, had originally come up as a result of "a [long] conversation with Trevor and Sandy ... chatting about musicians and music, and out of that, by the end of the night, it was [like,] 'Let's form a band' – we decided that we would all like to do something together ... Sandy liked to have people around her – people that she liked, people she respected, and once she had that she would go to extraordinary ends to keep it like that." These extraordinary ends included shooting herself in the foot financially.

Sandy herself said, at the time, that she had "decided against going solo because I would have had to work with a backing group. I knew that relationship would have been no good ... I like to be part of a group." Part of the impetus for this 'realisation' was apparently the experience of seeing Judy Collins perform at a recent London show. Out in the audience a feeling came over Sandy that here was someone who "was definitely a solo singer, who just happened to have a very good backing group. But that's all they were – a backing group. I suddenly thought, If you're playing together on a stage you might as well be TOGETHER."

Already her desire for companionship was clouding her judgement. As she told a journalist, barely two months after her new band Fotheringay's formation, "If I had gone solo I would have been involved more with the business side ... that side doesn't interest me at all – I'm happy to leave it to other people." Perhaps the last other person she should have left it to was her boyfriend. For every old friend of Trevor who recalls his good nature, there's another who cannot surpress a wry grin at all the hare-brained ideas and grandiose schemes that came from Trevor's fertile imagination. As long as it was some record company or unsuspecting man of means that bought into his antipodean verbal hogwash, it remained a source of anecdotal amusement, Trevor as a Fulham *Broadway Danny Rose*. However, when Boyd returned from L.A. with a deal that could have put Sandy on a secure financial footing for the forseeable, Trevor was the man to ensure it would not.

Joe Boyd: A&M eventually came up with a $40,000 advance figure – twice what they paid for Fairport Convention albums – and an immense amount of money in 1970. [But] by the time I returned from California with this offer,

Sandy had already begun rehearsals with Albert Lee, Pat Donaldson, Gerry Conway and Trevor ... [and] said she was absolutely committed to the idea of this band. I said to her at the time, I'm not going to manage this band. I don't think it's a good idea. It's financial suicide. Whatever you call the band is not going to sell as many copies on the day of release as your name would. A&M is gonna be disappointed. No-one wants this. You're swimming upstream. At the bottom of it all, as I think we know, it was all about Trevor ... She wanted Trevor in the band, with her, 24 hours a day, and the only way to ensure that was to make him an equal partner. She understood that that was the only way that she could have at least the semblance of a balanced, professional relationship with Trevor. I believe we kept the money in the Witchseason account, and Roy Guest became the manager, and was able to draw on money that was in the account. [But] Roy was not the sort of person to say No, and so absolutely every one of my worst fears was realized – they bought a Bentley, they bought [a huge PA they christened] Stonehenge, everything that Fairport would never dream of doing.

Boyd, for all his endeavours on Sandy's behalf, knew he had returned to a *fait accomplis*. He also knew she had a streak of stubborness as wide as Wimbledon Common, aligned to an inner determination to prove him (and others) wrong. Initially at least, she did just that. Less than three months after she had abandoned her solo plans, formed a band called Tiger's Eye, replaced the guitarist, rechristened it Fotheringay, rehearsed a whole new set, and recorded the bulk of a quietly impressive sleeper of a debut album, she was on the road with her new five-piece. As the new band toured the UK reviews spoke of "Fotheringay ma[king] the kind of debut artists usually only dream about," playing to "tremendous acclaim," and referring to Sandy's own new numbers as "excellent."

The original Chipstead Street conversation, involving Trevor and Gerry Conway, had come about in part because the days of their own band, Eclection, were numbered. Trevor had for some time been trying, in Conway's words, "to keep together something that didn't want to be together." If Sandy now acquired the Dorris Henderson role in the new collective, she asked Thompson's opinion as to the best guitarist around (present company excepted) and went along with his recommendation, recruiting Albert Lee and, via him, Pat Donaldson on bass, with whom Lee was playing in the short-lived Country Fever.

This line-up lasted long enough to be profiled in the music press, and photographed at the common near Sandy and Trevor's flat by their landlady-turned-photographer Linda Fitzgerald-Moore. Albert Lee may have been happy enough with the Gordon Lightfoot and Bob Dylan covers but when it came to the Fotheringay originals his way of picking did not gell all that well with those folky time-signatures. After a fortnight, the others began to observe a certain taciturnity bordering on disinterest.

Gerry Conway: Eventually Trevor said, "I don't know if Albert's happy, we'll have to tackle him." ... So we asked him and he said, "Well, I've been meaning to say..."

If rehearsals with Albert Lee occupied much of January 1970, rehearsing with his replacement, Jerry Donahue, recording the results for Island and playing a five-date tour, occupied February, March and April. Donahue, a New Yorker by birth, had come to England in 1961 with his parents, where he joined a band called the Zephyrs, though, according to Fotheringay's program notes, "it was not until he joined Poet and the One Man Band that Jerry came to prominence." No Richard Thompson, he was nevertheless a versatile guitarist and team-player. If Donahue believes Fotheringay "wasn't enough of a vehicle for" Lee, it suited him just fine.

The pretence of a democracy within the band had been maintained by the simple expedient of giving Trevor a couple of favourite covers to add to his own 'Ballad of Ned Kelly'. Sandy had enough songs up her sleeve to concentrate on her own material, though she reserved her finest vocal on *Fotheringay* for the one and only traditional song in their early repertoire. 'The Banks of the Nile', like the equally epic 'Bonny Bunch of Roses' currently being performed by Sandy's previous ensemble, was another of those long litanies on the Napoleonic wars that filled the English broadsheets in the early nineteenth century. In her hands, though, it became the second act in the trials and tribulations of military sweethearts, as poignant as 'A Sailor's Life', though not as easily caught. Indeed, when it came time to record the song, it stood in stark contrast to the studious arrangements that occupied the remaining session-time.

Gerry Conway: We [had been] rehearsing in the music-room at Chipstead Street, and as far as I can recollect, we just went straight in the studio ... [Sandy] had songs that she had written, and I think what she really wanted to do was perform her own songs. Nobody in the Fotheringay line-up even questioned that. She would guide if she didn't think [an arrangement] was right, and encourage if it was. She knew what she didn't like ... Things like '[The] Pond and the Stream', we rehearsed it and that's how we played it on the record, [Most] songs were like that. [But] 'Banks of the Nile' was different – we rehearsed it but it never really settled, and when we got the studio it was still in a state of flux. We came to record the song and did quite a few takes of it, and it wasn't happening. It was a long song, a lot of verses. We finally got to the point where it was getting a bit frustrating, so we went to the pub and in a conversation we decided that we were just gonna go in and busk it. And that's exactly what happened. It was a first take, everybody doing what they felt, and that became [the album cut].

Despite Boyd's antipathy towards the Fotheringay collective, he proceeded to produce their self-titled debut, by his own admission applying himself when he felt the songs merited the effort, believing 'The Sea' and 'The Pond and the Stream' to be "two of the most unbelievable, fantastic songs." But his memory is that, "they weren't a tight band. With Fotheringay everything was a struggle." Jerry Donahue reaffirms that Boyd "clearly didn't take a personal interest in it. We were pretty much left to get on with the job ourselves." Recorded in just seven days of sessions, and with most songs barely blooded on the road, *Fotheringay* was a surprisingly strong album. Even Trevor's contributions more than held their own.

If the tensions in the studio impinged on the band, everyone save Sandy (and presumably Trevor) remained blithely unaware of the precarious financial precipice on which they were balancing. Gerry Conway recalls, "feel[ing] somewhat intimidated by the political side of it – my intuition was saying, 'I don't think everybody wants this'." However, he knew Sandy well enough to know that, "having decided to do it, [she] was gonna stick with it and see it through, regardless of how everybody else felt about it."

When Richard Williams concluded, in *Melody Maker*, that "'Banks of the Nile' is probably the best rock arrangement I've ever heard, simple as that, and the rest of the album isn't far behind ... this is the way that British music must go," it must have seemed Sandy had been fully vindicated in her decision to form Fotheringay. The first tour, which concluded at the Royal Festival Hall on March 31, six months after Fairport's triumph, was also well-received and though the album, on its June release, only hovered nervously around the lower twenties on the charts, the foundations seemed to be in place for a sustained assault on the record-buying public.

Of course, the album may have fared somewhat better if Fotheringay had toured to support it – rather than three months prior to its release. It must have seemed to some at Island (and Witchseason) that, after the brief flurry of excitement that came with something new, Fotheringay had all but disappeared off the radar by the time of the album's release. There was certainly some whispered resentments expressed by Sandy's old band, for whom Fotheringay represented a draining of resources at their expense.

Dave Pegg: I used to get pissed off about Fotheringay because we'd be doing about 200 gigs a year, the Fairports, we all got paid from the Witchseason office. We all got the same [but] when Fotheringay got put together, they seemed to us to do nothing at all. I think they only did about six gigs, but we knew they were getting paid the same as we were getting. And they'd got a better PA system than us. There was a bit of rivalry, mainly because of Trevor. Trevor always had these huge, grandiose plans but he usually pulled them off, or he'd get somebody to fund it, and we'd be like, "Bloody Trevor, seen what they've got!" They're driving around in chauffeur-driven cars and we're stuck in the back of a transit. It was a very smooth, slick production ... whereas Fairports it was like, "We'll do the vocal when we get back from the pub."

Slightly embroidered as Pegg's recollections may be, it *is* true that between April 23 – when Fotheringay, Fairport Convention and Matthew's Southern Comfort shared a unique bill at the Roundhouse – and October 2, when Fotheringay headlined, over Elton John, at the Royal Albert Hall, Fairport toured America twice, as well as playing their own mini-tour of the UK, to promote their first post-Sandy offering, the superb *Full House*. Fotheringay, on the other hand, played nothing more than the occasional European festival date.

Sandy's distaste for the road, and craving for companionship, instead resulted in a happy summer spent in a farmhouse in Wittering, near Chichester, on the Sussex coast. Chaffinches Farm, which journalist Michael Watts described as "a neat brick building with a grove of shrubs and trees on its right," seemed like a quite deliberate recreation on Sandy's behalf, part Farley Chamberlayne, part summers in North Wales with her cousins. Replicating the Farley methodology, time passed slowly, as Fotheringay reinvented itself in *Liege*

& *Lief* mode. Even if Donahue recollects that "we didn't get *a lot* of work done," he felt that the time at Chaffinches Farm allowed him to find "a way inbetween" the band's country influences and "the Celtic goings-on."

> **Pat Donaldson:** We spent a long time playing through most of the songs. It was a good band from that point of view. We were always arranging songs – it was a pleasant thing to do because everybody was in the same frame of mind, nobody wanted to be the 'superstar' of the group. [CD]

Fotheringay could be an insular outfit. When Shirley Collins and Ashley Hutchings came to visit one day, they found the quintet off-hand, wrapped up in their own world. Still, their occasional forays into the real world, to play the Holland Pop Festival, the National Jazz & Blues Festival or the Yorkshire Folk, Blues and Jazz Festival, reminded fans of the band's strengths and, whatever the economic wisdom of this hiatus, the months of splendid isolation turned Fotheringay from a gauche outfit, unsure of their place in Pop, into the sort of solid, dependable musical backbone needed by England's finest female singer.

On September 19, 1970, the day after Jimi Hendrix choked to death on his own bilious vomit, Sandy even found her paramount position being recognised in the most prestigious of the various annual readers' polls run by the English music weeklies. Unexpectedly voted the Top Female Singer in the *Melody Maker* poll, Sandy then found her name attached to a leader in that tabloid favourite *The Sun*, which announced that 'Unknown' Sandy is our top of the pops'. It may have seemed newsworthy that a singer like Sandy could supplant the likes of Lulu, Cilla Black and Sandie Shaw, let alone Dusty Springfield, but it also proved that the increasingly album-oriented readers of the music weeklies shared almost no common ground with single-buying teenyboppers or TV-guided parents.

Though the gap in musical tastes had been growing for some time, to put the result in context, the previous year's winner of the *MM* poll had been Chicken Shack's Christine Perfect and, sandwiched between Lulu and Cilla Black, at six, had been one Sandy Denny. And it wasn't like Sandy had actually won the International Section for Top Female Singer, which had been won, for the second year running, by the raw-nerved Janis Joplin. Though Sandy would surely have voted for Dusty Springfield, whose early 45 'Silver Threads & Golden Needles' occupied a prime position in the Fotheringay live set, she equally aspired to emulate Janis, at least vocally, something she had admitted to herself in that surprisingly confessional excerpt from her 1969 diary where she "had decided to experiment with [a mixture of gin and Southern Comfort] to see if I, too, could produce the shattered effects which Janis Joplin seems to acquire as a result of drinking it." The posed photos of Sandy taken at Fotheringay's inception, by Linda Fitzgerald-Moore, also seemed to suggest a persona quite consciously modelled on Janis's.

That the silver-tongued Sandy sought to replicate "the shattered effects" of Janis Joplin's vocals seems to beggar belief but, in keeping with many aspects of herself, Sandy didn't want what she had – this 100% pure vocal tone – she wanted the stripped-raw rasp of a boozy blues singer. What Sandy could not have known at the time was just how alike the two of them were. Nor can she have imagined, the day she attended the *MM* shindig to collect her award, and be photographed with her male equivalent, Led Zep's Robert Plant, that Janis was just a couple of weeks away from the sordid finale of a life spent looking for love in all the wrong places.

David Sandison: The parallels between her and Janis are quite interesting. Janis was absolutely convinced she looked like a dog but she could be luminously beautiful. She'd get on stage and grow six inches. She was incredibly self-demeaning, she just thought she was worthless. Sandy ... was just desperate to please her parents all the time. She always thought she was less than she was. I just found parallels with Janis, having known them both. This business of drinking the same cocktails as she'd read Janis had; the immersion in the rock thing – making friends with [Pete] Townshend and Don Henley and Zappa – she wanted to be a rock singer, and Trevor was never going to let her do that 'cause Trevor didn't know that world.

Three weeks after Janis was found dead in a New York hotel room, having chased one dragon too many, Sandy was being asked about her own influences in *Melody Maker*. Leavened with her usual self-deprecating wit, Sandy gave a surprisingly forthright insight into how she saw herself, "My influences? Alcohol – no, not really[sic]. I tried to model myself on Twiggy but that didn't work. I'm basically a coward and people are very important to me. I really like to be with people and if I find myself alone in the flat, I won't stay there, I'll go out and visit someone."

On her return to London, after a summer on the coast, Sandy immediately threw herself back onto the circuit of afterhours Soho clubs then catering to

West End party animals. The Speakeasy, where Mario the maitre d' could be relied on to keep her stash of brandy at the ready, the Mandrake, the Buxton, the Colony, and the Scotch had now definitively supplanted the Cousins (now closed) and the Horseshoe Tavern as homes away from home.

Sandy, it seemed, was determined to reinvent herself as a hard-drinkin' rock chick, all the while preparing to make her headlining debut at the Royal Albert Hall, fronting the gentle folk-rock of Fotheringay. Sandy on the brandy at The Colony, though, was destined to remain a quite different lady from her stage-trippin' alter-ego.

Linda Thompson: We went to the Speakeasy together. She had these rock friends, like Pete Townshend and Frank Zappa. She had this life away from folk music, which I didn't. She was earning reasonable money, and she was incredibly generous. "I can't go to the Speakeasy, the drinks are seven shillings." "Don't worry about that. I'll pay." She also used to go to Muriel's place, The Colony in Soho, a between hours and afterhours drinking place. Lucien Freud, Jeffrey Bernard, Peter O'Toole, all these people. I went once, and it wasn't my cup of tea. It was for serious drinkers. Sandy could drink people under the table, but I didn't last at The Colony ... She used to hang out with [the likes of] Keith Moon, serious wild people. She was years ahead of her time. She wasn't an apologist for feminism. She just was it. She didn't make any diffentiation between her and the boys. And she didn't put up with any shit.

Part Two
THE SOLO YEARS

8

1970–71: FAREWELL FOTHERINGAY

Outtake from the *North Star* cover photo sessions.

"We'd reached a peak in our careers at that time. Joe Boyd decided that Sandy should break into a solo career, so he aborted the second [Fotheringay] album when we were about halfway through recording it. No-one really agreed with him that it was the right time for it, including Sandy herself. She was in tears when she told us. She'd never been happier. The way things were going, the second album was likely to do even better than the first. It was all so sudden and there were no warning signs ... When you see what happened in retrospect, it greatly affected all our careers, and Sandy's probably more than most. It didn't enhance her career as Joe had said that it would." [CD]

Jerry Donahue

"You can have all the abstract conversations about finances you want, and [Sandy]'s not hearing it because she's got another agenda. But a year later, the money's running out and Roy Guest is explaining it to her, 'When this next advance comes in, all it's going to do is wipe out your debts.' The whole issue of what was said to whom is a red herring."

Joe Boyd

O n October 2, 1970, Fotheringay resumed touring activities, with a show
at London's most cavernous emporium of sound, the Royal Albert Hall.
Having departed from received wisdom by prefacing their autumn tour,
not climaxing it, with their London date, the new songs they had in mind to
debut were still in their embryonic state. Nor was the circular acoustics of the
venue suited to Fotheringay's type of amplified gentility. When Sandy
attempted a heartfelt 'Wild Mountain Thyme', dedicated to her attendant
father, it was all but lost to the rafters. Compounding these problems was the
support act that night, Elton John, on the verge of great things and newly
chartbound (with 'Your Song'). Sandy's band were ill-suited successors to
Elton's boisterous trio.

Jerry Donahue: That was a terrible miscast. It was our fault. He asked if
[he] could do it. Actually Pat, Gerry and I had to talk Sandy and Trevor into
[it]. Elton, Pat, Gerry, I, and Linda Peters were all enlisted by Joe Boyd to
go in and do fourteen tunes in one day. We did all the backing tracks, and
Linda and Elton stayed on to do vocals after that. We'd done these
[publishing] demos and the way he was playing – he was a wonderful piano
player – [we thought] he was sensitive enough. We knew very little about
his stage-show. We thought he'd be a really good opener for us. But we
had no idea what he had in mind, that he was going to do the most
incredible rock & roll show ever. He pretty much blew us off the stage
before we even got on the stage. [And] unfortunately it was not one of our
best gigs. Both Sandy and Trevor were very, very nervous.

Inevitably, the reviews chose to contrast Fotheringay's perceived failure of
nerve with Elton's new-found edge. Suddenly the tour on which the band was
about to embark was overshadowed by a series of post-mortems in the media.
A usually taciturn Pat Donaldson was prompted to snap back, "It [has been]
made into such a big thing, that Albert Hall gig. That one gig [has been] made
into like the end of the group."

Whatever forces were at work to dissolve Sandy's happy band of musical
recluses had indeed taken the slightly shambolic nature of this single set as
their cue. Trevor Lucas, happy enough coming offstage – "I felt that the group
had actually played very well" – found that "a day later people started saying
blah blah blah and I was a bit taken aback, because I didn't really understand

it." It was Sandy, though, who bore the brunt of renewed pressures imposed by those determined to upset the band's precious equilibrium.

Sandy Denny: We really get heavies laid on us. You wouldn't believe the things that I went through after the Albert Hall concert. I kept getting approached by people who were telling me things about this member of the group and that member of the group, and like you'd do much better without him and him, and why don't you do this or that ... Listen, you could be a superstar! ... I don't even want it. In the end I said to people that I was just one member of a group, and if they wanted me without the group then they could piss off. [1970]

Nothing if not audacious, Fotheringay had elected to assign as much of the set to songs they had been working on over the summer as the now-familiar *Fotheringay* fare. Fronted by a notoriously unpredictable performer, and with anything upto three guitars to integrate into the mix, Fotheringay were bound to occasionally flounder. But by the time they closed out their autumn tour, at Oxford Town Hall, two months to the day after the Royal Albert Hall disaster, they had again achieved a remarkable makeover, the new songs and arrangements having successfully taken on lives of their own. Most notable were two new songs from Sandy's pen that showed a new allusive quality she was now bringing to her lyrics.

The more personal, and therefore more lyrically oblique, of the pair was called 'Late November', seemingly a reference to the time when Sandy decided to leave Fairport, though its original point of reference was a dream "all about the tall brown people/ [and] the sacred young herd/ on the phosphorous sand." This was the same dream in which she had seen herself hurtling along an icy road with Fairport roadie Harvey Bramham at the wheel. The prose version in her commonplace book, dated February 21, 1969, contained both 'the tall brown people and the sacred herd':

"Before long we stopped, although I don't know why, beside a beach. I got out of the van and wandered along the water's edge among a heard [sic] of cows. Also on the sea shore I found many strange objects (apart from the cows – I seemed to accept the presence of those). These things resembled parts of internal organs of some animal, but they were dry and salted, sort of preserved by the sea. I poked one of them to verify my first thoughts of what they were, and then stood up and asked one of the cows about these strange things. "They are all that is left of the human race

as it was many years ago, and this is a place of sanctity," said the cow in reply, but he seemed kind. I said "Oh" and went to walk away but that feeling of "somebody behind you" crept up my spine, and I turned suddenly. In front of me were two very tall people; I'd never seen the like of them before. They dwarfed me incredibly. There [sic] skins were light brown, their hair vaguely fuzzy like a negros, but not so tight, and it was brown. Grey eyes, wide open. There [sic] robes were brown. They were both male, and I thought they could have been brothers – they looked so similar. They seem surprised to see me but concealed it better than I did, for I felt myself trembling. "Where do you come from," said one of these two. "Wimbledon!" I blurted out...."

Brought to the place "where they lived" – presumably the temple that, in 'Late November', was "filled with the strangest of creatures" – Sandy found herself being "walked up stairs, passing many similarly clad people, all with the same kind of features as my two escorts. Many paused on the stairway, and stared at me, but turned away as if they realised it was impolite to stare. I came to the conclusion that, to them, I was some kind of freak." The dream, and its import, remained a mystery, even with it occupying eight pages of one of her notebooks. However, as *Rolling Stone*'s Steve Morse was informed a couple of years later:

"Several months after the dream [Sandy] was coming back from St. Andrew's in Scotland when she stopped to walk her Airedale, Watson. They went out to a beach which she realized, walking along, was the same one as was in the dream. A jet pilot suddenly came out of nowhere and began swooping down to the water and climbing back up. She watched him idly for a while until she realised that it was not the dream and he was in some danger, flying so low. About the time that became clear, the pilot disappeared."

The moment on the beach at St. Andrews evidently marked some kind of epiphany. The dream-like Sandy seems to be disregarding information about the fate of others, seemingly part of the song's initial concerns, in order to come to terms with her own "ill-fated day" (surely a reference to the M1 accident). The vision of "the pilot [who] flew all across the sky and woke me" in the final verse brings back the previous vision, which in turn reminds her that she must move on, even if it must be at the expense of "the insane and wise."

Having applied "the pathos and the sadness" to her own predicament, she proceeded to dissect the "methods of madness" that lead men to war, in her other major work of the summer, a song that dealt head-on with mankind's wilful rush to destruction – 'John the Gun'. Whether or not Sandy was directly inspired to write her own anti-war song by hearing Fairport's epic workout, 'Sloth', 'John the Gun' remains the darker work, a lyrical evocation of the AntiChrist in the guise of the title character, a figure driven mad by the thunder of guns until he pours scorn on those whose "ideals of peace are gold/which fools have found upon the plains of war – I shall destroy them all." The song had been debuted back in August, when Sandy and the boys recorded a session for Dutch radio, and it was evidently one of that small band of songs that made her proud. In an October press interview, she called it her personal favourite, and insisted it would definitely be going on the next album.

'John the Gun' was also one of five songs Fotheringay chose to preview to their listening fans on two BBC radio sessions, recorded on November 12 and 15, less than a week before sessions were due to begin on 'that difficult second album'. It had been barely seven months since the sessions for *Fotheringay*, but Sandy seemed unduly anxious to make another vinyl statement, insisting that, "the next album can't fail to be better than the first ... [which] ... was the preliminary effort of the group." Not that she had a surfeit of songs to bring to the sessions. Despite the undoubted quality of 'Late November' and 'John the Gun', it would appear that Fotheringay, one album late, were now set on making a more natural successor to *Liege & Lief*. The other four songs debuted on the Beeb comprised two Scottish ballads ('Gypsy Davey' and 'Eppy Moray'), a highland lovesong ('Wild Mountain Thyme'), and an Australian 'bush ballad' ('Bold Jack Donahue').

The egalitarian model, tenuously maintained on the debut platter, was all but abandoned on these sessions, with Trevor's resonant tenor confined to 'Bold Jack Donahue' and the opening section of 'Eppy Moray'. Otherwise, it was to be all Sandy's singing. The choice of which songs they planned to record also seems to have been largely hers. Aside from the two self-penned compositions, there was 'Two Weeks Last Summer', a Dave Cousins song she had last recorded with the Strawbs back in 1967. Also rehearsed with Fotheringay, and probably pencilled in for the second album, was a powerful arrangement of the English ballad, 'Bruton Town', long a personal favourite. Along with a beguiling 'Wild Mountain Thyme' and a broody 'Gypsy Davey', Fotheringay had the makings of a very strong album, albeit not the largely original work that might have been expected from its predecessor. Sandy, it seemed, again preferred reworking traditional fare to the more painful self-examination that songwriting required of her.

As it is, the situation may have been largely forced on Sandy. Quite simply, the financial footing on which Fotheringay had been conceived now required a major injection of cash if it was to retain any grip on reality. Money they could ill-afford had been squandered on a PA system designed by Trevor, which because of its scale had been christened Stonehenge. Unfortunately, as Gerry Conway recalls, "you had to stand next to it to hear anything, it didn't really work, and the size didn't make any difference. We had this thing built, it cost a lot of money, and ... it was all on a grand scale. [Then] WEM [had] to store it, because it was so big."

Two months of gigging had only returned Fotheringay to break-even point, and the only other obvious way of generating a significant input of cash was to get the A&M advance on the second album of Sandy's recently-negotiated contract. Island money was seemingly already spoken for, and with Boyd's management/production company on the verge of being sold to Island, the Witchseason weekly retainer system was also about to go by the board.

Joe Boyd: A lot of the issues to do with Fotheringay were financial. Technically, according to the contracts, the deal was always cross-collateralized. If I'd gone crazy and spent $100,000 making a John and Beverly record, which had been unrecouped and Fairport had had a big success, theoretically Island would have been in a position to recoup the money that I'd spent on the [former] from the income that was coming in from the [latter]. In practice, [Blackwell]'d give me whatever I needed to pay the artists what they were entitled to individually, so that the crunch never came. But there was never really that much of a credit for anyone ... When Witchseason was [being] sold to Island, there was a big toting up and there was a position arrived at for every individual signed to Witchseason, and the idea was that everyone would do a new deal with Island directly, and their account balance would be transferred ... The only reason [Fotheringay] had any financial solidity as an entity was the advance that was due on delivery of the second record from A&M, which wasn't as much as $40,000. So they weren't even gonna have as much as they'd had the first time [around].

If the atmosphere at the sessions for the first album had been a little strained, it was as nothing to the vibe that permeated the sessions in November and December. Boyd had agreed to produce the album, despite being, in his own words, "under tremendous pressure to get all these projects finalised before I left for California. Sound Techniques studio was block-booked, I was there every day, working with Fairport, Nick Drake, Mike Heron and Chris McGregor." Juggling Fotheringay sessions in the sliver of time he'd allotted himself before taking up a job at Warner Brothers, he seemed quite unwilling to give 's ban the benefit of the doubt.

> **Joe Boyd:** I probably shouldn't have been producing the [second] record. My lack of respect for the group was clear, and couldn't have helped the atmosphere. We'd put out a record that had sold disappointingly, A&M was unhappy. Sandy's tracks on the first record are among the best things she ever did – the rest of it, who cares? And the artwork, Trevor's sister, was terrible. It would have been one thing if I'd been unhappy with it and it sold, and the group was working all the time, making money, but that wasn't the case ... I knew what Sandy was capable of, and it was very upsetting to me.

Boyd has given a number of accounts over the years as to his role in the break-up of Fotheringay, and it is to his credit that even now he is prepared to expose his version of events to a sceptical biographer. However, this version is not borne out by the memories of the other participants, nor by something as historically irrefutable as the studio log-sheets. According to Boyd, the culmination of his personal despair at the way the album sessions were going "came on the 42nd take of a basic track for a tune, where I ended up standing in the middle of the studio with a baton, trying to keep the rhythm section in time." He thinks the song in question was 'John the Gun'. The track sheets for the sessions that still reside in the Universal/Island vaults find no evidence to support Boyd's recollection. According to the files, 'John the Gun' was recorded in three takes. The other original Sandy title seems to have been cut in a single take, something Gerry Conway distinctly recollects.

> **Gerry Conway:** The first thing we went in and did was 'Late November' ... it was either a first or second take – that was it! – so we started on an up. Everybody was a lot more confident. That very first session went very well, and we all felt that we'd improved. I don't think the band had any idea about what was going on behind [the scenes].

Assuming that this is the 'New Title 1' listed on a Sound Techniques reel,

dated December 18,* 'Late November' was indeed cut in a single take. Sandy
alluded to the same sensation as Conway in a later interview, "[we] put one
track down, and ... we did it in two takes (sic). It was a song we'd been playing
for about a week, and it was really great. I suddenly remember getting up from
the piano and thinking 'Wow, that was really great,' and when we listened
back to it, it was. Then we broke up about a week later."

Jerry Donahue also remembers feeling "that the second album was going
better than the first. It was gonna sound much more unified, probably would
have been a much more interesting album. [We were] loving the direction,
and we were all playing much tighter as a unit." On the evidence of the tape
logs, Fotheringay worked through at least six songs, two thirds of an album, in
just three days' worth of sessions. Hardly tardy. And yet, Joe Boyd, in
correspondence with the *Hokey Pokey* fanzine in 1989, insisted he was not alone
in his despair at the way things were going.

Joe Boyd: With Fotheringay it was very frustrating, we were getting
nowhere fast and nobody was very happy with what was being recorded
... Sandy, Trevor, and I think Pat Donaldson and I, ended up having a meal
in the pub opposite Sound Techniques the week before Christmas ... We
hadn't finished our target for that day's recording. We sat there eating our
lamb chops, chips and peas. Sandy was very upset. She was despairing of
what they were going to do. The record wasn't going well, it was taking
longer so it was costing more, and the group was running out of money.
Sandy was saying, "What do you think I should do?" I replied that she
should do what I said in the first place: disband the group and be a solo
artiste. Sandy said, "If I [was to do] that would you stay in Britain?" This is
the most contentious microsecond of the whole story. I recall that I said I'd
already sold the company, and been appointed director of music services
at Warner Brothers, [but] if there was anything that could make me want
to undo those steps, it was what she'd just said. The next morning I got a
call from Roy Guest, Sandy's manager, asking me to a meeting with Sandy.
When I arrived, she said, "I did it. I've broken up the group." I said I thought
that was good and that I would try and arrange to come back and produce
her record if she wanted me to. We could do part of the record in London
and part in Los Angeles. Sandy said, "You mean you're not going to stay?"

*It was not the first session, which had been at least a month earlier.

I said I would love to record an album with her, but I couldn't unsell Witchseason.

Again the evidence is against Boyd. The December 18 session yielded finished takes of two new titles, one in a single take, the other in nine. Possibly there was a bad day in the studio, where nothing had got done (a December 29 session is listed in the Island records, though no tape has been located). Jerry Donahue thinks not: "We'd been to a Christmas party only a few nights before Sandy broke the news to us, and she'd been really enjoying herself and saying how well things were going."

Not surprisingly, the Boyd version that seems to fit the facts closest comes from an interview given before the long-term consequences of the decision on Sandy's well-being had become apparent. Back in March 1973, he admitted in *Rolling Stone* that he "did pressure [Sandy] into that breakup, and then I left her with the results of that breakup ... We had long, emotional meetings; I told Sandy she should break up the group ... During one of the meetings I said if she would break up the group I would think about staying in London to produce her. The next day I told her I couldn't; that I had to go to L.A., and she shouldn't base her decision on me. The amount of time spent under that rash commitment of mine was about twelve hours."

Certainly the other members of Fotheringay are of the opinion that Boyd had committed himself to Sandy's future. As Donahue recalls it, "Sandy [told] us that Joe Boyd had been offered a big job with Warners, and that he'd turn it down if she'd go solo ... she finally thought that if he had that much faith in her, then she ought to go along with his plans." Conway thinks that Boyd was there in the studio when Sandy announced the breaking up of the band.

Gerry Conway: It was another day in the studio – everyone was there except Sandy and Joe, and then Sandy turned up with Joe and they announced, That was it! ... She was very upset. After the announcement was made, it was [a question] as to whether we would carry on as a band without Sandy. I know that my reply was fairly instant.

However much Sandy may have misconstrued Boyd's offer, what she saw as his desertion – when he took the job at Warners – shook her to the core. Donahue remembers a Sandy who "was very bitter ... afterwards." Even four years after the fact, when interviewed about the break-up, her bitterness could still break through, "The management... just didn't want to know about us really, and they made life totally unbearable, and in the end we just broke up. [I] couldn't take it anymore." She would continue to resent the idea of fronting her own band all the time it took for her to rejoin a hybrid Fotheringay/ Fairport in 1974.

Though Trevor's role in the decision process seems to have been minimal to non-existent, Boyd prefers to believe that the break-up of Fotheringay was a combination of financial realities imploding and "this ... conflict and torment [on the part] of Sandy, [who] on the one hand was this emotional, needy female who had this normal desire to make a go of her relationship; but the other side of the coin was a fantastically intelligent, tasteful, brilliant musician who knew perfectly well how mediocre a musician Trevor was, who knew that what I was saying to her was right ... She saw, in my departure, that she was gonna be alone with these doubts and these fears, and as she was facing the reality that I was leaving ... she panicked ... [and] leapt on an opportunity to get herself out of this mess." Trevor refrained from commenting on the fateful decision at the time but some years later, when Steeleye Span's Maddy Prior was on the verge of going solo, he advised her, "Stay in front of the band. Don't start getting into all that thing of it being shared. Just get stuck out front and be done with it."

On January 30, 1971, Fotheringay officially said farewell at the Queen Elizabeth Hall in London. The show – which included three brand new originals, as well as 'Eppy Moray', 'Gypsy Davey', 'Bold Jack Donahue', five *Fotheringay* favourites, guest appearances by Long John Baldry, Martin Carthy and Ashley Hutchings, and even a version of 'Let It Be' sung by Sandy at the piano – was certainly a fitting epilogue.

The same afternoon, a Radio One special related the story of Fotheringay and rebroadcast a number of the songs performed at the November BBC sessions, songs from an album that was no more. It was a very emotional farewell and though Sandy would work with each and every musician in the band on a regular basis, the unique chemistry that could in the fullness of time have made financial imperatives moot was suffocated, if not at birth, then before it could put on its walking shoes. It would take Sandy a long time to fully come to terms with the significance of her decision. Though she told one journalist she envisaged making a record "and see[ing] how that goes for a couple of months," she later summed up how she really felt, to the trusted Karl Dallas, "I was very dead in a lot of ways. I felt almost defeated in a strange sort of way."

That feeling of defeat would last some time. Sandy's first solo album contains a number of lyrical chronicles from a vanquished soul. 'Wretched Wilbur' seems to have been composed in the weeks after the decision to break up Fotheringay. It was certainly debuted at their final show, and the lyrics suggest another example of Sandy writing about a traumatic personal event – this time the break-up of Fotheringay – in code:

"Misers mise [sic] and compromise,
I know what I have seen,
The wanderers are in the east,
That's where I should have been.

But I did not go there,
I couldn't find the way,
I do believe I made a try,
But I couldn't really say."

In the battles that were to come, Sandy would look back on the hazy days of Fotheringay with a sense of regret that would not go away. She had lost another surrogate family, and been thrown back upon her own resources at a time when she felt particularly vunerable.

The seeming surety with which she was being feted as the 'next big thing' was only reinforced by her first post-Fotheringay studio activity. The biggest rock band in the world wanted Sandy to duet on a ballad they had composed for their fourth vinyl outing, destined to become one of the biggest-selling albums of all time. Jimmy Page and Robert Plant were both huge fans of Fairport Convention, Page even going on record, in an interview in *Zigzag*, as saying *Liege & Lief* was for him the best album of 1969. When the pair of them penned a typically Zeppelinesque surrogate stab at tradition, 'The Ballad of Evermore', they decided it lent itself to the call/response mode of traditional expression, and requested Sandy lend her soaring tones to the experiment.

Sandy was now being pushed into coming up with more songs of her own, both by the powers-that-be and by her ever-persistent partner. The prospect of a solo album by a singer-songwriter in 1971 was generally perceived as some kind of artistic statement in the first person. The aborted Fotheringay album had offered slim pickings from her own pen. Trevor, in particular, knew Sandy well enough to know that songwriting did not come easy to her, and that given the choice between a night on the town and an evening spent in self-absorption at the piano, the fight would always be an uneven one. He also knew what she was capable of, and was not prepared to settle for second best. Unfortunately, his not-so-gentle proddings caused their own resentments on Sandy's part which, after a glass or two, could bubble to the surface.

Bambi Ballard: I remember going over to their house one time and Trevor was going somewhere, and I think I stayed the night. Trevor said to me, "She's got to sit and write some songs tomorrow," and he said it in front of her. In other words, she is not self-determining, she will use you as an excuse not to do it. You only do that if you have absolutely no sensitivity ... He might as well have said, "She's got to do the washing-up before she goes to bed." ... And Sandy was terribly upset. And she said, "I get five thousand pounds a year retainer for writing these songs, and I'm keeping him. That's the money that pays the bills, 'cause that's the one that comes in not because we're doing a gig or because we're doing an album, that's the hardcore of our bank account." She was the breadwinner, and was very, very conscious of it and the minute she got drunk and starting talking about Trevor, that's what she'd talk about.

Initially, Sandy proved reluctant to make the first release in her own name an essentially original statement. Interviewed when she was barely halfway through the sessions, she told a journalist, "There's far too much emphasis being put on 'writing my own material'. That's why so many bands are making bad albums. They think it's expected of them to compose the lot themselves, whereas quite often they haven't the talent in that direction." The comment was clearly directed at a self that had, as yet, failed to come up with enough songs to fill out an album, even with the additional six months the demise of Fotheringay had brought her.

Part of the problem stemmed from the fact that Sandy still had a tendency to slip into the kind of stock imagery that came so easily to her. Asked at this time about the inspiration for her songs, she opened up enough to admit that, "when I write songs I often picture myself standing on a beach, or standing on a rock or a promenade or something. I just put myself there sometimes and, without even realising it, I find myself describing what I'm looking at." The results, no matter how sincere and affecting, rarely placed Ms. Denny in the Wordsworth mould, forcing her self-editing side to kick in. One such example, perhaps the very one she was alluding to was a lyric called 'The Glistening Bay',* the second verse of which took her descriptive inclinations to the max:

"And I do recall I took a stone and felt it with my hand
I sat there on the high cliff top upon the incoming land
I hid that precious stone I held inside a weathered tree
The perfumed cedars caught the wind which blew in from the open sea
A handful of small coloured flowers were nestling in the grass
I tossed them to the blustery sky and watched them as they danced
Oh the fickle sea I've always loved and to this very day
I'll see those flowers come floating down towards the glistening bay."

In the same notebook Sandy had also written a number of traditional song titles, and a set of lyrics to one of them, 'Lord Bateman', an English broadside ballad which, according to legend, was based on the exploits of Gilbert Beket, father of St. Thomas, during the Third Crusade. The other songs listed were 'Blackwaterside', the Irish drinking song 'The Parting Glass', and Scottish elegy 'The Flowers of the Forest', already recorded by Fairport for the *Full House* album. Though no record exists of the latter two being recorded by Sandy, 'Blackwaterside' would be the first song recorded for *North Star Grassman & The Ravens*, as her first solo album would be known, and 'Lord Bateman' would occupy a number of early sessions, without ever making the final cut.

Even as some original songs began to come – 'The Optimist' and 'Next Time Around' were both laid down at sessions at the beginning of April – Sandy continued to cut a number of covers, unsure how many of her own strange new lyrics she wanted fixed in time. Richard Thompson recalls, "it was always hard to get Sandy to change pace in her material, so an untempo cover was sometimes attempted – which [invariably] tended to sound rather glued on." Sandy duly ended up reviving Dylan's 'Down in the Flood' from the *Liege & Lief* live set, Brenda Lee's 'Let's Jump The Broomstick', for which her vocal style was singularly unsuited, and Ernest Tubb's 'Walking The Floor Over You'. Having begun the album in early March, it would be the end of May before the final, and perhaps oddest, original of the lot – the title-track – was added to the master-reel.

---

*This is possibly the song listed on November 1971 session reels as 'Sitting On The Cliff'.

Containing some of her most difficult lyrics, *North Star Grassman* was never going to come out as an easy listening experience. At the time, not surprisingly, Sandy proved slightly defensive about the material, insisting that the original songs on the album "are biographical, [though only] about ten people can understand them. I just take a story and whittle it down to essentials ... I wouldn't write songs if they didn't mean something to me, but I'm not prepared to tell everyone about my private life, like Joni Mitchell does. I like to be a bit more elusive than that."

The songs Sandy was now penning were more than a little elusive. If 'Next Time Around', which had the even more cryptic working title of 'Only Just Impossible', was 'about' Jackson Frank, and 'Crazy Lady Blues' was apparently written for the soon-to-be Linda Thompson, each and every song on *North Star* seemed borne of personal experience (when 'Crazy Lady Blues' acquired an extra verse in February 1974, it was directed back upon itself: "Now give her a chance to sing, and she'll give you anything ... even 'Matty Groves', as you come here in your droves."). Talking at the distance of another, more successful album, she admitted that the results were not entirely satisfactory:

Sandy Denny: I think I was a bit depressed at the time, and the songs tended to be very introverted. In fact they got so turned in on each other that sometimes I had difficulty finding out what they meant myself ... I thought, "God! I've got to do this album," and I started rushing all these melancholy songs out. [1972]

Feeling compelled to make her first solo album without adequate respite, Sandy's biggest problem proved to be not so much the songs as the sound. Having known only the light touch of Joe Boyd as producer, she craved a similarly sympathetic taskmaster. Asked about possible candidates at the time of Fotheringay's final concert, her only comment was, "I think I'll have to work with someone on the album that I know and respect musically." Fortunately Richard Thompson, who had released himself from the relentless treadmill of gigging that had been Fairport's post-Sandy lot, was more than happy to provide input, though he found that "she couldn't quite face up to the idea of selecting a producer, so we rolled into the studio with Andy Johns engineering, and recorded a few things in a haphazard manner. It needed a little more direction, so we brought in John Wood ... but there still wasn't a firm hand on the tiller, and I think that reflects in the final production."

John Wood had worked on most of the sessions produced by Boyd, and knew the studio Sandy well. His technical capabilities, and ear for music, were second to none. However, he had been obliged to choose engineering as a more realistic alternative to the diplomatic corp. As Gerry Conway says of him, "If he's got something to say, then he'll say it." With Sandy, some foreign office experience might have come in handy.

> **Philippa Clare:** John Wood used to have Sandy in tears a lot ... He was difficult in the studio, very bad socially. John didn't nurture. "Wrong, do it again." [Not] "Lovely, Sandy, it was wonderful, can we try it one more time." ... She was always nervous in the studio ... I don't think you ever get Sandy really great on record, and of course John Wood was [always] engineering, so she was always on edge ... She would get very tearful when she'd feel insecure ... There was once when we went around and we collected seventeen lit cigarettes. She even put a burn in John Wood's fridge.

If (wo)man-management was not John Wood's strong point, his instincts as to the type of instrumentation that suited Sandy were equally out of kilter. Sound Techniques, Wood's studio, had an enviable reputation for its tonal quality when it came to strings, indeed acoustic sounds in general. This reputation led him to forge a relationship with a film-score arranger named Harry Robinson, whose services he sometimes recommended to his clients. Sure enough, he advocated adding some strings to 'Next Time Around' and 'Wretched Wilbur'. The results were truly wretched. Though Sandy would accuse Wood of being "a terrible string freak" who "if I leave it just to him to mix [the album] it'll come back swamped with strings," she was as fascinated by Robinson's arrangement ideas as her erstwhile producer, and Harry would become a regular fixture on her remaining albums, often to the detriment of her songs' simple purity.

As it is, the released *North Star Grassman* sounds like an odds'n'sods collection culled from a number of unfinished projects – an alternate *Liege & Lief* ('Down in the Flood' as a duet with Richard), the aborted Fotheringay album ('Late November' is the Fotheringay take with guitar/vocal overdubs), an album of traditional songs ('Blackwaterside') and a string-drenched diva's debut, to name a few – bearing out Thompson's assessment that, "there [really] wasn't any producer."

Richard Thompson: She'd do anything she could to avoid recording. Talk mostly. She'd give really half-hearted performances, and then come along to the mix and say, "That's a terrible vocal," and ... someone would say, "Well, fix it," and because it was the last chance, she'd do a good one. Always postponing the real performance until the absolute eleventh hour. [JI]

Even the sequence, which with its powerful one-two opening volley of 'Late November' and 'Blackwaterside' promised so much, was a last minute decision. The reviewers could not hide their disappointment, Derek Brimstone asking pointedly in the newly formed *Folk Review*, "What's the good of laying down such lovely words if you have to strain to hear them?" Satisfying neither her mainstream fans nor the folkies, *North Star Grassman* failed to chart, a commercial failure that was thrown into even sharper relief by Sandy's second consecutive win in the *Melody Maker* readers' poll, seemingly on the back of a single vocal duet on a certain chart-topping album.

The disparity between critics' expectations and those of the fans who filled the halls and bought the albums was further highlighted at Sandy's London concert debut as a solo artist. The show at the suitably intimate Queen Elizabeth Hall was scheduled for September 10, coinciding with the album's release, unavoidably forcing her to forsake the powerhouse trio who had been by her side in the studio, i.e. the Fotheringay rhythm-section behind, Richard Thompson leading from the front. When Sandy had debuted eight of the songs at an almost impromptu set at the Lincoln Festival in July, she had been able to rely on Richard and Gerry Conway to not only recall the songs in situ but, in the former's case, to open out the likes of 'Blackwaterside' and 'John the Gun' with some trademark licks.

Unfortunately, the September London show coincided with a fit of other commitments on the parts of Thompson, Donaldson and Conway. The result was an unscheduled bout of Fotheringport confusion, the Fairport rhythm section and Jerry Donahue being drafted in to play a set of songs they knew not. The concert began in a classically disastrous way, and rarely returned to an even keel.

Philippa Clare: Sandy's first solo gig ... she [usually] used to wear t-shirts and jeans, and she and Trevor had gone out and bought what I call the Mermaid Dress, it was this pale blue, sequined job, long, with sleeves that [hung down]. She's absolutely scared rigid, she comes up the steps, trips over the dress, puts her hand on the piano, knocks a glass on the floor, and then she trips over a wire, finally gets to the microphone, she puts her guitar over [the dress] and with the long sleeves she can't play it. She [goes,] "Trevor." Went off. Comes back on, jeans and t-shirt. Standing ovation.

Though the audience stayed with Sandy throughout the hour long set, the media proved less forgiving, *Melody Maker*'s Michael Watts complaining that, "She had difficulty adjusting to the piano, there was a period of several minutes when she was unable to find a guitar in the right key, and she generally could not establish any great rapport with her three backup musicians. This amateurishness had a charming naivety about it at first, but after a while became irritating." Other, more discerning critics, whilst giving Sandy the benefit of the doubt, agreed that "the lack of rehearsals often sounded painfully obvious," and that her "troubles were due, in the main, to lack of cohesion between the rhythm section, as a result of [too] few rehearsals."

The show only took off when Sandy and Jerry Donahue revived their arrangement of 'Wild Mountain Thyme' as the final song, and when Sandy returned for an encore alone, confessing to the audience, "We are so unrehearsed I'll just have to sing you a song unaccompanied, 'cause we don't know anything else." The resulting 'Lowlands of Holland' finally lifted the rafters, and perhaps suggested that an album as devoted to traditional material as originals should have remained the preferred option. It also implied that she might have been better advised to leave the band in the studio, and put the sole in solo. Two sessions for the BBC, one for TV (the only TV footage extant), one for radio, in August and October, confirmed as much. Sandy, though, was determined to persevere with perming a band of musicians from the remnants of two interchangeable surrogate families, even fronting an extended Fotheringport Confusion on her next recorded work.

9

1972: MAID OF CONSTANT SORROW

HP agreement Sandy received from Steinway & Sons.

"There's a lot of money coming in and going out, so I'm constantly grabbing onto a bit, and then having to give it away again ... If I was on my own, I would be rich." [1972]

Sandy Denny

Hankering for some of that old rapport she had had with Fairport and Fotheringay, Sandy took to the road in October 1971 with her old friend Richard Thompson and a pick-up rhythm section, to promote *North Star Grassman & The Ravens*. Though Timi Donald was a light-handed drummer, and Thompson remained a sympathetic wizard, her stage-fright was only exacerbated by the pressures of fronting a band. The tour, which certainly had its moments, concluded with another of those nights when, in the words of *MM* journalist Colin Irwin, "all her nerve ends [would be] showing ... [and] it got worse and worse, 'cause she knew she was doing badly, and that made her even more nervous. Everyone was sitting on the edge of their seats. I really felt for her." Unfortunately, it came again in London, at University College.

It was a perhaps unconscious longing for the days of Fairport that led Sandy to begin work on her next album, just a fortnight after the college tour ended, with a song discarded from *Liege & Lief*. 'The Quiet Joys of Brotherhood' was a Richard Farina lyric she now set to the Irish lovesong, 'My Lagan Love'. Recorded by Fairport in four takes, it took considerably more work to create a whole series of multi-tracked Denny vocals set to the stark accompaniment of Dave Swarbrick's violin. The results, though, put the lush in luscious.

Eight days later, Sandy (and Richard) joined Swarb and the remaining Fairporters for an extended encore at the legendary Rainbow Theatre in London's Finsbury Park, and found herself remembering just how good familiarity felt. The encore took on truly epic proportions as Sandy and the boys worked their way through the likes of 'The Weight', 'Silver Threads & Golden Needles', 'Country Pie', 'Blues In The Bottle', 'High School Confidential' and 'Sweet Little Rock & Roller'. It took Trevor Lucas, standing in the wings, to realise that an album which captured the spirit of that encore could yet turn the Fairport family's slightly po-faced reputation on its head, and even turn a career or two around.

Trevor Lucas: I saw Fairport doing a gig at the Rainbow ... and Sandy and Richard got up, and did some rock & roll things. And I thought it would be a nice idea to get that down on record – things that groups play that knock audiences out but never get recorded. So [that was how] we had the idea of doing The Bunch. And that was the first thing I did as a producer. [1972]

The bluegrass/country flavour of the original encore was largely jettisoned in favour of something more suited to a three-piece rhythm-section comprising Pat Donaldson, Dave Mattacks and Gerry Conway. The ensuing album, attributed to The Bunch, was appositely named *Rock On*! The line-up, almost a who's who of folk-rock, on closer inspection most resembled a list of callers at Chipstead Street. For the first time on record, Sandy got to sing with Linda Peters, Richard got to sing Hank Williams and Dion songs, and 'Tyger' Hutchings took his finger out of his ear long enough to give Chuck Berry's 'Nadine' a good stomping.

If The Bunch album was planned as a party record, the sessions became a party unto themselves. Having managed to persuade Island to fund such an indulgent venture, Trevor had secured the recently-constructed Manor Studios, the first studio venture from Richard Branson's Virgin label, for a couple of weeks at a cut-price rate, this being a dry-run for the studio's facilities. Dry, though, the sessions themselves were never likely to be.

Philippa Clare: God, that was bad behaviour. We had a ball! That was a great party. There was creaking floorboards everywhere. Branson wanted somebody to come along, and just try it out, and get all the glitches out. In the control room, they were drinking Fosters, and Trevor made a complete steel curtain with these [pull] rings. When he sang 'Don't Be Cruel' he was lying flat on the floor. Everyone was so stoned!

At the time, The Manor was unique. Set in picturesque Cotswolds countryside, it was a live-in studio, offering full board. The logic was that, rather than recording on an *ad hoc* basis at London studios, as and when time allowed, bands could block book the Manor and, two weeks later, return to the record company with the 'multis' for a new album. Needless to say, the sheer novelty and the combination of personalities comprising The Bunch meant that work gave way to play more often than not.

Linda Thompson: It was a startling concept, you were staying there and sleeping there, and having your food there. It was absolutely fantastic. And we were young. Because it was a big house, there was loads and loads of bedroom hopping. It was like the Duke and Duchess of Fonfon's weekend party. These were pre-herpes, pre-AIDS days, [so if] somebody said, "That was quite a good vocal," you thought, "I think I'll sleep with you. That's a very nice thing to say."

Not surprisingly, Sandy wanted to sing everything, from 'Peggy Sue Got Married' to 'The Locomotion', and occasional subterfuge on Trevor's part was required if his concept was going to be preserved. Thankfully, Sandy's proclivity for partying hardest gave him enough downtime to slip on a vocal overdub or two from the then-Linda Peters. Even so, the Manor sessions were never going to result in a finished record, and a whole bunch (sic) of overdubs were needed back at Island studios. Not that the return to London seems to have unduly impinged on the party-mood.

Linda Thompson: In those days [Richard] was very supportive of me. I was always terrified of singing with Sandy, and he'd say, "Now, don't let her [intimidate you]." ... And Trevor ... would be very helpful with my vocal. When Sandy wasn't around, he'd say, "Let's nip in and do this vocal." She was fabulous, but she was definitely competitive ... [ ] ... Sandy and I had a bit of a clash over who was going to sing the harmony and who was going to sing the tune [on 'When Will I Be Loved']. Sandy was a bit cross at first because I sang the tune, and she said but the harmonies [should be] higher, and I said, 'Come on, you [can] sing higher than me." ... [ ] ... Trevor and I did 'Locomotion' when Sandy and Richard were in respective loos in Island being sick. He literally couldn't stand up ... In those days we took it for granted [that] there was unlimited studio-time. We'd be in the canteen, sitting chatting to Bob Marley, and then he'd go into one studio and we'd go into another. He'd sell eighty million records, and we'd sell eight! [CH/CD/CH]

Island (and indeed A&M's) strategy for selling The Bunch album extended to a press release anonymously penned by some maverick, who signed him or herself simply Subjective, and called Sometimes It Pays To Be Subjective. The tangled prose insisted that, "the biggest surprise on the album ... is Sandy Denny's singing, which although not really all that much as a rock and roller [Huh!], has a hell of a lot of soul and expression. For me Sandy singing 'That'll Be The Day', 'Love's Made A Fool Of You', 'Willie and the Hand Jive' and 'Learning The Game', makes the album fat, rounded and complete." Notwithstanding such subjective praise, *The Bunch Rock On* – an enjoyable enough curio from the days before vinyl shortage – sank like a cracked oil-tanker.

In an attempt to add some U.S. sales, Sandy committed herself to playing a series of shows at New York's Bitter End and L.A.'s Troubador – where she generously offered up renditions of 'Love's Made A Fool of You' and 'Learning the Game' – almost as soon as the twenty tracks recorded had been wittled down to album-length. A brief promotional tour the previous September had barely impinged on the American psyche but A&M were pushing *North Star Grassman* hard enough to warrant this second assault; and the musical trio in tow was as close to Sandy's perfect ensemble as she would come in her solo years. The ever-reliable RT was ably supported by Timi Donald and Pat Donaldson, and the shows themselves were almost universally impressive, even if Sandy's promise in the music press, that she would "take all the new material [she had] over to the States and do it for about a month, and then come back and record it," proved illusory.

Perhaps Sandy was originally planning to record versions of 'Maid of Constant Sorrow' and 'Bruton Town', both classic weal and woe songs represented in the shows, and prefaced in the latter's case by the observation that this "is about a poor lady. They all are, you know. 'Cause men are so rotten." Sandy seemed to be surprisingly willing to draw on the impressive traditional repertoire she had acquired over the years, even singing a sprightly 'Matty Groves', an acapella 'Reynard the Fox' and an explosive 'Blackwaterside', that showed just how potent the Denny-Thompson combination could be.

One night she returned to her hotel to find Richard ensconced in a discussion with an American fan about Bert Jansch's version of the Scottish ballad, 'The Twa Corbies', and when the fan admitted the meaning of the words eluded him, "Sandy sang the song ... unaccompanied, sitting on the floor leaning against the bed, stopping to explain the lines here and there." It was one more reminder that this material still held up for her. Almost the first track she cut on her return from the U.S. was another Jansch favourite from the old days, Anne Briggs' 'Go Your Own Way, My Love' but Sandy once again passed over it, admitting "I've always thought it a lovely song, but when I think about it, I listen to Bert singing it, and I don't know, I don't think I'd better it somehow."

Refraining from trying out her new songs, save for an occasional 'Listen, Listen', on the small but appreciative American audiences, Sandy still returned home with at least half a dozen originals she hoped to record. There had been something of a change in her songwriting, brought on in part it appeared by the flak the lyrics on *North Star Grassman* had generated. Talking shortly before leaving for the States, she owned up to the need to open up more in her lyrics.

Sandy Denny: If I wrote blatantly about something it would be going against my character ... I don't like people to know what's happening in my head. And this is a fault ... My songs are a bit devious, and perhaps weird ... I like doing little clever things in songs, with funny chords ... [But] I [do] want to write songs which make people understand what I mean, without having to lead them on. [1972]

One of the results of the rethink was a set of lyrics, in Sandy's handwriting, included in the next album centrefold. Another was some of her most accessible songs – 'Sweet Rosemary', 'The Music Weaver', 'The Lady', 'Listen, Listen' – and, perhaps inevitably, one of her most oblique, 'For Nobody To Hear', a song listed on the studio track-sheets either as 'Brahms' or 'The Ballad of Brahms', evidently a reference to the Brahms symphony that prompted the song:

> *"A symphony I learnt at school,*
> *In pigeonholes so clear,*
> *It made me for to write no songs,*
> *For nobody to hear."*

Having bedded the band in, Sandy decided to return to the Manor to complete the album begun at Island's London studios, back in November. The producer was again Trevor Lucas, who saw Sandy's second album as the perfect opportunity to present his own credentials as sympathetic-man-at-the-helm, but who in Thompson's view, now "pushed the records a little towards pop, with the danger of losing [Sandy's] uniqueness." John Wood was again called in for engineering duties.

With none of the usual time-pressures of a session at Basing Street or Sound Techniques, sessions at the Manor, scheduled for two, unerringly started at five or six, and the side of Sandy that, "in the studio ... could be lackadaisical," came to the fore. There were also technical problems Wood simply did not encounter at the London studios (Thompson recalls, "it was not a great sounding room [even after] John Wood hung a few blankets around").

John Wood: [*Sandy*] was started one way and then a lot of it scrapped and then we made it quite quickly ... We went to The Manor to do it, and we had a great deal of technical difficulty, and it was basically a total waste of time. Sandy wasn't a disciplined worker. At least when you went into a studio in London you went in at a set time and you got on with the job and everybody was there to do the job at a specific time ... There wasn't an urgency to get on with anything ... There wasn't the discipline of getting on with it. So not much was achieved. [PW]

Despite Sandy's familiarity with her musicians, a whole week in March yielded just two usable cuts, 'Bushes and Briars' and 'Sweet Rosemary', the former of which Sandy wrote at the Manor, inspired by an empty church she chanced upon on a Sunday stroll. The other six songs attempted that week were left in various states of disrepair, some just as backing tracks, some as solo performances by Sandy. 'After Halloween' and 'Go Your Own Way, My Love' would be left firmly at the wayside, whilst the others awaited the Sound Techniques touch.

Asked about the experience the following month, Trevor Lucas insisted, "it's good for a producer to know someone so well that they see them as both a person and as an artist. Sandy tends to be fairly introverted and sensitive in her writing and lyrics, so it is easier for me [than most] to understand what they are about." That introverted side, though rarely seen in public, made Sandy prone to bouts of uncertainty in the studio, for which Trevor was the ideal counsellor, even if sometimes his presence became a key factor in the negative energy emanating from the studio.

John Wood: Sometimes you'd get nowhere. She did have mood swings, to put it mildly. Sometimes, if Trevor was in the studio, she'd be so uptight it would end up in some domestic fracas. A lot of it was a lack of self-confidence which is very common in people who bluster, which she was very good at. She certainly had black moods, where she would drink a lot. She really needed to be the centre of attention. She was larger than life, but ... more than once ... she'd be doing an overdub and couldn't get it right, and would completely go to pieces and run out of the room. [JI]

There had evidently been some form of altercation involving Sandy at Sound Techniques, back in March 1971, at the start of the *North Star Grassman* sessions, which had prompted her to look further afield for the right sound. However, on her return to 46a Old Church Street in early April 1972, she was forced to admit, "I put these two vocal tracks down the other night, and there's just no comparison with anywhere else." The remaining seven songs, aided and abetted by a couple of Manor backing-tracks, were completed in a handful of Sound Techniques sessions through April and May, intersected by a dozen or so dates on the college circuit, to keep the coffers intact.

At least half a dozen of the new songs were debuted at these shows, as Sandy revelled in the opportunity to play with the closest she had come to a standing band since Fotheringay. That sense of celebrating song carried over onto the album, where 'For Nobody To Hear', 'The Lady' and 'The Music Weaver' all placed music at the centre of the singer's soul. The forces of nature also reappeared, on 'It'll Take A Long Time', 'Quiet Joys of Brotherhood', 'Listen, Listen' and 'Bushes and Briars', harnessed to the same joyous sound. Sandy even tried, for the first time since Fotheringay, to write in a consciously traditional style, perhaps inspired by the songs Richard was now writing for *Henry the Human Fly*. The results – 'Sweet Rosemary' and 'It Suits Me Well' – fell easily on the ears. 'It Suits Me Well' was a particularly successful evocation of departed values, Sandy adopting three male personae for whom "the living it is hard/ oh, but it suits me well." Interviewed about the album on its release, Sandy put her finger on a key transition.

> **Sandy Denny:** It's a much more forthright album than North Star Grassman and the Ravens, because I was just in a completely different frame of mind. My [new] songs are much more positive. They are more like statements than the withdrawn, tentative things [on the previous album] ... I'm quite pleased with the record as a compilation ... it encompasses a lot of the things which have influenced me. [1972]

For her most honest album to date, Alexandra Elene MacLean picked her most straightforward title – simply *Sandy*. Given the opportunity to tour with the same band on the album's release, the possibility of good radio airplay for the first single, and the sort of album reviewers could at last respond to, it seemed that England's maid of constant sorrow could yet get a mass audience to listen, listen. Island seemed as enthused as Sandy and suggested a simple portrait to go with the terse title, all parties agreeing that the olde worlde feel of the *North Star Grassman* cover had not worked. Sandy, though, remained desperately self-conscious about her looks.

> **Pete Townshend:** Her appearance was a problem for her. We shared this. I remember telling her I couldn't understand how I'd managed to marry one of the most beautiful women from my school days, and she told me I was beautiful. She obviously meant it. When I returned the compliment, I could see she felt I was horse-trading. But I found her quite lovely.

A line-drawn self-portrait, nude at her favourite piano, from one of her notebooks, shows both a mordant wit – the halo and jug ears (presumably intended to illustrate her musical ear) – and, in its typically exaggerated depiction of her girth, the sagging self that Sandy believed she saw in the mirror. Even when a photographer was willing to prove otherwise, capturing the glaring beauty inside, she would immediately want to reach for the dimmer. When Linda Fitzgerald-Moore took a series of portraits in the winter of 1970, the transition from frumpy wallflower to irridescent flower-child (and back again) was quite startling.

Sandy's mindlock was such that the better the portrait, the greater the sense of misrepresentation. As she admitted, at the time of her most memorable portrait, "If it's a good one I think 'Oh God, everyone'll think I'm prettier than I really am,' and if it's a bad one I think 'how can they print those awful things' – it's incredible, incurable paranoid." When the opportunity came for her to be photographed by the world famous David Bailey, for her album cover, Sandy took refuge at her friend, designer Bambi Ballard's, for the couple of days it took to work herself into the state of calm necessary for Bailey to do his job.

Bambi Ballard: I was living two doors away from David Bailey and so she came to stay. And she was very funny about him, too. She liked him. [But] I think she was slightly disappointed that he didn't make a pass at her. He was really nice to her. She got a buzz out of being photographed by Bailey. [It] gave her an enormous fillip.

The cover-shot to *Sandy* presents a classically beautiful portrait, even if none of Sandy's real spirit is captured. There is not even a trace of a smile on her lips, or that twinkle that came into her eyes at her most rambunctious. But it presented, to Sandy herself, as much as to her perceived audience, a necessary affirmation that she could *be* that sculptured face. That she could both despise the surface beauty of others, and envy those to whom it came easily, was something that prompted some of her most pointed barbs.

Bruce Rowland: Sandy had a wicked sense of humour. [She] had a coat made like a Gladstone bag, out of carpet, which weighed a ton. She and Trevor went to a party somewhere, and just inside the door was a sofa, and on this sofa was this 'model' – matchstick girl, very, very pretty, with long, straight blonde hair. Sandy sweeps through the door, and takes this coat off and just drops it over this girl, who collapses under the weight of it. Trevor lifts it off, and Sandy says, "Oh, I'm so sorry. I thought you were a pile of coats."

The night of Bailey's session, with the pictures developed, and her relief clearly visible, Sandy returned to Bambi's, who was allowed to see the image crack. Bambi, who designed stagewear for the stars, had been introduced to Sandy by Anthea Joseph, perhaps in an attempt to spruce up her 'country barmaid' image. Initially, Bambi admits, she was intimidated by Sandy's presence, "My first impression of Sandy was that she was so confident that I felt completely crushed by her. It wasn't until I got to know her better that I realised that actually 40% of the job of being a friend of Sandy's was to prop [her up]."

The aura of assurance Bailey caught so effortlessly began to fall away as Bambi and Sandy uncorked their way through a fine selection of wines but in its place was a Sandy eager to please, and receptive to that state of 'emotional recall' (Al Stewart had a similar experience, around the same time, having "invited her for lunch ... [and] made the mistake of offering her a cup of tea. She looked very wistfully at a bottle of wine on the top of my fridge, and said, 'Can we have that instead?' and proceeded to drink it, then play[ed] my piano for a couple of hours"). As a result, Bambi was offered a wholly unique preview of an album that finally made Sandy proud.

Bambi Ballard: Of course, we got pissed [that night], and at one in the morning she said, "I'd love to play [the album] to you." I said, "Let's go to the Howff. They've got a piano." "Oh, you're not gonna want to hear my music." "Of course I am." I drag her down the road. Roy Guest is just leaving and says, "Just slam the door when you leave," and then she sat down and she started to play, and then she said, "You don't want to hear this. It's not very good." But finally she played me the whole album. It was sublime. I had tears running down my face. I was the one member of the audience and she sang them for me. But between every song, "You don't want to hear anymore, do you?" And you'd have to build [her up]. "But of course. I loved that one." "You did? Really?" There was nothing false about that. She so needed the praise.

Unbeknownst to Sandy, her little one-woman preview of the new songs also christened a new solo persona. Through the summer, as Island readied *Sandy* for release, the real Sandy was subjected to a number of pressures to drop her band. It would be autumn before another UK tour would be viable. Also, Richard Thompson had just about finished his own statement of intent, the deeply English *Henry the Human Fly*, and was angling to tour with his feisty new partner and fiancee, Linda Peters.

An insistent Sandy told more than one journalist, "I really like having a band. I've said this so many times, it sounds like I'm going over old ground. But people don't believe me ... I could be making a lot of money if I was working on my own. I can understand their point of view, but I really like to be with a band." When Karl Dallas came to call, to discuss the new album, he found the conversation constantly returning to the question of 'the band'.

As Dallas wrote as the time, "I began to realise that her need to have them with her was a human as well as a musical thing, and her determination not to have them taken away from her was rooted as much in what happened before she performed as in what actually occurs on stage ... But somewhere, some time soon, someone is going to start polishing that Rolls Royce for her. And though it's got acres more space than a Ford Escort, there's not going to be room in it for her band. A pity, but it's inevitable." Sandy fiercely resented Dallas's inference. Though she never admitted it to him, Dallas now suspects that "the violence of her reaction against what I was saying might have indicated that it made more impact on her than she was saying."

It must have seemed that she was being forced to relive the Fotheringay split in real time. This time, though, when her manager, Steve O'Rourke, began to lay out the economics of a band, she summarily fired him. When a replacement management team reiterated the same arguments, she simply ignored them.

Gerry Conway: I never quite understood Sandy's motives, why she did the things she did. She certainly would only do things on her terms. She gave managers a terrible runaround – they'd suggest that she did this and that to further her career, and if she thought it was crap, she just would not entertain it. Eventually they'd give up the ghost.

Sandy's determination to hang onto the band this time around seems to have resulted in a couple of curious soundtrack assignments, presumably undertaken to shore up the finances. At the beginning of August she found herself recording a ten-minute suite for a short TV film entitled *Pass of Arms*. Though she evidently threw herself into the project, despite having to "virtually [make] up the tunes to fit the words [they] gave me on the spur of the moment ... [and then] race around all sorts of really hammy studios, eventually ending up with Island at Basing Street," she found "the film ... incredibly atmospheric, especially all the effects of the wolves and the wind." Not so, the next film job, a four-song assignment under the auspices of Manfred Mann, for a lame slap and tickle feature by the name of *Swedish Fly Girls*, which was purely one for the money. With words and music already supplied, and without a credit to her name, Sandy delivered surprisingly unself-conscious vocals to songs with titles like 'Are The Judges Sane?' and 'What Will I Do With Tomorrow?'. Their kitsch content, though, resisted even her best endeavours.

Sandy now turned to perhaps the one person capable of the necessary acquiescence, her brother David, to help her in her weakness – management of money. A qualified civil engineer, he planned on taking a year's sabbatical from Taylor-Woodrow to help get Sandy's finances straight, and to put his own head back together. His marriage to a German nurse had recently run aground and, according to his father, "Sandy took him in and more or less picked him up when he was in a very low state – and [then offered to take] him into the music business."

Neil and Edna were not exactly thrilled to lose their aspirational son to the same precarious industry as their daughter, but David's presence on the road was a necessary adjunct to the inevitable disbandment of Sandy's own combo, and the need to do a solo tour on the back of *Sandy*. It coincided with Richard Thompson coming to Sandy to tell her it was time to move on. As he remembers it, "I don't think I gave her too much in the way of advanced notice ... but I felt I was treading water and I wanted to do something a bit more for my own music."

In a way it must have come as a relief. Soundtrack assignments and a resolution of her managerial conundrum wasn't about to dig Sandy out of her ongoing financial black hole. The release of *Sandy* had only added to the pressures, with reviewers again focusing on the damage Harry Robinson's strings had inflicted on what was basically a welcome return to form. Karl Dallas's *Folk Review* review told it like it was:

> "*There are so many lovely things on* [Sandy] *that I could spend the whole of my space listing them but instead I would like to consider in what respects it falls short of being the even more superlatively excellent album [sic] it might have been ... What is needed now ... is for the sort of sparseness [found on certain tracks] to be applied to the overall sound of Sandy's records ... After all, her voice is rich enough without having to be lushed up with*

strings and brass and such. I would like to hear a whole album as restrained in its backing as 'The Music Weaver'."

A couple of solo radio sessions in the months leading up to her first solo tour only served to reinforce a commonly-held view that a full ensemble remained ancillary to the music weaver's needs. At the first of these sessions, a *BBC In Concert* back in March, Sandy self-consciously introduced herself by saying, "As you've probably noticed I haven't got my band with me tonight ... I thought I'd try and do it on my own. I'd like to announce right now that I don't know much boogie-woogie, so you'll just have to put up with *this*." Though the set starts hesitantly, with a muted 'North Star Grassman', the *North Star Grassman* material in this context begins to make sense, and the two concessions to tradition, 'Bruton Town' and 'Blackwaterside', fit comfortably alongside the likes of 'Sweet Rosemary' and 'John the Gun'.*

In her mind's eye, though, Sandy continued to associate singing solo with singing folk. Asked that September what sort of set her fans might witness, she admitted, "I haven't got quite together what sort of things I'll be doing on gigs in the future. What I would really like to do is go out and collect some really beautiful traditional songs to sing. You know, the way Martin Carthy goes to the ends of the earth to find exactly the right sort of material. I really admire that." And yet, as Karl Dallas notes, "If you criticised what she was doing, and it was 'non-traditional', then it was because you were a boring old tradie." The contradiction would remain, as she moved ever further away from her perceived roots, and towards the mainstream.

The more upbeat material and beguiling melodies on *Sandy* again made the disturbing spectre of commercial success hove into view. When Radio One's daytime darling, DJ Tony Blackburn, picked 'Listen, Listen' as his single of the week, in September 1972, it seemed a chart entry was assured. Sandy's reaction to the prospect was typical of the times, "I remember the feeling of panic – thinking 'What on earth am I going to do if I get in the charts? I mean, how could I go on *Top of the Pops*?' ... Anyway, the single got nowhere and the panic passed." And yet, on another occasion, at the Speakeasy with Island's PR man David Sandison, she responded to Carly Simon's 'You're So Vain' coming on the sound system by telling Sandison, "God! I hate that, I really hate that."

---

*'Bruton Town' appears on the boxed-set, the remainder of the set opens the deleted BBC Sessions 1971–73 CD.

When he asked her why, she freely admitted, "'Cause it's so fucking good. I wish it was my record."

As Linda Thompson observed to Jim Lloyd, during a 1988 Radio Two tribute to Sandy, "I think in a way she had a bit of a self-defeating clause built into her contract, as it were ... We were very snobbish. We'd look at *Top of the Pops* and think it's gruesome. Nobody made singles in those days, it was the days of albums. Who would want to be popular? We were arty." Sandy's feelings were considerably more ambivalent than she might have been prepared to admit: yes, she wanted success, but on *her* terms, and saw no reason why that hadn't, or shouldn't, happen. When it didn't happen, even with an album as strong as *Sandy*, she began to fear that her time had passed, something that began to gnaw away at the foundations of her artistic instincts. Old friends found it increasingly hard to find 'the old Sandy' in this confused soul.

Heather Wood: Sandy was not a secure person, she didn't seem to trust her own genius and I think she was frequently a very unhappy person. She obviously had a drive to write and to perform but it never really seemed to give her what she wanted.

John Renbourn: She seemed to be quite determined to be famous ... In the early stages I didn't notice that in her, but it became pretty intense later on ... [But then] when I did run into her ... she seemed to be getting progressively more miserable ... It hurt to see her sometimes.

Unfortunately, Sandy's perception that she had something unattainable to live upto continued to feed into her performances, queering her self-confidence and letting in the ghost of previous stage-fright. The greater the burden of expectation, the more likely he would come a-knockin'. Not surprisingly, most of her more erratic performances were in London, on nights when friends and reviewers were on hand to remind her of her 'destiny'. Her solo debut at the Queen Elizabeth Hall, on September 6, was one such occasion.

Sandy Denny: I feel really bad about the Queen Elizabeth Hall concert ... I could feel that the audience were staying with me and I hate putting people through that drama ... sitting on the edge of their seats, thinking is she going to make it ... Audiences like to be entertained as well as listening to the music, but I'm the same person offstage as I am on. I'm not an actress. [1972]

Actually, it was Sandy's determination to keep that offstage person at bay that created that initial infusion of fear – what she labelled, "this whole 'oh God, am I going to be able to play?' thing." The irony is that, as Gina Glazer remembers the wily ol' manager Herb Cohen observing to her back in 1968, "You know, I like her singing but what I would love to see is her personality injected into her singing."

The upbeat personality evidenced in some of the *Sandy* songs was only rarely allowed out at the shows, as if Sandy had forgotten how endearing that "off-hand, off the cuff" singer who "maintain[ed] a dialogue with the audience," could be. Solo, the voice could now be heard in all its resonating purity, driven by an unerring instinct, but the secret Sandy remained a deeply unhappy person, for whom the songs remained her only release.

10

1972–73: ALONE AGAIN, NATURALLY

Naked piano playing woman, as drawn by Sandy.

"All I know is that things aren't going as well as I feel they should be. That's as far as I'll admit it's going wrong – the fact that it isn't going right. But I don't know how right I want it to go." [1973]

Sandy Denny

"She is more than just a singer. In a far more interesting sense than rock stars like Carole King or Carly Simon, she is a songwriter – her gift for language is unmistakeable. That so marked a gift can become a casualty seems to me a fundamental problem. Is it just that the rock audience can't tell chalk from cheese, and so discourages those who can from going on caring about the difference? Or is it that the beautiful singer, lacking limitations, is turned aside from art by having no obstacles to overcome."

Clive James, *Let It Rock* 3/74.

Clive James' piece in *Let It Rock*, published when Sandy's solo career had again been placed in suspended animation, in the winter of 1974, accused Ms. Denny of "content[ing] yourself with merely becoming a British rock queen, instead of nurturing a world-class songwriting talent into the revolutionary force it once bade fair to be." Damning with faint praise a woman whose "open-space, low-volume, high intensity vocal style" afforded Fairport's "spellbinding electro-folk sound" the opportunity "to develop into a new rock idiom," she had apparently almost single-handedly allowed "that special rock idiom [to] now show signs of regressing, of once again becoming solely a folk style."

James' article hit a number of targets but missed the point – Sandy was no longer interested in recrafting any folk style into a rock idiom. Denied a gesture as iconoclastic as Dylan going electric at Newport, and forced back into playing solo, Sandy's increasingly personal work found itself compartmentalized by critics whose vocabulary floundered in the face of such uncompromising individuality, even as she was insisting that she, "wouldn't like to mislead the folkies by saying [*Sandy*] was a folk album, and I wouldn't mislead rock fans by saying it was a rock album."

Sandy had been everything critics had insisted was required for the lady's commercial potential to be realised. The problem, as Stephen Holden suggested in his glowing *Rolling Stone* review of the album was that, "a fine solo album [like] *North Star Grassman* ... didn't get anywhere," and though he hoped, "the fate of *Sandy* will be different ... if this can't do it for her, nothing can." Sandy concluded that only a clean break from her traditional roots, coinciding with a daring raid on a new audience, was likely to achieve what *Sandy* had not. In the interviews on *Sandy*'s release she asserted a new agenda, "I like romantic songs. I'm a romantic at heart."

The album Sandy would begin recording in the spring of 1973 would be her first collection of songs from the heart, but it would be all but discarded by her record label, and the moment would not come again. The album in question, *Like An Old Fashioned Waltz*, would be described by Sandy, at the time of its completion, as "simpler and more romantic than the last ... more direct ... it's pure romance," and in concert notes to a mini-tour of Japan she expressed the hope that, "the feeling of some of these songs ... will evoke some of the romance of the Thirties, for these are also time[s] when a touch of the romantic may be just what we need." In fact, Sandy's jotted thoughts on each of the seven originals that make up the bulk of the album, in the same

Japanese programme, make it clear that the overriding theme of the album was loneliness, set against a backdrop of frayed love:

"Solo – *A song which depicts that knowledge we all have inside, which is, that nobody can live your life for you....*

Like An Old Fashioned Waltz – *...Two dancers alone in an enormous deserted ballroom. But where does the orchestra hide?*

Friends – *This is about some people I know and love – even with their faults and all.*

Carnival – *...When the summer is gone, and all the laughter and frivolities which go with the summer have mellowed, all at once the autumn is with us...*

Dark the Night – *About lost love perhaps, and being alone with your memories, wishing that things may have been different, if you had your time again.*

At The End of The Day – *Anyone who has ever been away from home for a long time, and has felt a little homesick, will understand the sentiment behind this song...*

No End – *The story of two friends, one a person who loved to travel and the other one to paint. They persuade each other back into their respective vocations. A strange song perhaps, but we all lose our zest for life at times, don't we?..."*

That sense of aloneness largely stemmed from the fact that, for the first time since they had moved into Chipstead Road together, Sandy and Trevor found themselves leading increasingly separate existences. Ironically, this had come about because Trevor had recently joined that endlessly evolving outfit, Fairport Convention. Seemingly on its last legs in the summer of 1972, retaining just two members from the groundbreaking *Full House* line-up – the two Daves, Pegg and Swarbrick – and not a single original member, Fairport found itself putting an album together at the same time as Trevor was wrapping up the *Sandy* album. In their haste to co-opt Sandy and her musicians onto their own album, Swarb and Pegg found out Trevor had ambitions of his own. The resultant album, *Rosie*, was cobbled together using the talents of Timi Donald, Gerry Conway, Richard Thompson and Sandy herself, but then Island expected 'Fairport' to tour on the back of it. So it was that Trevor Lucas, Jerry Donahue (Trevor's suggestion), Dave Pegg, Dave Swarbrick and a reconciled Dave Mattacks took to the road in the winter of 1973, with a schedule to play and an album to sell.

Perhaps Trevor was looking for respite from the role of Sandy's Other Half, a demanding job at the best of times. Not that he was looking to end the relationship, just that, as Philippa Clare recalls, "Sandy's mood swings were

Sandy's father, RAF pilot Neil Denny

Sandy's mother, Sgt Edna Jones

Sandy aged 5

Sandy and brother David on a family holiday

Sandy and David at Worple Road, Raynes Park

Sandy as a teenager in Trafalgar Square

Early Sandy promo shot

Fairport Convention

Sandy and David

Sandy takes time out in Denver to relax during
the mixed experience of her first US tour

Sandy and Trevor at the Cambridge Folk Festival, 1973

Trevor and Sandy marry at Fulham Registry office

David Denny takes care of Watson while Sandy poses for more wedding pictures

A&M promo shot

Sandy in the 70s

incredible, [and though] Trevor had amazing patience ... he'd get to a point where the steel bolt down the spine would lock, and it'd be like Enough. And that's usually when Sandy would go off the rails, just to punish him ... I think she would have been *completely* off the rails if Trevor hadn't been around. There were times when he was absolutely magical with her, when I've seen her in a complete state and Trevor would calm her down."

One such instance came the following summer when, in a rare respite from the road for the pair of them, Sandy and Trevor decided to check out that year's annual Cambridge Folk Festival. Not surprisingly, Sandy's presence generated a certain interest verging, in one case, on the voyeuristic.

Karl Dallas: Cambridge Folk Festival, mile-long queue to the toilet, Sandy decides she's gonna take a pee under the hedge. While Sandy's doing this, somebody takes a photograph of her. And she was absolutely distraught. She was in a terrible state, "Oh Karl, how could people do such a thing?" She was in tears, and we were all gathered around her, "There, there, point out the person" – we'd bought into her hysteria – and Trevor turns up, and he goes, "What's the trouble?" She told him and he [just] laughed. He said, "People are sick, aren't they?" And in five minutes he had her laughing about it. And I thought this was a relationship made in hell but it works, because he understands her better than any of us ... Sandy was a very difficult woman ... When I heard about problems between her and Trevor, I always assumed it was her fault just because I knew her, and I knew she [could be] a stroppy, very emotional person.

Trevor felt he had something of musical worth to contribute to Fairport, and his voice certainly lent some much needed texture to the vocal mix. But others tend to take a more cynical view of Mr. Lucas, extending to his motives for taking up with Sandy in the first place. Heather Wood remains firmly convinced that, "he wanted to be a star. Why he took up with [Sandy] I don't know, 'cause somebody who really, really wants to be a star, taking up with somebody who is a star, [does so for] one of two reasons, either you think that they can make you a star, or you're happy just to bask in their presence. But then what he seemed to delight in was putting her down." Others who knew both Sandy and Trevor concur with Heather Wood's assessment.

David Sandison: [Trevor was] an extremely amenable and completely untrustworthy man. I think he was a chancer. I think he was a man of some ability, not much, an adequate musician, and I think he was very ambitious ... I don't know about the productions he did with Sandy because wisely he got some of the best players, and some of the best arrangers ... [But] I just found him too slick. There was something about Trevor that was sneaky ... He was a master at subtly putting her down. I was with her one night at the Speakeasy, and she asked Mario, who was the MD there, for her bottle of brandy and he brought it out, and she held it up to the light, and she called Mario back, she said, "It's down." He said, "Oh, Trevor was at it." She said, "Fucking Trevor, he knows he's not allowed to touch my fucking brandy." She was really uptight.

Not surprisingly, it was mostly Sandy's small band of close female friends who were on the receiving end of the Sandy version of Trevor. And yet she couldn't imagine life without him, admitting in a letter to one of those friends in 1976, "if I hadn't bumped into Trev. I often think who would have [had] me." But her lack of self-esteem made her especially susceptible to the well-chosen putdown, something Trevor had readily at his disposal.

Bambi Ballard: I never sensed that he supported her as a musician. My take on [their relationship] was that Sandy was with a man who was using her, who was spending her money, who despised her and who didn't desire her. There are men who only see themselves reflected in a woman's eyes when they're in bed with her. He was one of those ... He was always not quite laughing at her, but [was like] the kind of father I'm very glad I didn't have – the kind who [when] you make a cute remark, they laugh, but they have to cap it. Sandy didn't need that kind of person. Sandy needed either the classic power-behind-the-throne figure, or somebody with whom she could have a really good creative relationship, and I don't think that Trevor was a good enough creative artist for this. Trevor did in a sense have what she wanted, 'cause he was down to earth, [and] not volatile intellectually, so even if Sandy was drunk and talking nonsense, Trevor wouldn't have known the difference ... [but] his view of women, and this woman in particular, was, "Oh God, she's doing that again," rather than, "Why is she doing that?"

Sandy needed someone who bolstered, rather than eroded, her fragile self-confidence. She herself admitted, in an interview prior to her first solo tour, that she "needed to get a bit of confidence back; I seem to have lost a lot in the past couple of years, been undermined by lots of things." Going out on tour was a rare opportunity to remind herself that she needed "to get out there and sing, and know that people really want to hear me, and enjoy what I do." In this, at least, Trevor was as supportive as ever. But Sandy was also increasingly guilty of not communicating, not only with her partner but with everyone around her. Bambi Ballard remembers the reputation that Sandy had begun to acquire even before they first encountered each other at the turn of the decade.

Bambi Ballard: By the time I met her I had heard so many negative Sandy stories, how difficult she could be. And she was somebody who if she drank too much there'd be that moment when she ... didn't communicate anymore. And she was a great drunk. But at the same time there were moments when she sort of shut off, [and] you really felt that she'd left the room. As I got to know her better, I felt that these shut downs were often because she'd kinda lost confidence in herself. Almost as if she was mentally [as well as physically] staggering.

And yet, even when boorish, Sandy remained someone who treasured friends, old and new. Maddy Prior, then riding high fronting an increasingly commercial Steeleye Span, remembers someone saying, one time, "'Oh you're a friend of Sandy,' and I said, 'Well, I wouldn't say I was a friend. I know her.' And the next time I saw her, she was really offended, ... She obviously thought of us as friends ... [But] her and Linda [were] a formidable team, [who] used to terrify the life out of me, 'cause they were devastatingly witty. I'd always felt slightly that they thought I was a bit of a clown."

The increasing distance between Sandy and her old singing companions – as the likes of Maddy Prior and Linda Thompson established their own niches; while Val Berry and Gina Glazer brought up families – only served to remind her of her new-found solo status. It perhaps even prompted the occasion, one afternoon in 1972, when after "a happy afternoon sitting around drinking and trying a few songs," Sandy suggested to Heather Wood, Linda Peters and Todd Lloyd that they form a singing group together.

Sandy's craving for companionship had never confined itself to her own sorority and now, in her hour of darkness, she had need of a true friend of the male variety. One experience prompted the first song in recent times that didn't attempt to get "as far removed as I could get from the real subject matter ... [just because] I didn't really want anyone to know what I was really like." 'Friends' dealt specifically with an unhappy liason with Pete Townshend, an old drinking-partner from the Speakeasy, at a time when Trevor was away. Townshend now admits that, though he enjoyed Sandy's company, and though her "albums of those days, 1973–1976 ... seem to me today to have been seminal, essential ... I was rather strange about British folk [at the time]."

Pete Townshend: I liked her tremendously. She was, to my eyes, very pretty and compactly voluptuous. I was very attracted to her. Adding fire to this chemistry was the fact that I found her intelligent and assertive as a writer. When she sat to play the piano ... she had a strident, purposeful attitude. One night we nearly slept together. She had come several times to the Who studios and I ran her home in my chauffeured Mercedes 600 stretch limousine. The driver sat in the street while we talked. She had been crying at the studio. I had no idea about what. I had some notion that she had parted company with her man ... She had a lovely flat in Parsons Green with a huge grand piano and an even larger double bed with lace and linen sheets. I kissed her, but she insisted that I should stay all night, otherwise I could not touch her. I took my driver's presence as an excuse and left. I was married, and very rarely unfaithful to my wife at the time. I remember Sandy and I were both drinking a lot, but she seemed, like me, able to handle it physically. I feel very dim not to have realised that she was reaching out to me so urgently, in need not only of some physical love, but also some ... of my spiritual strength perhaps ... She [later] rang and told me she'd written me a song.

The song certainly pulled no punches. Though the identity of the figure who has "lost everything/ but what money can own," is never overtly stated, the last two verses suggest just how cut to the quick Sandy felt by Townshend's change of mind:

"My love is not here, my love is away.
You've caught me alone, but you've nothing to say,
And it's time to leave now, and you know the way [x2].

Go and live in the country, and I'll stay in the town,
I have everything but what money can own,
And I'll be just fine now, so long [x2].
So long."

Townshend is not alone in believing that Sandy had at some point temporarily "parted company with her man," a view alluded to in lines scattered through *Like An Old Fashioned Waltz* ("I can't communicate with you/ and I guess I never will" certainly implying irreconcilable differences). The difficulties Trevor's new career presented may have had less of a bearing on this than a more mundane explanation – Sandy's belief that the fire had gone out of their sex-life. Bambi Ballard remembers one particular heart to heart about "the fact that Trevor didn't find Sandy as attractive [as he used to]. She was beginning to sense that he was going off the boil, so we had a long chat about sexuality ... [and] what began as a heart-to-heart talk about perhaps not being sexually attractive to Trevor the way she'd want to be ... [became,] 'He oughta like me as I am.'" A certain bitterness swept over Sandy on such occasions, manifesting themselves in lyrics like:

"Whatever you did for me
Save that which helped your company
Beguile and cheat behind my back
So that no one ever can keep track.

You expect me to be famous
And you despise those whose help I seek
While you grew rich on someone else
But can't afford the time for me ....

Your friendly voice
which one time swept away
my bitter thoughts
of kings and courts
Will now no longer make me see
For while you speak, the echoes say
What did you do for me?"

The reference to somebody who "grew rich on someone else," but remains incapable of figuring out a way to live, reoccurs in another lyric probably written around this time, which begins with a line later used in 'Solo':

> *"What a way to live*
> *What a day to die*
> ~~*You may think it easy*~~
> ~~*With all your piles of money*~~
> *When you've got the right idea.*
>
> *I'm a singer, I'm a woman*
> *I'm together and alone*
> *But I wish I was a hobo*
> *with a freedom of my own,*
> *in the heart of me.*
>
> *In the heart I wish I knew which is the way to go*
> *Do I run and hide [in the undergrowth]."*

The impending prospect of a lengthy sojourn in the States – a time when she would have to be both "together and alone" – was clearly playing on Sandy's mind, even as she was insisting to Steve Peacock, "I don't want anyone saying, 'ah, poor old Sandy', because [touring] is just something you either choose to do or you don't. And if you do it, you just have to become strong and get yourself together." Her more acid assessment, in 'Solo', was far closer to the sentiments expressed in the second verse above:

> *"What a wonderful way to live,*
> *She's travelling all over the world,*
> *Why, the fame*
> *And all the golden opportunties unfurled."*

With the idea for 'Solo' already germinating in her mind, and in surprisingly confessional mode in the days before her six-week trip Stateside, Sandy revealed to Steve Peacock some of her deepest fears:

Sandy Denny: It's when I'm sitting in hotel rooms on my own that I tend to get a bit morose ... Men have different ways of entertaining themselves on the road, and no way could I get into entertaining myself in that way, it's just not part of the way I feel, and it only messes you up anyway. I think women get very emotionally attracted to people – blokes have the ability to entertain themselves for an evening and then forget about it. [1973]

Sandy's solitary female companion on the road was the friend she once described in her diary as "quite intolerable ... no wonder I get on with her," Miranda Ward. Miranda confirms the chaste nature of her charge, "She would just feel so rootless, that's what would mess her up. I was there as her sort of anchor ... but Sandy ... was not promiscuous at all."

Sharing the same room throughout the U.S. trip, Miranda witnessed a woman who had indeed 'gone solo', not, as Sandy later explained, in the sense "that I went solo, as it were. It's more the way we live within ourselves." On the other hand, if, in the quote above, 'Women' was a cipher for Sandy, for 'Men' read 'Trevor', and the idea that Trevor might "have the ability to entertain [himself] for an evening and then forget about it," clearly ate at her. On her previous tour, Sandy had asked Miranda Ward to "keep an eye on Trevor, and we went out for dinner, and we were having this lovely dinner and this great flirt, and then I suddenly realised Trevor was fucking serious ... The guy was amoral." Though Miranda never talked to Sandy about the incident, the opening verse to 'Solo' suggested a growing distance between Sandy and her man:

"Good morning, good afternoon,
and what have you got to say,
Well, I'm waiting, but I can't stay long,
it's such a lovely day.
There's a time to be talking
and a time when it's no use,
Right now I think the things you say
are liable to confuse."

'Solo', perhaps Sandy's most complete song since 'Who Knows Where The Time Goes', could as easily be seen to deal with the break-up of a relationship as the prospect of touring, its key admission coming at song's end, "Ain't life a solo." Thrown back upon her own resources for the first time in a long time, Sandy knew that this was "a bit of hard work coming up – and I don't often admit that." How hard, 'Solo' can only hint at.

The jaunt across the pond, due to begin on March 31 and run through to May 14, involved a whole series of support slots on other artists' bills, and just two shows, at the intimate Main Point, on the outskirts of Philly, as a headliner. Required to 'wow' fans of Loggins & Messina, Steve Miller, Shawn Phillips and Randy Newman, Sandy found the whole shebang tough going. Barely a week into the tour, after two sets at Constitution Hall, in Washington, on a bill with the terminally staid Loggins & Messina, Sandy told a Georgetown journalist, "If this is what it means to get three thousand people to come and listen to you, I'd rather go and play to my best friends." Even supporting Randy Newman, with whom she shared most of the shows, the audiences seemed unusually inattentive and boisterous during Sandy's set. Miranda later found out "that Randy had a rider in his contract that no drinks were allowed to be served [during his set] because of the noise of waiters and chinking glasses, and so everyone was stocking up on drinks during Sandy's set."

Sandy later told an English journalist, "I found it very heavy ... There were only three of us ... a sort of assistant ... and David, my brother." Miranda, who had taken a sabbatical from school to be with her friend, did her best to bolster Sandy's spirits, with picnics in the Rockies and tracking down old friends like Gina Glazer and Paul Simon. But sometimes it was only the prospect of meeting up with Trevor and the Fairport gang in L.A. – where the three of them were scheduled to find themselves in early May – that kept her going.

As Sandy admitted in one of her notebooks, "When you are with the one who loves you, you want to get away somewhere, yet no-one else is quite the same when you do, so you run hell for leather home to him, and swear to yourself you'll never leave again." It was in just such a state of mind that she began to idealise her relationship with Trevor in song, penning her own 'Moonlight Mile', under the title 'At The End of the Day', on one of the endless plane journeys she was forced to endure (though not, as she would later claim, "on the plane journey home, after an extensive tour of the U.S."):

"Just miles and miles of rosy sky,
I'll fall asleep, by and by.
I'm crying now 'cause you're so far away
But I'll be home at the end of the day."

Finally – after shows in New York, Toronto, New Paltz, Washington, Bryn Mawr, Boston, Upper Darby, East Rutherford, Passaic, Detroit, Chicago, Denver, Chico and Berkeley – as well as enough air-miles to qualify for her own pilot license, Sandy found herself in Los Angeles, at a Hollywood 'motor hotel', on the afternoon of May 5, 1973. Don Henley of the Eagles had offered her the more salubrious surr-oundings of his Laurel Canyon home, but Trevor and the boys were at the Tropicana, a legendary stopover at the West Hollywood end of Santa Monica Boulevard.

First page of Sandy' 1973 U.S. tour itinerary.

Before six nights of two sets at the Troubador with The Association wrapped up another U.S. Tour, three days had been set aside for Sandy to get some recording done at A&M's fabled studios, the self-same studios she had enthused about on her first visit, back in the summer of 1969. Reunited with two-fifths of Fotheringay, adjoined to the trusty Fairport rhythm-section, she had four songs she was ready to record – 'Friends', 'Solo', 'At The End of the Day' and 'No End'.

'No End', the oldest of the quartet, was another song about the intrusions of the road – "It's strange how time just seems to fly away/I can't remember things." It had already been quite beautifully captured back in December by a mobile truck, solo at a vacant Walthamstow Town Hall, an attempt on Trevor's part to capture Sandy singing and playing in a classical music environment. It is tempting to view the painter who is asked by the traveller, "Why don't you have no brushes any more? I used to like your style," as the person Sandy felt she could have been, before her dreams "like autumn leaves ... faded and fell so fast." Certainly, no real-world confidant seems to fit her depiction here.

The four songs recorded in L.A. suggested Sandy had a very wintry album in mind. Only a handful of dots were now needed to complete the circle from

'Solo' to 'No End'. The album's major statements were in the can. Her voice had also stood up surprisingly well to the demands of a week of two-set shows. At the Troubador, though, tired from the sessions and struck down by that smog-induced condition, 'L.A. voice', she was grateful for the occasions when Fairport's schedule permitted a little musical support. Dave Pegg remembers the audiences "being very polite to Sandy, but I don't think she was enjoying herself very much." For Sandy, when Fairport "got up on stage with me, ... and we did some looning about ... I felt a sudden sense of relief when they started playing, it was just really nice to have them all behind me." That "sudden sense of relief" felt a lot like coming home.

Unfortunately, come the end of her tour, whilst Sandy took the red-eye via New York to London, Fairport were required to head onto Trevor's homeland for their first Australian shows. With a few more weeks ahead before Sandy could be reunited with Trevor again, it was perhaps 'Dark The Night', her personal 'Tomorrow Is A Long Time', that was really written on the plane home:

> *"Parting comes too soon,*
> *My weary tune has lost its pleasure.*
> *Waiting for the time,*
> *This lonely wine has lost its treasure.*
> *Dark to me the night,*
> *and dim the morning light tomorrow.*
> *How could I not see*
> *the simple melody of sorrow?"*

Such wistfulness carried over into the two remaining originals on the album, 'Carnival' and 'Like an Old Fashioned Waltz', recorded along with 'Dark The Night' at sessions in August at Sound Techniques. As Sandy told a journalist at the time, "I'm a bit of an old softie at the moment. I'm going to have to get myself some boxing gloves." The seven original songs, as they stood without their "fur coat on" (as Sandy liked to call the strings), would have made a powerful statement, by a strong, independent female singer-songwriter at the peak of her songwriting powers. And, with two six-and-a-half minute works reserved for side two, the seven songs constituted a good thirty-four minutes of material (six whole minutes longer than Nick Drake's 1972 offering, *Pink Moon*). Unfortunately, Sandy had another side to her personality, one that she had surpressed throughout a seven-year career.

Joe Boyd: Sandy wanted to be a diva, she wanted to be a pop star. But she had too much good taste to follow those impulses too far. Trevor I don't think was a strong personality as a producer. He had ideas which were okay, but you don't feel that there's a really strong vision unifying the records from beginning to end. It's not a consistent feeling.

When Sandy suggested recording two songs from her childhood radio days, at the end of the August sessions, Trevor's lack of a strong alternative enabled the idea to reach fruition. As John Wood remembers it, Fats Waller's 'Until The Real Thing Comes Along' "came up quite accidentally. We were sitting around somewhere and Fats came into the conversation and she just started singing the song, and it grew from there. We decided to record it partly because she wasn't writing an awful lot of material at the time." If a dose of Waller was bad enough, then the Inkspots' 'Whispering Grass', complete with 'whispering brass', was ten times worse.

Philippa Clare: If in doubt, Trevor would put on a lot of strings – wanting her to be the great, grand diva ... Trevor wanted Sandy to be a huge star ... Trevor was always Mr Showbiz, and he knew that Sandy could really do it. But I think Sandy was fairly ambivalent ... about it.

If the ambivalence was real, so was Sandy's love for a certain type of schmaltz. Dave Pegg remembers one occasion in 1974 when Sandy and Fairport were in a revolving restaurant in America, after a show, "and there's a trio in the middle of the restaurant ... we're going round, but they're not moving. Sandy's a bit refreshed and the first time we go past, she misses them completely. The next time we go past them, she goes ... 'I'm gonna sing with them.' So she gets up and she goes, 'Do you know 'A Foggy Day in London Town'?' '[Sure.] What key?' Maybe C. Off they go, and she's there, giving it all the cabaret bit. And it was sensational."

What had usually held Sandy back on record was, as Boyd suggests, "too much good taste." This time, though, concerned that her new album might be too downbeat, Sandy elected to break the mood. Though an album of such covers, in and of itself, might have proved a grand idea, both 'Whispering

Grass' and 'Until The Real Thing Comes Along' remain thoroughly distracting occupying the middle of sides one and two of Sandy's third solo album. The remaining songs were also given their fair share of fur-coats, and that extraordinary seven-and-a-half minute solo rendition of 'No End' from December 1972 was discarded in favour of the A&M recording, duly bathed in Harry Robinson's strings. Only in performance was it stripped to its essence, ready for a vocal for the ages.

At the beginning of September, with the album in Island's hands, Sandy definitively proved that the way to record her was with a mobile truck, and a few friends on hand. It was probably after this one-off concert, at the Howff in Camden Town, that John Wood asked Sandy, "Why don't you sing like that in the studio, then?" and she replied, "You try. Where's the audience?" Sadly there was no truck on standby that night, though the crowd was, in Al Stewart's words, "sort of like a Who's Who of the English folk scene." Stewart also recalls a Sandy, "paranoid with stage-fright. She did not want to go on that stage." It was the first time he had seen Sandy perform in some time and he remembers noting that "she didn't [previously] have stage-fright ... when she was with Fairport ... [but] at the Howff she was really shaky."

When she finally mounted the small stage, Sandy threw herself into the material as if only performing itself could offer her temporary remission from her progressive stage-fright. The after-show Sandy, though, high on relief, inevitably over-indulged in alcoholic refreshment.

David Sandison: She came off [at the Howff] so up and so thrilled, 'cause it had worked, and the audience reaction was everything she could have wanted, 'cause it was a brilliant, brilliant show ... but she was drinking really heavily afterwards. And she wasn't an amiable drunk; she got belligerent and argumentative ... My take on it at the time was that Trevor had said something just to cut away from the triumph. I'm pretty sure that Trevor blew the evening for her, and she got horribly upset, screaming and tearful. It was awfully sad. It shouldn't have been like that. It really was a wonderful night.

Still, she had finally delivered, in front of all her secret admirers in the mainstream press, generating a series of reviews quite unlike anything she had ever experienced. If *Guardian* reviewer Martin Walker suggested that "the only woman I have heard who could compel an audience in this blunt and harshly loving way was Janis Joplin," and Karl Dallas, in *Melody Maker*, called it "a completely flawless performance," it was Robin Denselow's *Daily Telegraph* review that most evidently crossed over into helpless hyperbole:

"It was one of those happenings that critics dream of but rarely experience, when a good but hitherto erratic singer suddenly takes off, carrying her audience with her on the kind of trip that singing is really all about. It was, in fact, Sandy Denny's moment of truth ... In some of her songs tonight ... talent became genius and there were glimpses of depths which few other singers have revealed to us."

Once again, though, external events were to conspire against her. Just as Sandy was preparing to reach for the sky, her previously dependable record company was quietly removing the landing-gear.

11

1973–74: RETURNING TO THE FOLD

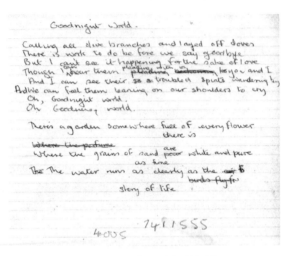

Lyrics from 'Goodnight World'

"There was just this immense capacity for reaching people. And it was just kind of drifting. I mean, she was making good records, but nobody was channelling it properly. Nobody was. I mean, Island were doing their bit. They were releasing them, they were promoting them, but there wasn't anything constructive going on in career terms, in terms of tour planning or putting a band together or any of that stuff. It just wasn't going on. And my knowledge of meeting her off and on socially was that increasingly she was a wreck. She was confused, she was wandering, she was drinking. And she and Trevor clearly weren't happy together." [PW]

David Sandison

Whether or not Trevor himself precipitated the tears that followed the Howff gig, he was soon ushering Sandy into a cab home, where over the next few days they sat and read the glowing reviews of her triumph. Together again, at the end of the day, they made a snap decision to finally exchange wedding vows, after nearly five years as a cohabiting couple. The two months in the States had convinced Sandy that she needed Trevor. As she insisted in 1977, when their marriage was at its rockiest, "it was either that or [nothing] ... the final thing that breaks up people [is] when they don't see enough of each other."

Neil Denny had previously been assured by Edna that there was no possibility of their daughter marrying this lumbering Australian, and was mortified to hear the news on their return from a holiday in Scotland. He had never taken to Trevor and refused to give his only daughter away, or to even attend the ceremony, scheduled for the afternoon of September 20 at Fulham Registry Office. Edna, though, decided to face his rebukes, attending what was meant to be a largely private affair, Sandy having invited just her parents, her brother David, and two of her oldest and dearest friends. Even then, Miranda nearly took the Neil way out, having to be persuaded by her parents, with whom Sandy was a firm favourite, to lend her moral support.

Miranda Ward: I nearly didn't go the wedding 'cause I didn't think it was right move. It was my father who actually said, "No, you've got to because she's gonna need your support when it all falls down, and you can't turn around and say, I told you so." ... I think they got married to save the relationship ... [But] if you suddenly realise that it's half day closing and you haven't got a bloody wedding ring [it's pretty unplanned].

Adding to the impromptu nature of the exercise, not to say the slightly surreal air to the day, was Sandy's choice of 'maid of honour', one of the great loves of her life and the closest she could come to a surrogate father, Danny Thompson. Thompson even found himself acting the chaperon on an unscheduled honeymoon, after berating Trevor for being 'unromantic' at Paddington station, where he proved less than willing to carry his new bride onto the train.

Danny Thompson: She said, "We're getting married, will you come and spend the night at the flat in Fulham the night before we go to the registry office." I said "What, be best man?" She said, "Well, whatever." So I got Trevor's suit ready and everything, cleared up all the fag ends that were lying around the place – because she was notorious for lighting 200 fags a day and leaving them burning and standing them up like candles. All these cork tips on the mantelpiece ... I remember doing all that in the morning, getting them off to the registry office and saying "All the best," genuinely chuffed for her, that she'd got a relationship, that she was getting married, not one of those relationships where the woman gets bounced about, a fairly stable relationship. But then she said, "Well, you're coming on the honeymoon, aren't you?" I said, "Don't be ridiculous." And she said "No, go on."I think she thought, "Oh, if Danny comes it'll be a laugh." Trev never said anything. I suppose he didn't want to rock the boat. Fairport had a TV appearence in Plymouth. So I went with them. [JI]

The irony in Trevor's gesture of arranging for a press photographer to snap the happy couple on the steps of Fulham Registry Office must have struck anyone who had heard the opening track on Sandy's latest album, which she had only just delivered to Island two weeks earlier. She seemed very happy with the album, christened *Like An Old Fashioned Waltz*, and envisaged a prompt release, making for her third album in three years, and set about assembling a small combo that could accompany her when she resumed touring activities.

Sandy had only just informed a journalist that she longed "to be [back] in a band, so that I [don't] carry all the responsibility ... I kind of miss the slight anonymity of just being a member of a group ... [But] I'm going to be playing with Pat (Donaldson) and Gerry (Conway) – just them to start with, until we get something else happening." In fact, Jerry Donahue recalls the five members of Fotheringay having dinner that summer and "Pat, Gerry and Sandy want[ing] to restart the band ... I said, 'What do you think, Trevor?' and he said, 'I'll do whatever you do.'" Donahue, though, was happy playing with Fairport and the idea came to naught. When Gerry Conway went off with Cat Stevens, Sandy was obliged to assemble a trio around Pat Donaldson.

The new band – which made its debut and, as it transpires, farewell performance at a BBC radio session on November 14, where they performed two songs, 'Dark The Night' and 'Solo', from the 'forthcoming' album – comprised Pat Donaldson, Hughie Burns and Willie Murray. On the admittedly slender evidence of their two-song session, this three-piece was as close to a rock combo as Sandy had ever come, the sound of these tracks leading onto the unabashed mainstream musical vocabulary in evidence on her next album *Rendezvous*.

Unfortunately, Island no longer considered the Witchseason acts a priority and, despite scheduling a number of dates in November on the college circuit, Sandy found her new platter had been delayed until March, thus negating the point of a tour. Though publicity manager David Sandison says he "never picked up on any lack of willing on Island's part ... everybody at Island adored all the Witchseason acts," he admits that the label was slowly reinventing itself, at the expense of their more traditional roster, and that "things had started to get kinda skewiff at Island. [Chris] Blackwell was away most of the time, he was making the Jimmy Cliff film, *The Harder They Come*. Although [David] Bettridge was running it, in A&R terms it was always down to Chris ... It [had been] a wonderful company. I was talking with Chris one time [about a new signing] and he said, 'They've got four albums to make it' – which is a hell of a luxury – but ... getting decisions made [had become] impossible, certainly crucial artistic decisions."

Sandy needed a Joe Boyd, someone who was part of the creative process. Supportive as her brother David was, he was no Boyd. As she admitted to a journalist back in September, "I'm a bit numb about the way things are going at the moment. When you're a bit indecisive about some things it becomes such a strain to make a decision ... one gets into a sort of mesmeric state about where things are going." In this context, it is perhaps not surprising that she made a decision to temporarily subsume her artistic identity within the communal confines of Fairport Convention, who had a Far East tour booked after Christmas, and into the New Year. Without committing herself to any long-term reunion, she was giving herself the opportunity to recharge some batteries, as well as giving her husband the opartunity to enact some of those wedding vows.

Sandy Denny: [When] I went on tour with [Fairport] ... I wouldn't have done, actually, if it hadn't been for the fact that the released album was late. I decided that the gigs I did hold for myself were a bit superfluous ... Fairport were going to be away for two months, and as I hadn't seen Trevor very much, I thought I'd go with them. [1974]

That summer Sandy had been bemoaning the fact that Trevor was "off on the road again for a couple of months, at the end of September, then he's off again after that ... it's obviously a bit of a strain, [even though] he's really got into it," betraying the self-same doubts that had led her to tie the knot. Joe Boyd, now merely an interested observer, considers Sandy just one of a number of "women who [were] very successful in this business, [where success] create[d] a certain distance between them and the men that they're involved with." He now saw Sandy again "set up a situation where they wouldn't be too separate from [each other] in the way that they advanced in their careers."

However, Sandy's return to the democracy that was Fairport was no *fait accomplis*. As Jerry Donahue remembers it, "Swarb and DM were the last to go along with that, for completely different reasons. I felt DM figured she might be difficult, too high-strung. Swarb, his reservations were that she would steal some of the limelight. I guess he was probably the last to be convinced that it was a good idea. The rest of us were all ready to go." Even Swarb knew that Fairport were never going to revive "that special rock idiom" without a force like Sandy, whatever whirlwind her addition might reap.

Dave Swarbrick: I wondered a little bit about possible ructions. It's never been easy being in a group with a woman. If you got a woman in a group, she pines for home more than a bloke does, and chances are you're gonna have more of a difficult time on the road. It is harder on the road for a woman than a bloke. If you're surrounded by fair dinkum blokes who like having a good time all the time, things can get hairy. There would become times when she would despair. I guess I was worried in case I wasn't going to get as easy a life as I'd been having. I don't know whether I made those worries vocal, but what was the matter with the group was it didn't have a singer. [No-one] had the depth that Sandy had ... The only thing that happened, was the sets got longer.

Sandy's membership also afforded a good deal more commerciality to Fairport's next project, a live album they planned to record at two shows at the Sydney Opera House at the end of January, both of which had about sold out. The band had recorded a number of shows with the *Nine* line-up, and back in 1970 had recorded three nights at the Troubador, but they had never released a live album as such, despite a formidable live reputation. With Sandy on board, a whole slew of possible numbers could be restored to the set, including some originally conceived with those Fotheringay half-breeds.

Dave Pegg: The reason [Fairport Live] was like [it was] was because we didn't have any time to rehearse any stuff. We went to Japan, and we went to Australia, and [Sandy] really wanted to come along, 'cause she didn't like being on her own, and Trevor being away. So she came along with us and we said, "You have to get up. [We] can't just be in Tokyo, and have you sitting at the side of the stage. You have to sing." And that's how that album came about. It really was just busked on the day of the gig ... When we got to Sydney, which was only a week or so later, we got John Wood out and just recorded it. We did two shows in one night ... It was very much thrown together. Things like 'Something You've Got', which is a cover number, [was] a bit of a novelty.

In fact, the *Fairport Live* album, drawn from London shows given by the *Nine* line-up in December, as well as the Sydney shows in January – and all the weaker for it – carefully maintained the pretence that the Fairport democracy could, and would, survive the addition of Sandy and her songs. In truth, once the decision had been made that Sandy should rejoin the band on a full-time basis, the set acquired Sandy solo material at the expense of some of the weaker work that separated the new band from its halcyon days.

'Quiet Joys of Brotherhood', 'Solo', 'It'll Take A Long Time' and 'Like An Old Fashioned Waltz', the last of these usually performed solo, filled out Sandy's half of the show. By the time she and the boys arrived in Los Angeles for a residency at the Troubador, a week on from the Sydney shows, her slot had already expanded to two-thirds of the set. In the mood to experiment, the band attempted to follow the music weaver through the likes of Dylan's 'Knockin' on Heaven's Door', Buddy Holly's 'That'll Be The Day', Padraic Colum's 'She Moved Through The Fair' and Sandy's own 'Crazy Lady Blues'. The likes of 'John The Gun' and 'Solo' also began to take on a life of their own.

The tapes were rolling on all four nights at the Troubador, capturing performances which with a little judicious editing could have made for a potentially strong live offering. Unfortunately, in classic Fairport fashion, having happily booked the famous Wally Heider Mobile Truck to record the shows, they found out that, in Jerry Donahue's words, "we had run out of money and couldn't pay for the tapes. They were held for a long time by Wally Heider's Mobile until Island eventually bought them back."

By which time, the Sydney/London tapes had already been reduced down to the single album offering, *Fairport Live*. Though Colin Irwin's generous review in *Melody Maker*, on its release in June, insisted that Sandy "has never sung better," in truth she had rarely sung worst. Whether it was her need to prove that she could still hold her own at the ubiquitous after-gig drinking sessions or simply the fact that, in Sandy's own words, "it's a great strain to go right over an electric band" – something her years singing solo, and the larger venues and P.A.s combined to make into an issue – the Sydney shows and a couple of the Troubador sets audibly featured a lead singer fraying at the edges.

Trevor Lucas confirmed as much, years later, recollecting an occasion, "at the Troubador in Los Angeles – [when] we played three shows in one night – and Sandy happened to fall off the stage. Just like that. But the audience, who were fantastic, just caught her and stood her back up. And she didn't miss a note." (It was presumably as a tribute of sorts that Trevor sang an arrangement of 'Down Where The Drunkards Roll' on the second night.) Though the final night found Sandy again struck down by 'L.A. voice' – hence the shattered vocal on 'Who Know Where The Time Goes' on the boxed-set retrospective – the residency also found Sandy playing a couple of inspired sets, culminating in some wonderful vocal and lyrical gymnastics on an extended, semi-improvised 'Crazy Lady Blues' and a no-holds-barred 'John the Gun'.

For the first time, Sandy needed to ensure that she kept her voice in the best possible shape. As she admitted to an American journalist at the end of 1974, "Playing on my own is easier on the voice. That's the only thing I've got against a band ... Up until now I haven't really suffered that much from laryngitis." Principle asset or not, Sandy continued to treat that voice in a million with scant regard. The wear and tear it had been subjected to in her solo years was as nothing to the effects of gigging night after night in front of the loudest folk-rock band in Christendom.

Still, barely a week after the six-piece returned home, *NME* were reporting that Sandy Denny had officially confirmed she was rejoining Fairport Convention. It also announced a hectic schedule of dates, beginning in Scandinavia in April, onto the States through May, and then back in the U.K. for the end of June.

Dave Pegg's later account to biographer Patrick Humphries implies it was Sandy who was pushing to make the association permanent, "We'd done these few gigs with Sandy, she wanted to come back into the band ... Nobody was sure whether it was a good idea or not, because we were quite happy as a five-piece, but there was a bit of domestic strife in their household." Sandy, talking at the time, suggested it was she who had been asked, back in November "but I had so many commitments to fulfill [that], although personally I wanted to say yes, I couldn't make an immediate decision. Besides, I didn't know whether our musical ideas would clash or not" – an admission that, stylistically at least, she feared that the band and her might have grown apart in the intervening years.

If the five-piece Fairport were content to play things by ear, Sandy had returned from America to the depressing news that Island had again pushed back the release of *Like An Old Fashioned Waltz*. Initially, they had offered the solace of a rush-released single of the title-track, backed by a *North Star Grassman* outtake she had reworked at the *Waltz* sessions, 'Walking The Floor Over You', but even this failed to transpire. By the time the album was released in June, it seemed almost like an archival release, something that reviewers like *Melody Maker*'s Colin Irwin found hard to accept at the time:

"Ironic that just as she's rejoined Fairports she comes up with easily the best thing she's achieved since leaving them in the first place ... Her vocals are better than ever, full of subtle embroidery and perfectly timed pauses. Yet it's the material contained here that really makes this record outstanding. We always knew Sandy was a good writer when she produced 'Who Knows Where The Time Goes' but the songs here maintain a constantly high standard throughout."

With her A&M deal about to end, and sliding down the priority pole at Island, Sandy's decision to reattach herself to Fairport begins to make some sense, even though she continued to talk about a show with an orchestra at the Festival Hall, to coincide with the album's June release, a grandiose scheme that was never likely to prove financially viable. And, however expedient her decision, it was inevitable that most of the compromises were going to have come from the other five members of the band, something bound to ferment a mild dose of discord.

Dave Pegg: [Swarb] was a bit compromised in terms of what he had to do musically. He may have felt he was pushed a bit into the background, as we all did, 'cause it was Trevor and Sandy versus the rest of the guys. Obviously, if Sandy's in the band you're gonna do her songs, and you're gonna let her sing. Which meant that there were some elements of Fairport stuff that kinda disappeared. Swarb didn't get much of a chance to show off, and may have felt bad about that. But it wasn't like he was gonna leave the band.

Sandy's contribution to the live set now solidified into a block of ten songs, of which just 'Matty Groves' and 'Who Knows Where The Time Goes' were culled from her previous stint in the band. The remaining songs all derived from her post-Fairport work and, save for 'Quiet Joys of Brotherhood', there was not a traditional melody in sight. Sandy also tried to conjure up some band spirit with a rousing new ditty, 'Rising For The Moon', a self-conscious attempt to trammel 'Come All Ye' territory one more time. It quickly became a feature of the spring shows.

Talking about the songs she had begun writing at this time, Sandy confessed, "I set off by thinking I must write with Fairport in mind. I consciously tried to do that, but I often got right back into my own style, whatever that is." At some point she gave the band three demos of songs she had written, the first of which, 'Rising For The Moon', was clearly written with Fairport in mind.

The second demo, 'The King & Queen of England', probably began life as an attempt to write something traditional-sounding, maybe in the *Nine* mould, but went "right back into [Sandy's] own style." The demo features one of Sandy's finest vocals, though she had returned to writing in dense allegorical code, where "the glory of what might have been/ Is all she feels," and the song doesn't appear to have been attempted by Fairport. The problem with certain of Sandy's demos, much like those of her friend Pete Townshend, was that they were so precisely directed that there was very little room left to rework them. 'The King & Queen' was such a song.

Dave Pegg: Nobody's going to alter her approach to the song, really. You can maybe stick a string arrangement on top of it, but you're not gonna change the way that she approaches music, and the way that she writes her songs. It's a very old fashioned way. She's not sitting there improvising a few chords, then she's gonna put a few words to it afterwards. It comes out like a song. It always came finished. A song like 'Rising For The Moon' would be her sitting at the piano at Byfield and she would just set the metronome up, the Bentley Rhythm Ace. Her demos were [all] like that.

Whether or not 'Rising For The Moon' and 'The King & Queen of England' began as songs Sandy felt obliged to write, 'One More Chance' was clearly a more serious proposition. It had begun life as a clarion call from some cradle of love, lambasting those who might want to cry goodnight world (its original working title):

"Calling all olive branches and layed off doves
There is work to do before we say goodbye
But I can't see it happening for the sake of love
Though I can hear them pleading with us, you and I.
And I can see their troubled spirits wandering by,
And we can feel them leaning on our shoulders to cry,
Oh, Goodnight world
Oh, goodnight world."

Though few laid-off doves seemed to respond to the call, Sandy's driving vocal on the demo suggests hope still springs – as does the original opening to the second verse:

"There's a garden somewhere full of every flower there is
Where the grains of sand are white and pure as time
The water runs as clearly as the story of life..."

The advent of such florid imagery seems to have coincided with the acquisition of a garden, part of a house Sandy could call home – not in London, but an hour up the A40, past Oxford's ancestral towers, unto the Northamptonshire hamlet of Byfield, where some of the Fairport clan were now settling. Perhaps Trevor had his own agenda in making the move – as Linda Thompson puts it, he "may have been thinking ... 'she won't get hold of drugs, or whatever'" – but it did not initially impinge on the thrill of it all.

A country house had always been an enduring wish of the still-young lass, and initially she delighted in the opportunity to escape London's oppressive environment, recording in her notebook, "I love flowers. I congratulate them often. Watson [Sandy's Airedale] thinks I've cracked. I feel better in the garden. Even the weeds are ok, if you give them a wink and say, 'Watch out, I've got my eye on you.'" In the original draft for 'No More Sad Refrains', written a few months later, Sandy would ask for, "the summer sunlight/ to shine upon the garden that I love."

However, as Linda observes, "it really wasn't Sandy ... it *was* inaccessible." Gerry Conway also considers the move, "a mistake, 'cause the flat at Chipstead Street was a bit like Piccadilly Circus, everybody dropped in all times of the day and night, and I think she liked that, [but] suddenly she was out in a village somewhere ... wrong enviroment." Whilst her life was full of tours, sessions and more tours, Sandy's boredom threshold was only sporadically reached, but as isolation passed from an occasional state of mind to a mindset, so she would begin to ask herself the question at the end of the completed 'One More Chance' – "Is it too late to change the way we're bound to go?" – on an almost daily basis.

By the time it came around to recording these songs in the studio, at the end of an exhausting tour of America with Traffic, Sandy's voice was already acquiring a layer of sandpaper. The sessions in November 1974 were the band's first time back in the studio with Sandy and, as Dave Pegg prophetically informed *NME* prior to the sessions, "it can't be a filler, everyone feels it has to be a monster." However responsible they may have been for the temporary termination of Sandy's solo career, Island had decided to place themselves foursquare behind a tenth Fairport studio offering, even providing the necessary funds to acquire a 'real' producer for the first time since Boyd took a hike. Jerry Donahue believes it was, "Swarb and myself in particular [who] wanted something [with] a little more expertise – we thought we were a band that deserved to have the very best. And Trevor agreed. It was Trevor's idea to bring in Glyn Johns." Johns certainly didn't go out of his way to endear himself to his new charges.

Bruce Rowland: One of [Glyn']s first comments was, "Right, let's hear what you've got, and I don't want to hear any airy-fairy folk bullshit." His brief was to make a commercial album for them. That was Blackwell's instruction. "This album is make or break for Fairport as far as Island Records go," that was told him in confidence, so he goes in and starts being Glyn Johns all over everybody.

Perhaps Sandy was delighted by the choice – she may have had some input into the decision, having worked with Glyn's brother Andy and seen him recording with The 'Oo. Rather than responding to the new studio regime with her customary petulance, Sandy knuckled down when Johns cracked his whip.

Sandy Denny: Working with [Johns] is incredibly easy, as he's very strict in the studio. It took all the weight off the rest of us, especially Trevor, who'd done the last two, and was finding it really difficult to say or even suggest something without us all jumping down his throat. Glyn just put himself by the console and told everybody to shut up. [1975]

The remaining men were not quite so responsive to their paternal taskmaster. Donahue remembers it being "a lot easier with Trevor to get him to agree to something ... With Glyn you'd really have to fight hard." There was almost immediately conflict between producer and musicians.

Dave Pegg: There was a lot of aggravation. Glyn Johns was given the job and Glyn is an absolutely incredible producer, and he got so much out of everybody. [But] he was really vicious and really hard to everybody in the Fairport. We weren't used to this. We'd never had to take instruction from anybody, we really weren't used to being like whipped into some kind of shape.

The real problem, though, as Swarbrick is prepared to admit, was that the band "didn't really have any material ... We had to get material somehow, and I think that shows." When he rhetorically asks, "why didn't we open a few [folk] books?" it seems clear that the answer was Glyn Johns. Johns' preferred solution, as stated to Dave Pegg, was, "Right, I need another two songs by tomorrow. Go and write some songs," unaware just how painstaking a ritual that could be for Sandy, and how limited the results were likely to be if the band's other songwriters lent a hand.

The compositions brought to those first set of sessions speak for themselves. Trevor's pair of offerings, 'Tears' and 'Restless', were retreads from a familiar mould. The co-composed 'White Dress', penned by Swarb and Ralph McTell, and 'Dawn', by Jerry Donahue (with the help of Sandy), were songs specifically written as vehicles for Sandy's voice. Only on 'One More Chance' do those sonorous vocal chords really reach for the sky, as Johns pushed her to do it again and again. As Pegg notes, "You can hear her on the verge of losing it. She's so emotional in the studio [anyway,] and he's making her do it *again*." This solitary example of vocal jet-propulsion again hinted at a latent greatness awaiting regular channeling in the studio. Before Johns could hone it further, though, the sessions came to a premature end, when the dependably solid Dave Mattacks took umbrage at Johns' working methods and told him what he could do with them.

Bruce Rowland: Glyn Johns is a pedant. If it went to a third take, he'd say, "Look here, I didn't come here to listen to you rehearse." ... And you had to do it his way, or not at all. Which was both the making of him and his downfall. Where he understood what was happening, and took control, nine times out of ten you got it right ... [But] if he met anybody head on, as he [had apparently] done at the first set of Rising For The Moon sessions, then it was hell on earth ... The performance of DM on the title-track ... was masterful, and beautifully recorded, and absolutely right, but it wasn't what DM went into the studio with. DM made a few caustic comments, did it, and left the band.

It was probably just as well that DM's departure, and the onset of the holiday season, curtailed work on the album as, one suspects, Swarb would not have been far behind DM in reaching for his coat. As he caustically observes, Johns "didn't know bugger all about the tradition, that's for sure. He wanted Mattacks to play like a country and western drummer, nice off-beat rim shots." The hiatus also gave Sandy the opportunity to add some songs worthy of her name to the album. Whoever Johns expected to write songs overnight, it was never going to be Sandy. They never came easy, even when she had a subject in mind.

As it is, the subject-matter of the first song Sandy elected to write in this respite was none other than Swarb, a man she now described in song as a 'Stranger To Himself'. Placing herself in the third person, she insisted "she loved him, loved him like a lover should," even as she deconstructs his penny-pinching ("his money was his health"), covetousness ("richer was the other man's land"), and fear of change ("run for cover like a frightened hare"). The tempestuous nature of their relationship, particularly when placed in close proximity, disguised the fact that, as Dave Pegg's wife Chris notes, "they were very similar in many ways," and parts of 'Stranger To Himself' could as easily have been rewritten as 'Stranger To Herself'.

The other song Sandy demoed for the band that winter offered no pretence of detachment, being directed at a very personal quest to find 'What Is True?' Even the confessional interjection, "Oh please, my darling, do not make me sad," has the ring of authentic experience, as Sandy writes into the night, hoping to "find the one and only thing I've never had," articulated in the final verse as:

> "What is true,
> Even though it only ever whispers
> Part of what it knows,
> And it's never ventured
> Through the locks

Where the brazen river flows.
It's the fingerprint
Which is never made.
It's the perfume of a rose."

Again, it was the demo that captured the essence of the quest, leaving the Fairport arrangement to scrabble for shards of the same inspiration. The song was the first to allude to the presence of Trevor at the moment of composition, pushing her to write. A looseleaf in the back of the notebook containing the drafts of 'Stranger To Himself', 'What Is True?' and 'One More Chance' suggested that the nights were increasingly being given up to tears, as the proximity of her husband stood in stark contrast to her physical distance from old friends. The metaphorical rainbow alluded to in 'One More Chance', still a feature of her songs, had become one in a series of question-marks:

"Tears are falling in the darkness
Hearts are bleeding in the silence
From the widest ocean, who would miss this smallest tear
Then, might always be a bad time
Then, might always last forever
But these stormy clouds, we might see them all disappear.

Hope,
Has she really gone?
Will she ever come home again, my love?"

Sandy did not shy away from the type of self-analysis alluded to in 'Stranger To Himself', ever willing to see faults in herself. Nevertheless, she proved a most unwilling patient when it came to taking any necessary cures. As she had observed as far back as January 1972, "People say that if you know your faults you're halfway to getting better, but the other half is really difficult to get across ... [and] how often do you sit down and think 'I know I've got these faults and I'm really going to do something about them?'" It would take Sandy three years to take that first step. When she did, shortly after penning 'What Is True' and 'Stranger To Himself', the analysis, over two pages of her notebook, showed someone all too aware of what was true:

"Dear Sandy,

When did it all begin? This need to hide away.

It seems you like to stay in one place fast, and yet be everywhere else at that moment. And when everywhere else is a reality, all you can think of is home.

Where is home to you? When you're there you want to go, when you arrive you want to go back, when you get back, your memories are rosy of the places you seemingly hated whilst you were there.

When you are with the one who loves you, you want to get away somewhere, yet no-one else is quite the same when you do, so you run hell for leather home to him, and swear to yourself you'll never leave again.

At rehearsals.

I wish I was a real musician. I wish I could just sit and play anything going. Consequently rehearsals get me down but for millions of reasons not just that. It's the pianos I get. I must get a Fender Rhodes.

But mostly I'm lazy. I know I am."

Over the page Sandy then asks herself a series of questions at the heart of her predicament, for which she has answers to just three, two of them musical, the other a perennial gripe:

"Am I happy in the country?

Do I enjoy my job?

Is there anything I haven't done which is bugging me?

Am I musically up to my own standards? NO!

Am I in love with my husband?

Is the business side of it all getting me down?

Am I writing well?

Am I writing enough?

If anything what do I need to inspire me?

Do I rely too much on other people?

Am I a great singer?

Am I talented? Yes.

Do I need to lose weight?!? Yes."

Finally, in a flourish of enthusiasm, Sandy tells herself, "And guess who is going to solve all these problems. ME! ain't I great? Yes!!!!!" By now, though, she was not even sure how to begin changing the way she was bound to go.

1 2

1975: FAREWELL FAIRPORT

Turquoise Medusa heads sketch, by Sandy Denny.

"If you'd taken the music away from [the 1974] Fairports, all you would have been left with was one very fucked-up band. Personalities, management, business, finance, record company, [the lot.]"

Dave Mattacks

Mattacks' motives for abandoning the Fairporters to their fate at the end of 1974 did not entirely stem from distaste for their current producer. The financial precipice on which the band had been pivoting had begun to come away, and the problems were so longstanding that there seemed little prospect of a solution. Sandy admitted that they were still "paying off debts that had been incurred by ridiculous management we'd had," a thinly veiled dig at everyone from Witchseason up to the present.

With nary a sober business head among them, Fairport had always operated at a disadvan-tage in this department. To apply Swarb's colour-ful turn of phrase, "It's hard to keep tabs when you're lying on the arse-end of the bar with a drink in your hand." Inevitably, the fuck-ups reflected the state of "one very fucked-up band." Swarb recalls on their Far East jaunt, back at the beginning of 1974, that "somebody botched up the travel arrangements and sent all the equipment to Tokyo excess baggage, a three and a half ton PA – fifteen thousand quid." The solution was simple yet radical – do what even the innovative Witchseason era line-ups had failed to do: sell records.

The main stumbling block, band politics aside, was that, as Dave Pegg recalls, "there was such a backlog of outstanding things that had gone wrong that nobody who came in and tried to sort things out [could] ... [and] it was getting to a dodgy state in the music business, where people realised that we were never going to be big, and they were being very careful." Nevertheless, the band *had* been alloted another bite of the corporate cherry, just as soon as they had enough songs to finish the album they'd started before Christmas.

> **Dave Pegg:** It was [to be] our seventh tour. It was make or break. We did do a record for Glyn and we had supposedly got the record company their support. And they did spend a lot of money on it ... It was like a good final attempt ... We had a pretty good crack at it. It was the hardest we ever worked. Everybody got stuck in 100%. [PH]

Work began almost immediately, on their return from a bizarre, drummerless stint in the Low Countries. Auditioning a drummer did not come easily to these veterans of the stay loose School of Musicology. Not that Sandy was helping matters. Her distaste for rehearsals, voiced in her notebook a couple of weeks earlier, was as nothing to her distaste for auditions. Never known to suffer fools gladly, and intolerant of the slightest discordancy, the auditions became as much about how the drummers dealt with Sandy as how well they sat on the beat.

> **Dave Pegg:** We [must have] auditioned about thirty drummers in London, which was one of the worst weeks of my life. Some of them were good, but the group was so untogether ... It was mainly Sandy who was at fault ... She was getting difficult to work with at the time ... Nobody had any sympathy for Trevor. It must have been very difficult for him.

Finally, Glyn Johns suggested they use a session drummer with a suitable pedigree, and that they make this work as the sessions were imminent. Bruce Rowland had, in fact, all but retired from gigging. Turning up with a pair of drumsticks and a clear conscience, he was quite unprepared for the amount of psychological baggage that accompanied each and every card-carrying member of this ramshackle collective still passing for a band.

Bruce Rowland: I wasn't aware of who was in the band, and what they were doing. The first thing I did was I went to a rehearsal at Island studios, just to get the feel of what was happening. Glyn set it up, and then didn't show up. I walked into an atmosphere you could cut with a knife. Peggy is trying to keep everybody's spirits up, and putting his foot in it, time after time. I couldn't figure out why. They had been to some record company thing and had stayed overnight at the Cunard Hotel. Sandy and Trevor had [by this point] what you might call an open relationship, and Sandy's paramour was [their road manager] – with Trevor's approval, all very civilized. There's a burglary in the hotel, and the hotel is crawling with police at four in the morning. Trevor was out on the town, Roger was in with Sandy, and the police knocked on the door and said, "Mr Lucas." "No." ... Trevor came back at five in the morning, and walked into all this, and for some reason, as he did from time to time, took umbrage. So they'd had a terrible row. That's what I walked into, waiting for Sandy and Trevor to show up, which eventually they did, Sandy all in tears, and Trevor like, "G'day, sport. Nice to meet you. Shall we do something."

The fact that he was seemingly unfazed by these shennanigans probably counted as much in Bruce's favour as his dependable, on-the-beat drumming, and he was officially in, for the forthcoming sessions at least (after which, they planned to work on him some more). If Sandy in the studio could be as temperamental as any Mediterranean diva, Rowland was relieved to find that Glyn Johns' working methods kept the *in extremis* side of Sandy largely in check.

Bruce Rowland: Sandy was fine [in the studio] 'cause she wasn't doing live vocals. I could see she was a prima donna, but through the rehearsal and first day of recording she got me in the frame of mind where I would have forgiven her anything – some of those long notes! ... [Johns] could be incredibly spiteful, but he got performances out of Sandy that beggared belief. He really knew how to do it, [and] he always worked at Olympic.

The need for songs, though, had become pressing, as Johns continued to keep the band firmly focused on original material. His request for overnight songs had yielded the lamentable 'Let It Go' and the risible 'Night-time Girl', but nothing to match the intensity of 'What Is True?' or the sheer dynamics of 'Stranger To Himself'. Turning to her discards, Sandy revived the 1972 outtake 'After Halloween', to give Johns a sporting chance of sequencing a strong album.

Bruce Rowland, who was allowed to attend the final mix sessions, felt that Johns had done an impressive job. The seven Denny vocal tracks even suggested that this might be some kind of grand return, including as they did the likes of 'One More Chance' and 'Stranger To Himself', songs as strong as anything on *Liege & Lief*, though uniquely Sandy in conception. The remaining four songs, though, defined filler as, yet again, the politics of Fairport was allowed to triumph over the common good, even as band members sought to suggest a unity of purpose.

Trevor Lucas: The group is moving towards Sandy all the time, and she toward us. You don't just take two acts who have been writing and performing separately and put them together without any problems ... Our music alters, changes as we go along, that's the way Fairport grows, we always change a little with every change of personnel, and we always have a few problems of transition ... [But] we're getting farther away from more traditional music ... We're getting more into soft rock. In a way, the Fotheringay side of the line up is coming out stronger. [1975]

In fact, the band was wrenching itself apart, torn by the same divisions that had prompted Sandy's departure back in 1969. The week after the tenth Fairport album hit the shops, Sandy was informing those planning to come to a show on their forthcoming tour that they might be "very disappointed when they come along and find that, although the musicianship is better than ever, we're not going to do the same kind of stuff, the old songs they've been expecting us to do ... We did 'Matty Groves' until quite recently. [But] I got so sick of the actual story. I know it's a marvellous one, but I know what happens at the end – everybody knows what happens at the end – [Yet] they still want to hear it."

Certainly, what traditional elements remained in the two-hour plus set at the Royal Albert Hall on June 10, 1975, the day of *Rising For The Moon*'s release, were conducted without Sandy's participation, save for an abbreviated version of "Tam Lin'. She reserved her own dulcet tones for her three strongest offerings on the new album, four familiar faves – 'Quiet Joys of Brotherhood', 'It'll Take A Long Time', 'John the Gun' and 'Who Knows Where The Time Goes' – and three one-off performances: one from Fairport's past, a spirited 'Mr Lacey'; one from Sandy's past, a faithful 'Listen, Listen'; and from the immediate present, a brand new song dedicated to her father, and introduced as 'I Won't Be Singing Any More Sad Refrains'. After a ripple of laughter from her disbelieving fans, she asks, "Can you believe that?" before sitting at the piano and inducing a suitably mesmeric state. The crowd response suggested they were with her, even if what she had written was another song "right back in ... my own style."

The response to the new album in the press, though, was less laudatory. Colin Irwin's review, in *Melody Maker*, set the tone:

"Occasionally, just occasionally, listening to this album, I'm tempted to search for extravagant words like 'brilliant' and 'masterpiece'. There are also times when 'jaded' and 'unimaginative' spring more readily to mind, and in between it's just okay: pleasant, cosy and predictable. It certainly falls short of the promise of A Major Work muttered from the Fairport camp ... [Sandy's] presence has injected the band with some of their old spirit, but it's too Denny-oriented for it's own good and it would be easy to mistake the whole thing as a record of Sandy Denny with backing musicians."

Irwin found himself in the rare position of learning exactly what Ms. Denny thought of perceptions like this album was "too Denny-oriented for its own good," the day his review was published.

Colin Irwin: *Rising For The Moon* ... was very much her baby, and I think she had high hopes for that album – kinda her renaissance, and the band's renaissance, supposedly – and I had this interview arranged with her through Island ... and [*MM*] got me to review the album that week, and I actually didn't like it. It was a huge disappointment. So I slagged it off. Anyway, I turn up for this interview [with Sandy], and the paper'd come out that day and she'd arrived at Island and while she was waiting for me to come she read my review and threw a wobbler, just stormed out. I went in, saw Lon [Goddard] and he said, "Er, you just missed her" ... She did [later] explain [to me] that it had been an album that was important to her, personally, and a lot of the songs were quite personal to her.

By the time Karl Dallas got to offer his thrupennyworth, in August's *Let It Rock*, he was obliged to note that "the buzzards have started collecting around this album, suggesting that its occasional weaknesses indicate a band past its peak and running out of steam," whilst lamenting what he perceived to be Sandy not having "someone a bit tougher to fight against, artistically, as she did in the days of the old band." Fatally compromised, *Rising For The Moon* dipped into the charts at midnight and was out by dawn. Half a good album at this stage was never going to be enough. Its lukewarm reception only served to further loosen the stitches.

Dave Pegg: There were a lot of personality problems in the band then ... When the three of them [Swarb, Trevor and Sandy] got going, they could get fairly wound up ... There were times when it got very difficult and there was the occasional punch-up, and people went storming off, disappearing.

It is impossible, at this distance, to discern how much the disappointment at *Rising For The Moon*'s reception, and sales, ate into Sandy's eroding artistic assurance but her uncharacteristic action at the Island office suggested it bit deep. The fact that Island had committed significant resources to one last assault on a mass audience failed to help much. Sandy perhaps sensed the futility of it all long before she called it a day, hoping against hope that "it might just have sparked off like it did in the old days, which it was quite capable of doing." In fact, what happened is "most of the time we were so bloody worried about everything – and you lose a lot of enjoyment from that."

Her behaviour at the shows that came shortly before the album's release, on another antipodean tour, suggests that she was becoming increasingly self-destructive, even if it hadn't as yet destroyed her performing capabilities. Bruce Rowland recalls her being "pie-eyed for about three gigs on the trot, and it edged her performance. I thought it was riveting. There was an element of something unexpected in her demeanour." Nor did either of the men with whom she was having relations seem to know how to keep her on an even keel.

Bruce Rowland: [Sandy] was remarkable, a pathetic figure but with enormous balls at the same time. [With] everybody else, there was a lot of water under the bridge. Swarb used to lose his temper with her for being pissed and objectionable. All she was looking for was somebody to confront her. Nobody knew quite how to do it without at least two days of grief for everybody. When she was up, she was up, when she was down she was appalling. Trevor would just fire off one-liners at her. Trevor just wanted to have a good time ... I think Sandy was a little bit overwhelmed by the [psychic] energy of the band. I was very much finding my way so I wasn't gonna [push] it ... It was for them to sort out [their relationships], but it [just] seemed to be [creating] too many ripples.

The few tapes from the months after the Albert Hall show bear out the sheer unpredictability of Sandy's performances. One night in Chicago, on another support-slot September stint Stateside, her voice sounds shot, a boozy blur all but overtaken by laryngitis, and yet she forces herself through two sets, without regard for the long-term consequences. Archivist Ed Haber remembers another occasion when her determination to push herself through a New York show ended with her being rushed to hospital. Other nights, the voice could still torch up the night and puncture the stars, though only after her now nightly stage-fright threatened to envelop the entire backstage throng.

Dave Pegg: She'd have dodgy nights when she was playing a gig, and she did sometimes get a little over-refreshed, [but] we were all very guilty [of that] in the Fairports. When Sandy eventually rejoined the band again, there were no people who went to bed straight away after the gig. It was like a boy's club that she joined. Not that there was any problem with Sandy having any fun. She'd be the first person at the bar at the end of the night ... She would play badly some nights and sometimes she'd wet herself, she would have hysterics 'cause she'd played this really bad note, but the next night if it happened, we'd all have a snigger, and she'd throw a wobbler. You never really knew where you stood. One minute she was like a bundle of joy, the next minute she could be really depressed and really down.

As Chris Pegg observes, "Trevor [continued to] act as a buffer zone between Sandy and the outside world ... [Though] there were one or two screaming matches backstage before gigs, after which Trevor and Sandy would take to the stage wearing fixed smiles, they remained devoted to each other. But damage was being done – insidious, corrosive damage that would eventually prove disastrous." No matter how much their wedding vows had become a two-way sham, Trevor – and only Trevor – could and would subject himself to the nightly ritual of coaxing an increasingly debilitated Sandy onstage.

Dave Pegg: She'd never got the right dress on for the gig. Two minutes before you're going on she's going through this performance, "I can't possibly wear that." It's like when you're going out for dinner, except this is every night of the week and you're going on the stage, and you can't say, "No. It doesn't suit you, that." Then it's all over. And she would throw big wobblers. She was as good as any of the guys, if not better. If she was going to be stroppy, she was gonna be stroppy.

As Trevor started to distance himself from the great love of his life, he seems to have begun to see Sandy's own liasons as a form of temporary relief. Sandy had clearly forgotten her previous pronouncement that, "no way could I get into entertaining myself in that way, it's just not part of the way I feel," or the wisdom of her conclusion – "it only messes you up anyway." Some of the lyrics she would pen, after coming off the road, indicate how much she was now investing emotionally in her 'other men':

"I drink of the moment you nervously kissed me and ran away.
A night in New York, you stayed with me when I was lonely.
So wildly I hear the heart beating whenever I see you there
But the distance grows wider and now all ties are broken.
Love is so strange, but it has to be love that I had for you.
Stage fright and thoughts of you stir up the butterflies, just those two."

Sandy's use of drink was not confined to mere metaphor. Always a prodigious drinker, she had (re)joined a band for whom alcohol was the first, last and often only refuge from the tedium of the road, and the apathy of away-from-home audiences. The Traffic tour, the previous fall, had only fueled the problem. The Fairport contingent had been able to imbibe almost around the clock, at the expense of some hard-drinking headliners. Chris Wood and/ or Jim Gordon would invariably set up their own optics of brandy, whisky, vodka and gin in their hotel rooms, until finally, and somewhat belatedly, Island brought in an accountant to supervise their spiralling 'touring expenses'. When Al Stewart also shared a couple of bills with the six-piece Fairport, he was stunned by their rapacious consumption.

Al Stewart: I did play a couple of shows with Fairport Convention [in 1974], one of which was at My Father's Place on Long Island. I was partial to Bacardi & Coke, and I'd gone out to get a bottle of Bacardi, and [somehow] I didn't buy a bottle, I bought half a gallon. I bought it back, and somehow we drank all of it that night. Extraordinary quantities of Bacardi were disappearing. I was in a state of shock. I'd never seen anyone drink that much Bacardi in a single session.

Danny Thompson, relating his own alcoholism to Sandy's, observed that this "was the kind of environment Sandy was in, she wouldn't see that as being notorious or nasty or weird or blokish. She'd join in, and fall about laughing … When I was coming out of alcohol I refused to go to AA meetings, I found them very depressing, because some of the best times I've had have been drunk." Sandy showed a similar disinclination to detach herself from her hard-drinking friends, one of the heaviest consumers being her own husband.

Trevor's controlled substance abuse, though, stood in such marked contrast to Sandy's that he may not have realised how deep were her problems until the addiction began strangling the life out of her art. As Dave Pegg notes, "Trevor was an incredible party animal – you wouldn't believe what he'd put inside his system. He should not have been standing up, and you'd see him nine o'clock the next morning and he'd be cooking himself like steak and eggs." Philippa Clare also recalls how, "Trevor was the only person you could get a gram of cocaine for and … [he] would still have some three months later … None of us knew, though [about Sandy's condition]. We didn't understand what an alcoholic was, we just knew that some of our friends drank a lot and were a pain in their ass when they were drunk, and other people didn't."

The introduction of Goodtime Charlie's drug of choice, cocaine, into the equation, a sign of the times, only made Sandy push her constitution even further unto the brink. Charlie's capacity for clearing the head, allowing the user to party last and longest – bound up as it was with that rush of wellbeing

– had always given it a certain cachet among the chronically insecure. Sandy soon learnt to embrace it as a cure-all for the cripple inside.

The American tour that September brought each of these problems to a head. Even though the Fairporters were required to stagger, sometimes literally, through a 24-date tour on their return to the U.K., the fiasco that was their final U.S. stint represented a distillation of all the disasters to have befallen this line-up to date. Their biggest mistake was recruiting Jo Lustig as their manager, despite many a horror story in folk circles regarding previous mismanagements.

As Jerry Donahue remembers it, "we did ... a tour of the States where we had half of the promoters pulling out, apparently because Jo hadn't secured signatures to all the gig contracts. We ended up over there on a tour with a load of unconfirmed dates. We just didn't know what was going on, and we lost a lot of money over it. It wasn't our fault, it wasn't our department. We'd left everything up to Jo ... it was a king-size mistake and we didn't end our relationship with him on the best of terms." David Denny, as the new road manager, was also left high and dry by Lustig, and Bruce Rowland remembers, "many a time I had to hold David against the wall and say, Look here." David's duties inevitably included becoming an underpaid apologist for his sister's behaviour.

Dave Swarbrick: [David] was always a couple of steps behind her. He was quick, but he wasn't driving the same car she was. "Oh, Sandy!" you heard that a few times.

Lustig proved equally inept when it came to arranging press interviews, even though, in Pegg's words, "Island Records really had a go. They spent a lot of money, in America especially. There were billboards up on Sunset Boulevard for *Rising for the Moon*, and ... we lounged around [in America] for the first week doing nothing, 'cause Jo Lustig said, "Oh, you'll be doing like press and interviews for the first week." But there was nothing. There you are in Los Angeles for a week with nothing to do. By the time the first gig came around ... we could have been on the road for three months."

As for the tour itself, Dave Swarbrick's description remains the most vivid, "We travelled all over the coldest part of America, for months [sic]. I sat staring out the window of this car, looking at the aerial, which was encased in a solid block of ice. We did gig after soddin' gig after soddin' gig, got back to

England, and I got four-pence. I wanted to chew out [Lustig's] jugular vein."
By the time they got to New York for their final shows before Britain beckoned,
Swarbrick was not alone in wanting to chew somebody out. Sandy, in classic
Denny fashion, decided to pick the biggest target she could for her
pent-up wrath.

Dave Pegg: I've seen her do some incredible things ... Once we were in
New York and we'd been playing some dates with Renaissance. We did six
dates with them in Ohio, and they were supporting us – not that the
Fairport ever bothered if you go on first, you're in the hotel bar earlier, that
was our philosophy – then we got to New York and I get the *Village Voice*
and I look for the ad ... and it's like RENAISSANCE! With the New York
Symphony Orchestra, and then underneath it was like 'with Fairport
Convention'. David Denny was the tour manager. He said, "I forgot to tell
you about this but they're recording this Renaissance gig with the orchestra
for a live album. We're only doing forty-five minutes." ... We get there at
5.30 [for the soundcheck]. Of course, it's mayhem. They can't hear the
bloody violins. Sandy's like hanging around. But there's a grand piano.
Trevor's got like eight Ovation guitars which have all got to be tuned up, to
save him putting a capo on. We eventually get a soundcheck, for about
fifteen–twenty minutes, then we've got to get off. Sandy insists on going
back to the hotel [to shower]. You can't get a cab. It's ten blocks. Just time
for a shower. Twenty-five to eight, Sandy comes down, her hair's soaking
wet, she's not happy, not happy *at all*, and now we've got to leg it the ten
blocks to get to the gig. We go round the back, great big black security guy
on the door. We go, "We're the Fairport." "I need your passes." "We
haven't got any passes." "You're not coming in." David Denny's like, "I'll
go in and get the promoter." Sandy's like, "Fuck you." She gets her
handbag and she just hits the guy across the head with her handbag, just
physically starts hitting him across the head, and we're [going,] "Sandy,
Sandy..." But she wasn't having it.

The English shows helped to revive spirits somewhat, simply because
Fairport were playing as headliners, to people pleased to see them. Though the
album was already heading for the cut-out bins, the band pushed themselves
to remind paying punters of their pedigree. However, it was clear that Island's
injection of cash was one last roll of the dice, not an ongoing commitment. As

Pegg recalls, "We just thought, 'That's it. Nobody's gonna do this kinda promo job on us again. We've failed.' We kind of got an inkling, before this all started, that this was possibly going to be the case."

Life after Island was a prospect the Fotheringay half of Fairport preferred not to contemplate. After the tour, Jerry Donahue flew back to the States, where he was domiciled. He had already announced that he wanted out, "I just finally felt that no matter what we tried to do, there was always something that would go wrong ... [and] musically, I wasn't enjoying things as much. I really missed Dave Mattacks." As Sandy later told Karl Dallas, "When [Jerry] decided to leave, Trevor and I had a discussion about [the situation] – it seemed so endless, recruiting new members into the band and teaching them the old stuff." Admitting in 1977 that rejoining, "was a mistake, but ... my marriage is quite important to me, and I hardly ever saw Trevor," Sandy also acknowledged that there had been "a lot of musical conflicts. Swarb is an entity of his own, and we're both strong personalities ... I'm not saying we didn't get on, but we *did* have our moments."

Though they would remain the best of friends, and Swarb would be among the first to hear the new material she now set about writing, a band featuring both Sandy Denny and Dave Swarbrick in 1974–75 was never going to work. Swarbrick remained devoted to the folk world that Sandy had spent her years away trying to transcend. Attempting to take the 1970 Fairport where her and Richard's songwriting seemed to lead would have been a task unto itself, but the weary warhorse that was Fairport '75 was just as two-headed, and twice as lumbering. The English 'folk-rock moment' had come and gone, its demise passing the Fairport family by even as they presided over its wake.

AN INTERLUDE WITH WATSON

– Sandy Denny, ca. 1976

One Thursday afternoon Watson was taking a nap under the grand piano.

He has been fond of sleeping underneath things ever since he was a puppy, and of course when he was a puppy he was quite small. In those days it was a job to find him sometimes. We'd look under the chairs, the sofa and the beds. His favourite place was most often our double bed, but as Watson grew bigger and bigger–as Airedale terriers inevitably do–we would often have to lift up the bed and rescue a flattened and confused Watson from beneath.

Watson is not terribly clever, but eventually even he realised that the discomfiture incurred by being sandwiched between the furniture and the floor, for the sake of finding a bit of peace and quiet, was not worth the loss of dignity involved in the rescue operation. Watson valued his dignity very highly. So gradually he was resigned to abandon his by now famous disappearing act (not without a certain amount of reluctance) and settled for behind chairs, on top of current newspapers (preferably when they were being read) or diagonally stretching across our bed, thus making it impossible to get in ourselves without disgruntling Watson somewhat and presenting him with the perfect excuse for demonstrating bad vibes and disapproval at us both before finally getting down and stalking off to lie behind the curtains. Very melodramatic is our Watson, though I'm sure he believes he performs these scenes in a most convincing manner.

Thus when I bought my Steinway Grand Piano, which I cover with a beautiful piano shawl, Watson was thrilled to pieces. I could tell this was so only because I've known Watson some seven years now and one gets to recognise his peccadilloes.

Anyway, there he was on this Thursday, lying comfortably under the piano, gazing dreamily through the long fringe of the piano shawl. "Very comfortable I feel," thought Watson and self-indulgently stretched out his legs absolutely straight, right down to the very tips of his paws, then relaxed them back into their normal hinged position and completed this exercise with a groan of pleasure.

"Mm-Hmm" said Watson and licked his lips before resuming his afternoon nap. He always kept one ear cocked in order never to miss the Parish Magazine being pushed through the letter box. Watson and the Parish Magazine (amongst other postal deliveries) were mortal enemies, and he was unsurpassed as "Annihilator of the Printed Peril" whose method of breaking and entering the house never varied. "Huh," thought Watson, "always through the letter box! No imagination. It's always a pushover."

"As a matter of fact," he reflected complacently, "I might not even bother today – unless of course it's the 'Banbury Cake'. Yes, I like the 'Banbury Cake' – it's most diverting. It tears up well and makes the most satisfactory ripping sounds, and besides it's perfect for jumping and tossing loudly around the hall and front room afterwards."

13

1976: DARK THE NIGHT

Part of Sandy's letter to Miranda.

"I don't want to write miserable songs. Do you know how I feel after I've written a miserable, sad song? Something that's really hit me and hurt me? I feel terrible. I go and sit down, and I'm really upset by it. I always write on my own. It's like a vicious circle, being on my own. I tend to think of sad things, and so I write songs that make me feel even sadder. I sit down and I write something, and it moves me to tears almost. I'm fed up with feeling like that." [1977]

Sandy Denny

In much the same way as her fellow escapee from Fotheringport Con-fusion, Mr Thompson, Sandy had made songs of doom and gloom something of a trademark in the years since *Liege and Lief*. As she told a journalist back in January 1972, "I sit down to write, and I say, 'OK, I'm going to write some jolly little songs, with none of that doomy quality about them', and as soon as I get my fingers to the keyboard, or pen to paper, out they come in their thou-sands – doomy, metaphorical phrases, minor keys, weird chords." Miranda Ward recalls how even some songs that "came out of joy, she'd actually hook onto sadness ... she was [just] not the sort that was going to write 'It's A Beautiful Day Today'." Yet, at times, she clearly wanted that side to come out, perhaps simply to show the world that such a person existed.

> **Bambi Ballard:** She told me once she was trying to write a song about just how she felt about her life, her house, Trevor, her dog, all of it, and she said, with that wonderful laugh she had, "Of course, it'd be terribly boring if I just talked about the house and the table and the kitchen and the dog. But that's what I want to write about." So she want[ed] to put the emotion that she had about these terribly mundane things [into song]. Sandy was always trying to express that comfort [at home] that one has, a sense of love.

Of the handful of songs she was writing in her final months with Fairport, perhaps the most ambitious was one of those songs that chose to deal with "these terribly mundane things," and tied them to the passing of the seasons. 'All Our Days' was clearly conceived as a centrepiece of work to come, much as 'No End' had channeled the material on *Like An Old Fashioned Waltz* towards itself. Written in an autumnal mood, 'All Our Days' conjured up a series of "memories for saving all our days," devoting a verse each to winter, spring and autumn (summer having to share its verse with spring).

'No More Sad Refrains', as performed at the Albert Hall back in June 1975, seems to have also begun life as a declaration of intent. That sense of sadness it sought to expell, though, seemed to come from a pit of sorrow somehow divorced from "any tragedies that were." In the original draft, that pit occasionally opens up, as when Sandy celebrates the (female) morning and hopes that if she helps it "wash away the dust of yesterday," that it "will take away the constant pain of ..." (the source of this persistent agony is never given). In the finished song she seeks to "forget about you," a surprising volley from the emotional battlefield that had become her marriage, and which now inspired bouts of self-examination, purging pangs of guilt and reconciliation, and fierce assertions of independence, often in the same song.

Another song, written shortly after 'No More Sad Refrains', that sought to cast aside past miseries, focusing only on happy memories, from a present of uncertainty and infidelity, was 'Full Moon'. Taking as its inspiration a night just "like the night when we first met," the song is directed at the faithless second-person lover, insisting that "this is where I want to stay/ maybe it could always be this way." The final verse as demoed – along with 'No More Sad Refrains', 'All Our Days', 'Take Me Away' and 'Still Waters Run Deep' – in the winter of 1976, at their home in Byfield, made it quite clear that Trevor was the subject of this plea:

> *"Gentle music rock away the sadness in me,*
> *Rock away my lonely yesterdays,*
> *Like pennies on the ocean*
> *'Till no trace of them I see,*
> *'Till moonlight shows no ripples on the waves.*
>
> *Our lives will be so different from now on,*
> *Each and every good time will be longer,*
> *Full moon."*

The final three lines here, rewritten into something more poetical by the time album sessions came around, suggest a willingness to change, if only he would stay, or perhaps if only he would come back. Though the song seeks a romantic rekindling of first love, the despair underlying this very personal song is betrayed by an addenda to Sandy's written draft: "Say you feel the [?same]/ Why do I feel I love you? ... Maybe we will see another day/ I still want you back."

The ebb and flow of Sandy's relationship with her husband found a more even keel on another song written in those months, 'Take Me Away', a simple lyric of transcendence perfectly suited to that plaintive quality in Sandy's voice. With none of the ambiguity of 'Full Moon', it suggested life without her man unthinkable, a sentiment also expressed in a long letter she wrote to Miranda on February 23, 1976, a couple of days after she had a wisdom tooth removed when, unable to run up her telephone bill nattering into the night, she took up her pen instead:

"*Dear Miranda,*

...I shall definitely be down on Wednesday night and if not then I was thinking perhaps after the extraction of stitches I might wend my way Barnes-ward. It would be so lovely to see you again. I really haven't seen a soul for so long. It's amazing when I think of it – quite the hermit in fact. Just me and my piano working on into the night ... Congratulations on [finding] the Schaeffer pen and the fiver, and by the way I know just what it's like to suddenly discover yourself totally indulging in reminiscences and waves of nostalgia as you uncover drawers and boxes full of the past. We have John Wood, you know, of the engineer's breed, coming up to stay for a couple of days today. Trevor and he are proposing to discussing the ins and outs of my new album. For the first time, before a record has even been started I'm feeling so confident. I have as you know been writing a lot recently, and I keep reading through words and changing them all the time. It's great for me to take the time to do that. It means that I'm not in such a panic when I do go into the studio and the end result will be more satisfactory to my ears, which I think is probably one of the most important things.

...Linda [Thompson] had a little boy on Friday. From what I can gather her labour was about 24 hours, which I suppose was fairly unpleasant, as she had it at home. Her mother rang me about it but unfortunately because Friday was the day I had my small op. I was well out of it. Trevor took the call and you know what men are like when it comes to relaying any kinds of details of that nature with any accuracy. You quite took me by surprise with your startling red pages but I must agree that a fountain pen is the basis of true enjoyment in handwriting. Whoever invented the biro ought to be etc. What happened with that Time Out *escapade [a lonely hearts ad]? It sounds like it could be interesting. You know, although you have a tendency to self-mock, you can have some pretty bright ideas. Unless it's never occured to you before, I would be in the same situation as you if I hadn't bumped into Trev. I often think who would have me, or more likely, who would I have. It's a situation to be fussy over, and there's nothing wrong in thinking your standards are too high because I'd rather you stayed like that and eventually entered into a permanent relationship with which you are truly happy, but Miranda that doesn't mean you can't have a bit on the side. This is the age of women's emancipation so to hell with stuffy antiquated reputations which stem from the ever responsible (sic) Victorian era! So there, chum! Capricorns are in for a good month and February sees the end of recent disasters, which I read in* Vogue *I think I told you. I for one welcome this as 1976 so far has been one major catastrophe for me, and if you feel the same perhaps we're in for a good productive time ahead, and isn't it just about due!!!!*

... Cheerio, Love from Miranda." [Note: They both often signed each others' names]

The chatterbox Sandy, captured here by pen and ink, illustrated a side of the mystery woman that her songs barely hinted at. The enthusiasm with which she writes about her new songs and her new album also show someone who felt there was a way back up the slippery slope down which she had recently slid. The good news that had reached Sandy shortly after leaving Fairport was that, though Island Records had now parted company with her old band, they wished her to resume the solo career their previous prevarications had prompted her to abandon. The opportunity to return to making music her way, and her way alone, now pushed her to write a batch of songs and record a further set of demos that laid the groundwork for what promised to be a major collection.

Trevor continued to crack the metaphorical whip, even though his own songwriting remained still-born. As Bruce Rowland observes, "Trevor could be pretty unkind at times, and used to castigate her for not having written anything. 'That's no good, that sounds like this one.' ... and [he] was still writing 'Iron Lion'." Sandy knew it was necessary, writing a brief note of thanks one morning to her absent taskmaster: "My dearest one, I hope you are well, I worked until five o'clock this morning just to make you realise I meant what I said about trying hard. I think it is the best song I have ever written, maybe because I feel as if I know all those feelings in the song." The note precedes some stacatto images from the middle of the night, as inspiration proved fleeting and unwelcome thoughts about her husband's whereabouts crowded in:

"It's so late – it's tomorrow
There's nothing doing in my yard.
Early light – frosty covers
It's that first day that's so hard
The central heating pipes are banging
I keep thinking it's the car
But if I keep up with my singing
I won't be wondering where you are.
Oh don't stop singing till you drop.
The only way you're going to stop
is if a neighbour starts complaining.
And I won't hear them any way
Write a book – sketch my home town
Don't pick up the phone
It's out of bounds

Shortage of sounds
strange to be alone."

By the time John Wood arrived at Byfield to discuss Sandy's musical direction and ideas for an album, at the end of February, she had half a dozen demos to play him, and was flowing with ideas. Her most recent song was another product of the night. It was also perhaps her most honest self-portrait-in-song, even if the first-person Sandy had transposed herself into the third person for the tune in question, originally entitled 'Mystery Woman', but issued as 'Still Waters Run Deep'. The song later lost its introductory verse, in which she admits that "sorrow dwells beneath" her "witches hat," before asserting independence from her public persona – whatever that might be:

"I'm mystery woman
so keep well away
I spell trouble to you
if you get in my way.
But how could you tell
it's not like that
and sorrow dwells
beneath the witches hat.
How could you know me
You [who] never have spoken to me
Though you think you know me
Still river[s] still run deep."

If the narrator lost her witches hat, she remained "all dressed in black." The remainder of the autobiographical portrait was almost too revealing to sing straight:

She's got a thorn in her side
A chip on her shoulder
Heartache to hide
A lot of people to scold her
But no-one comes near
It's no place to be
They all live in fear

They might set her free."

A new bridge also conspired to leave some surprising insights on view:

"The darkness grows
and the lady does not sleep
It's so hard to lose
Now it's so hard to weep
While the river flows
Still waters still run deep.

The darkness was indeed growing, as was Sandy's insomnia, prompting a rewrite of her little lyric about lost hope from the winter of 1975, so that it read: "Sleep/ Will I ever sleep?/ Oh, to sleep in peace once again, my love?" In an attempt to paint some colour into those "shadowed lanes," Sandy wrote a song that looked forward to an evening when "we'll be laughing/ just wait and see/ all the changes there'll be", 'By The Time It Gets Dark'. Another attempt to inject some joy back into a relationship gone sour, the song was demoed on a 12-string at Byfield in the weeks leading upto sessions in April, along with 'Take Away The Load' and 'I'm A Dreamer'. The former, donated to Dave Swarbrick, presumably prior to the album sessions (it was never cut in the studio), suggested that blame was a two-way street:

"You are the one I love,
You are the one I touch,
And it's you who must not go
But it's I who must try
Not to send you away."

In fact, Swarb was privvy to most of the songs Sandy was now writing, desperate as she was for a kindly sir to share her worldly woes. Swarb remembers, "Sandy used to come round every day. Or I'd go over there. I knew her walk. I wouldn't even look out the window, I'd just let the door open and let her in ... [but] she didn't look well." A sounding-board for her new songs, Swarb was particularly struck by one that she hadn't even demoed yet, obliquely named 'One Way Donkey Ride'. Though the song seemed to have been written from the viewpoint of someone standing at the crossroads between a new and an old relationship, "swaying in both directions ... how do I make my selection?," it is hard not to see some religious import in the narrator's cry, "God bless the poor ones on that one way donkey ride," nor some messianic subtext in Sandy's description of someone who "stand[s] in your splendour and jewels":

"While we fumble in the darkness where once there was light,
Roaming the land of the ancients,
Oasis of love, sweet water of life,
God bless the poor ones whose patience never died ..."

Sandy's own capacity for suffering had assumed its own messianic tinge by now. Again, her notebooks caught her writing to herself in mock approbation:

"Sandy – why should you be unhappy?
Why be offended? Why get drunk?
Take away the brain, and substitute misery and sheer suffering torture
and you probably would accept it as your due."

As someone for whom religious allusion had rarely informed her bag of imagery, even something as ambiguous as 'One Way Donkey Ride' suggested some kind of choice on offer. Not that the messianic portrait in this song was unduly flattering. In fact, Sandy had only recently exposed herself to the teachings of one such false messiah, L. Ron Hubbard, founder of the Church of Scientology.

Linda Thompson: She became a Scientologist for a very short while, and then she left. And they hounded her, sending her literature. You weren't supposed to break out of Scientology ... She went to have some 'auditing', and the guy who was doing the 'auditing' was a really attractive guy. It's like two tin cans and [string] – [the] 'electric impulses' tell if you're lying, if things are bothering you. So she just reached over and grabbed his crotch, and he got this enormous erection, and she said, "Well, what are your feelings about that, then?" ... Anyway she became a Scientologist partly due to this guy, and then got very sick of it ... [But] I know what getting embroiled with cult religions is like, so I can't throw stones.

The vacuum Sandy felt in her life had only been exacerbated by the decision of Richard and Linda Thompson to become part of a Sufi commune, adopting the dictums of this Islamic* creed until it invaded every aspect of their lives. It would be unwise to underestimate her sense of loss. As late as April 1975, she had delighted in sharing the stage at Queen Elizabeth Hall with the pair of them on an impromptu encore of 'When Will I Be Loved' (after Sandy had mockingly requested 'Meet on the Ledge' from the audience and Linda had retorted, "Only if you come up here and sing it."). Sandy's embracing of Scientology may have been her way of asserting a dormant spirituality, it may have been simply another plea for understanding, but she was finding it hard to face up to her friends having their own lives to lead, their own paths to find.

Linda Thompson: That was very difficult because we'd become Muslims, and Richard became more distant than ever. If you were a Muslim, you weren't supposed to be throwing your arms around the opposite sex, and Richard really took that to the max. I suppose I did, too. I think that was quite hurtful for her. It's like when you're an alcoholic, and you stop drinking, you have to give up your friends. We had to give up Sandy – and people like that. However misguided it was, we were trying to better ourselves/find a spiritual side, and we couldn't hang around people who were sinking brandy and snorting coke.

That Sandy had successfully inoculated herself from her own bout of spiritual doubt is indicated by a brief piece of prose written into the same notebook as 'All Our Days'. This prose parable is subjected to a number of rewrites until it arrives at the following, with Sandy presumably playing the part of Reynard the Fox:

"A religion is too much like wire netting on either side of The Path, which it reveres, and to which it adheres. But the bright and wily fox will always search and find escape [... Any wily fox can find a hole in the wire netting ...] It must be there. For perfection is so rare. And then how different the aspect of the path becomes from the wide and boundless space without."

So much for Scientology. Trevor's reaction to the news of her swift

---

*The Sufi, as I understand it, are very dubiously orthodox in mainstream Islamic eyes.

conversion may have also persuaded her to recant – he apparently almost destroyed one of their 'centres' in an uncharacteristic fit of fury. The thought that Sandy's 'conversion' was a cry from a lonely woman, hurting from the heart, seems to have eluded Trevor, who blithely continued a series of affairs, most notably with singer Jackie Byford, the ex-wife of guitarist Andy Roberts, prompting a whole series of entries in those last few notebooks, suggesting that the open relationship they had allowed their marriage to become was shredding their vows one by one. In one outburst, Sandy had simply written: "No Deal/I won't write a song about the one I love/ even if he is a shitbag/I can't r[h]yme when I'm upset." The churlish tone hid a real, and almost constant, pain, which was only rarely allowed to spill over into song.

Preceding this note in the notebook is a lyric, 'Makes Me Think Of You', seemingly the song that Sandy described to Trevor in another note as "the best song I have ever written," though it is hardly that. It seems rather to be an example of "keep[ing] up with my singing/ [so] I won't be wondering where you are." Demoed at some point between February and April, though with the key line "before you fell in love with her" rewritten as "before you went with her," 'Makes Me Think Of You' is one of Sandy's most personal examinations of her increasingly strained relations with her husband, the false optimism of 'Full Moon' and 'Take Me Away' having been replaced by an all too real regret:

> *"No use knocking at my door*
> *I don't think I live here anymore*
> *[I live in the past you see]*
> *I think of the need to be by you*
> *I think of the last time you were here*
> *Before you went with her.*
>
> *All my letters lay unopened*
> *Along with calling cards and tokens*
> *I cannot read you see*
> *I only need to be with you now*
> *If I could only move somehow.*

The albums strewn without their clothes
Gather dust amongst the grooves
The only one I play is Blue
It makes me think of you."

The song would remain unreleased, indeed unrecorded save in demo form, perhaps because, as Sandy put it to Patrick Humphries a year later, "I adore Joni Mitchell but I do think she went around wearing her heart on her sleeve [on albums like *Blue*]. I adore listening to those songs but I wouldn't like it to be me whose painting it around for everyone to know. The last thing I'd want everyone to know is my business." As it is, when her own pain obliterated all sense of self, Sandy would simply stop writing.

The notebooks suggest that Sandy had a lot to hide from unknowing eyes, as instances when Trevor "went with *her*" became increasingly common. Though the official line was that Trevor was in London producing, very little product resulted from the tracts of time he spent away. Sandy herself was preparing herself for the worst:

"It's all very sad, and I won't stand there in the wings
And wait for the tragedy I know the last act brings ...

It's goodbye now for the very first time
It's hard to force a tear when you are numb.
It's hard to squeeze our lifetime into a simple r[h]yme
Where is the laughter now, where is the sun?..."

Even now, though, Sandy couldn't resist jotting another note to "my darling Trevor," insisting that, "I never write to you. I wish I was like you, and was with you always. Sometimes I feel that I am so far away from you..." The precise, generous arcs of her earlier penmanship have now given way to jagged edges and fierce angular lines, the after-effects of one too many.

With her anchor coming away, Sandy felt the need for some tender, loving care of her own. The 1976 notebooks are as riddled with references to a.n.other as to "darling Trevor." Whether Sandy's own affair/s began as retaliatory gestures, or were a unilateral recognition of Trevor's inability to plug this well of sorrow into which he had sunk so much of his energies, is impossible to say at this distance. Miranda Ward insists that, "Sandy twice turned up on my doorstep in an absolute state. One time she'd gone round to

Philippa's, Philippa wouldn't let her in, she got in and found Trevor in bed with somebody." Philippa herself paints a quite different portrait of the decaying relationship.

> **Philippa Clare:** Trevor looked after her very well, but he would stray. But then Sandy wasn't exactly a saint either. And they both thought the other didn't know! ... She certainly had her own excursions ... [At the time of] *Rendezvous*, she was having a scene with Pat Donaldson. She really fell in love with Pat. I gave 'em safe house here. [But] I think [Trevor] knew. It didn't go on that long, but it was very intense. Pat had [already] split up from his wife.

The notebooks suggest that Sandy's affairs failed to bring her any peace. If the void inside was too great for Trevor alone to fill, then long-distance liasons were hardly likely to provide the necessary gerrymandering. And yet, references abound in the notebooks of someone in the U.S. who Sandy is longing to see again:

> *"I'm going to call that number*
> *Though I don't really mean to wake you from your slumber*
> *While England is asleep.*
> *The hotel is just like yesterday's*
> *The city has no name*
> *It stands there in a grey haze*
> *My room is just the same*
> *I wonder how you're keeping ...*
> *I feel so tired and lonely*
> *I'm thinking of you, lover*
> *I wish you could console me*
> *But maybe when it's over."*

These lines were presumably directed at the same man who "stir[red] up the butterflies [that] night in New York." In the final couplet of that previous lyric, there had even been a suggestion that Sandy's marriage had become a form of method-acting, that the "pain in my heart/ puts a strain on the part I've been playing so well for so long." Her marriage was not the only charade being played out at this point. So was the pretence that she had a handle on her career. When she penned one of those bitter invectives at [the] one who had ended it, it became as much a rant at her own expense for the way she allowed life to treat her:

"I never thought about it much
But still I counted on you
And when you never got in touch
And never left a clue
I tried to find you, all in vain
I should have realised
You were out for what you'd gain
Knowing I would not complain
Leaving me the bare remains
As consolation's prize."

The charade itself became the subject of one of those lost lyrics that now filled her notebooks, but failed to fill out into song. At this point any sense of defeat at the prospect of another day could still be held at bay by the hope that "he'll come tonight." The question was, what might happen when that hope also faded to black?:

"Another morning
Another dreary day
Put [on] a face, it's not really there
I wonder if he'll come tonight
I wonder what he'll say
I'll make believe that I don't really care.

She had invited many in order to disguise
That she only wanted him to come
Hoping that the crowd would hide her beating heart."

The prospect of sessions back at Island, which held out the promise of better days, couldn't come quickly enough for Sandy. The first set of sessions for Sandy's fourth solo album were scheduled for the last week of April 1976, barely four months after she had quit Fairport. However much the struggle for content had brought out the old demons, the winter days had produced more than enough for an album of all original songs. As she later told a journalist, "I was writing all the time at home and [for the first time] I had virtually everything ready, including all the words, when I went into the studio."

And yet, Sandy was again reluctant to allow her own songs to become part of a single entity, determined to dispel the unity of mood that carried across all her home demos. On the first day of sessions, the freshly-penned 'One Way Donkey Ride' was paired with a Flying Burritos Brothers cover, 'Losing Game'. Also recorded that first week was Sandy's only ever cover of a Richard & Linda song, 'For Shame of Doing Wrong', as well as six of the eight songs she had previously demoed.

In the case of 'I'm A Dreamer', it was cut in a single take, which John Wood believes is, "why she sings it so well. She was very much put on the spot to do it, she just had to sit down at the piano." Lovely as the new vocal was, though, the slightly idealised self-portrait of this "schemer with an eye for a show" was again submerged 'neath the strength of Harry Robinson's ubiquitous strings, forsaking all the texture and tone so effortlessly captured on that simple home demo. Jerry Donahue still remembers her guide version, "'cause it was so much better than the one she chose. It seemed like she wouldn't state the melody enough first, she would start to overdecorate immediately, whereas on the original version it was a lot simpler, you could really hear the full melody."

'I'm A Dreamer' was one of three songs cut at one remarkable session, on April 25, 1976. Donahue cites, "'I'm A Dreamer', 'Full Moon' and 'No More Sad Refrains', those three [as being] done the same day, with the full orchestra in there, with us playing at the same time." John Wood believes it was his idea for Sandy to sing and play live in front of a full orchestra. As he told Pam Winters, "When I started making records, that's how people used to do it. I just thought it might be worth trying it. It creates a bit of tension. I think we did three tracks like that, and it worked very well." Though the voice had finally lost its virginal purity, most of the control and power remained intact, and augmented by a set of musicians that included Pat Donaldson, Timi Donald, 'Rabbit' Bundrick and Stevie Winwood, Sandy pulled out vocals that rode the strings effortlessly.

By the end of the first week of sessions, Sandy had recorded enough material for an album. She had only one more song, the classically conceived 'All Our Days', in mind to record. This, too, she wished to record live, with an orchestra. A larger studio, though, would have to be found as she also planned to record a choral version on the same day. Finally, they settled on CBS Studios.

> **Jerry Donahue:** She ... didn't have the rock band at all. It was just her and the orchestra, and she did that live ... I remember we were invited to come along and we watched her and I guess it was Harry Robinson, and he would have to nod to her when it was time for her to start singing again. I think they did it on like the second take. It was amazing, she was kinda nervous. She dressed up in a really nice dress for the occasion, [like], 'This is the real thing now.'

In Sandy's mind, though, the album still needed work. Part of her doubts seemed to stem from Trevor's vision of where she might be heading. Perhaps he knew the subject-matter of her own songs all too well, but he continued to imagine that he could effect her transformation into a mainstream act by not so much embellishing the songs as embalming them. Rather than being content with what he had, Trevor wanted to clock up more studio time, to see what more there was, and to apply some more fur-coats.

> **John Wood:** I think by the time she made *Rendezvous*, she was not necessarily doing what she wanted ... I think Sandy drifted away from some of the more, if you like, rootsier and gutsier feelings that she'd started with both in Fotheringay and in the next couple of albums. With the increasing influence of Trevor ... [she] started to get a little more pandering to the middle of the road ... She'd lost some of her individualism ... Although some of the tunes might have been good, there are a lot of songs that are a little sugary, saccharine ... [they] have a sort of sentimentality which I really shouldn't have associated with her, knowing her as a woman. [PW]

Sessions resumed again at the beginning of June. Whatever went down between Trevor and Sandy in the five weeks between, there had been a key transformation. Sandy's voice had lost another notch of tonality, but more signficantly she now became even more highly strung in the studio, and Trevor's presence only served to make her worse. Wood found himself being forced to acquire some skills as a personal counsellor.

John Wood: By the time [of the June sessions] she'd started having these very black moods, and it was a long time before any material came together, and her mood swings were much greater. ... She wouldn't turn up, or she'd turn up very late ... She was not in control of herself. Halfway through ... she turned up at 2 o' clock in the morning where I used to live in London, virtually battering the door down in a complete state of nervous exhaustion, having drunk too much, feeling unloved, unwanted. [JI]

The first session at Basing Street in June started promisingly enough. Sandy not only wanted another stab at a studio arrangement of 'By The Time It Gets Dark' but had brought a new song with her, 'Gold Dust'. Based loosely on her and Miranda's journey across America in the spring of 1973, the song had a subtext that suggested the golden promise of Hollywood dreams could easily turn to dust, or perhaps rather white lines of powder. Her exposure to the Laurel Canyon circuit of singer-songwriters had certainly not managed to dissuade Sandy from establishing her own direct line to Charlie.

If, as Miranda asserts, 'Gold Dust' "was the way her music was going," it set its own price. As if almost too aware of the levy, Sandy also recorded Lowell George's 'Easy To Slip' at these June sessions – "it's so easy to slip/it's so easy to fall..." Indeed. Sandy had been hanging out with Little Feat's Lowell George, by this time a walking snowman, in the days before the resumption of sessions, as George's low achievers awaited a brief U.K. stadium tour with The Who. Miranda and Lowell had had something going for a while when Sandy came up to Lowell's hotel suite to jam with him, and hang out. Though Lowell hardly needed to introduce Sandy to cloud nine, he was happy enough to let her share the view from the self-same foggy mountain-top. Enamored of the 'rock' lifestyle, unhappy at home, hugely talented but largely unrecognised outside her homeland, Sandy remained particularly vunerable to the promise of perhaps not a better, but an easier life out west, previously proffered by the likes of Mama Cass, Don Henley, and Jackson Browne. Possibly, Sandy conceived of making her new album more 'West Coast' sounding to smooth that passage. Its working title would remain *Gold Dust* for a long time, and, a note jotted in one of her exercise books suggested, "Go west young woman/ you need the change ... Smile and leave the losers behind."

West L.A. '76 was the last place a person like Sandy should have been. It had already eaten up the great Dusty Springfield, a stronger character and a better known property. But Sandy was already at the place where she was looking for external solutions to internal problems. When Miranda joined Lowell in Los Angeles for a few weeks that summer, she was surprised to receive a number of long distance phone-calls from Sandy who, when questioned, invariably insisted that everything was fine, and she was just phoning halfway round the world for a chat.

Work on her album now progressed at a pace even a snail might have regarded as tardy. Vocal overdubs, and a smattering of covers – including a rerecording of 'Silver Threads & Golden Needles' that would finally find a place on record, brass band et al. – ate up several weeks of studio-time, aided and abetted by a tortuous series of mixing sessions. As days were given over to overdubbing a clarinet, a fiddle, a guitar solo, or new vocals on songs not even destined to make the final album, like 'Full Moon' and 'By The Time It Gets Dark', it would be the first week in August before a final sequence was approved.

Despite the weeks of sessions in June and July, the bulk of *Rendezvous* would still come from that week of recordings back in April. The west coast covers would end up discarded. Of the album's eventual contents, just 'Silver Threads & Golden Needles' and 'Gold Dust' had not been recorded in basic track form in April. All that remained now was for Island to release the record and start recouping the substantial studio bill Sandy and Trevor had been allowed to run up. Once again, though, Island placed the album on the backburner schedule they reserved for their B-list artists, and the plans Sandy had for taking herself back on the road and really promoting the album again went up in flames.

Sandy Denny: It was finished about July … and I was supposed to go on [tour] in October with a band and everything. I had a big band lined up with a a lot of good people in it: Jerry Donahue, Rabbit, Dave Mattacks, Pat Donaldson, Andy Roberts, about eight people. I put the project to Island and they just didn't seem to want to invest an awful lot of money to put the show on the road … The next thing I knew it was coming out in October, then November, then December, and there was always another date and another date and another date. Eventually it ended up being May 14, when I was just about to think of giving the record a birthday party. [1977]

Forced again to put her career on hold for nigh on a year, while Island decided where they wanted her on their tired release schedule, Sandy found herself in a strange limbo, unable to tour without label support, unwilling to return to the boards solo, and without any incentive to work on her songs or her craft until Island deemed it appropriate. When *Rendezvous* was finally released, in late May 1977, she would find "it very difficult to talk about the record ... because I've got to renew my original interest in the album when, quite frankly, I haven't listened to it that much for such a long time now. I've got to get back into the way I felt when it was finished, which was excited."

The delay prompted Sandy to record a version of Elton John's 'Candle in the Wind', at a session in February, something that apparently required some twenty-five takes to come out right. In a strange move, that baffled even her engineer, she then proceeded to substitute Elton's paean to a female superstar who ran out of reasons to live for her own restless self-portrait 'Still Waters Run Deep', a curious move that smacked of Trevor and his diva complex.

Sandy's choice of song at the February session merely served to suggest that six months between sessions had failed to yielded anything in the songwriting department. The most shocking aspect, though, of her recording of Elton John's 1973 hit single was that voice. Sandwiched between 'Gold Dust' and the glorious 'Take Me Away' on the released *Rendezvous*, it largely escaped notice at the time, but the voice had all but gone. Unable to sustain her notes without a tell-tale tremulous waver, her lungpower greatly dimmed, 'A Candle in the Wind' was precisely what that extraordinary natural gift had become.

Doubtless Sandy told herself that her lungpower had become affected by the child she was now carrying, the child she'd longed for, and that she still hoped would turn her marriage around. Unfortunately, the grand promotional tour that was to have accompanied the release of her fourth solo album would now have to be deferred until after she had had the baby, due some time in August.

Island still seemed determined to ensure that the album was released when even a TV appearance or radio session would have been out of the question. In fact, her label was increasingly concerned at various reports they had been hearing, presumably from A&R and studio personnel, and there was a very real danger that Sandy would be joining Fairport in a label-less limbo. At one point, during discussions about an English-style *Trio* album, Island's Brian Blethyns asked Sandy's old friend Bambi Ballard if she would consider managing their would-be diva.

Bambi Ballard: [Sandy] was so keen on this mad idea that I had of putting her and Elkie [Brooks] and Maddy [Prior] together in a jam session. The concept was [songs like Fats Waller's] 'Honeysuckle Rose' ... Then I talked to Brian Blethyns and he said, "Great, Island's for it." But Atlantic wouldn't let Elkie go. Island [then] asked me to manage her, again through Brian Blethyns. He came to me and said, "Would you manage her, because if you do, we think she'll be okay." They were seriously concerned. With hindsight, I say, "Why didn't I?" ... It was for all the wrong reasons. Brian Blethyn's attitude was, We can't handle Sandy anymore. Island is thinking of blowing her out because there's too much friction, she's baulking at certain gigs, Trevor is too much of an influence, and Sandy needs serious management ... And then Sandy got pregnant, and everybody felt she wouldn't come out of this one being quite the person she had been.

That person had been, for most of a decade-long recording career, a singer of her own sorrows.

14

1977–78: NO MORE SAD REFRAINS

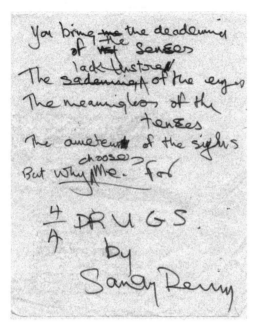

Only overt reference to drugs in Sandy's notebooks.

"I'll probably stop for a while one day. After all, children have to arrive eventually, don't they – otherwise, after a while you begin to wonder what you're here on earth for." [1974]

Sandy Denny

"In many ways I really needed a break from the business. I've been in it up to my eyes for over ten years, virtually non-stop, though people don't realise it because I'm not hitting the headlines every day. But when you're out working for ten or eleven years with not much of a break you can go completely mad without realising it at the time. It's taken me since last summer to get back to some sort of sanity – something I didn't even realise I'd lost." [1977]

Sandy Denny

On June 7, 1976, Sandy Denny recorded her last original song, 'Gold Dust', at a session at Basing Street Studios. Eleven months later, she returned to Basing Street to record a one-off version of a Bryn Haworth song, 'Moments', that she had heard him play one day in the studio, during the Rising For The Moon sessions. Eleven months after that, she would be dead. Whatever brick-wall she hit in her mind, even the formative lyrics that fill her other notebooks seem to have been all but stilled during those last twenty-two months.

Initially, it was doubtless a conscious "break from the business," prompted by the news, at the dawn of 1977, that she was finally pregnant (again – there had been an earlier abortion), and this time she was going to keep the child. Though Philippa Clare remembers that, "Trevor felt they should wait, and build her solo career a bit," Sandy perhaps sensed that it was now or never. Certainly Island's release schedule seemed to be setting aside ample time for her to sit out her pregnancy, and it was something she would talk about repeatedly as the hole inside her grew – as Philippa Clare astutely observes, it was "something from the outside to make her feel better inside."

Dave Pegg: She always wanted a child so much – we were all aware of the fact that she would love to be a Mum. She would say to my wife, "Oh, it's okay for you. You've got kids." And we'd go, "You wanna babysit 'em for a couple of nights." But I think she thought that would probably make her happy and fulfilled, as a person and as a woman.

Seeing friends with their children only served to make the hole bigger. When Gina Glazer, now residing in Berkeley, Ca., last got to see Sandy, at the end of the Fairport farrago, she recalls, "She was quite thin. She just didn't seem her old self. [But] she did tell me she wanted to have a baby." She had admitted as much to her closest friends and family. And yet, her father remembered, when "eventually she said I'm having this child, Mummy ... everyone was very annoyed, including Trevor, because it was going to upset their schedules." On visiting her parents at this time, Sandy was uncharacteristically inspired to jot down reminiscences about her own childhood, in terms hazy with hormonal pangs:

"There are children at the school, where I used to go
They are learning things I used to know

No doubt they'll see things just like me
Or else they'll dream of a degree
The sun sets on the pavement squares
On which the homegoing student stares."

Bruce Rowland recalls that Sandy "had a phase of responsibility" when she learnt she was pregnant. However, on the evidence of 'Candle in the Wind', it cannot have lasted long. It had certainly come to a grinding halt by the Thursday in March when she caught one of the great unwashed combos then filling the London pubs in the wake of punk's revisionist template. Having missed that all-important window of opportunity in the autumn of 1976, Sandy was not the only Island artist now peering out on a changed musical landscape – "No Elvis, Beatles or the Rolling Stones in 1977."

Galvanized by a cussing two-minute interview with the Sex Pistols on a local current affairs TV programme, punk's 'keep it simple, stupid' credo left record company A&R divisions feeling thoroughly disoriented. The Only Ones, though, had taken the novel route of learning to play before adopting the credo and, in drummer Mike Kellie and Alan Mair, had a rhythm section fully conversant with Sixties verités. It was almost certainly Kellie, having known Sandy from his Spooky Tooth days, who invited her to come on down to the Greyhound pub in Fulham and catch one of the better examples of the new vanguard.

Sandy, who was, in guitarist John Perry's choice phrase, "a little wobbly on her pins ... like a much-loved aunt who has had a few too many," was greatly impressed by Perry's guitar-playing, called him "a young Richard Thompson," and invited him to work on her next record (though, when it came to record 'Moments', she forgot to make the call). She returned to see the band on a couple more occasions, in the company of her well-connected coke-dealer. Unbeknownst to Sandy, his supplies were actually coming from the lead-singer of the band she was so impressed with, the shamelessly amoral Peter Perrett.

It was probably on one of these occasions, whilst the Only Ones were carving out a reputation, that Sandy called at her old landlady's house, in Chipstead Street, no more than a hop and skip from the Greyhound. Linda Fitzgerald-Moore recalls, "she was pregnant and she was smoking, and I said, 'You shouldn't be smoking.' And I think she was upset about something. She came round quite [late], about midnight." They chatted into the night, before Sandy weaved her way back to Byfield, or perhaps crashed at Miranda's in Barnes.

On another occasion, with Sandy clearly more than a little the worse for drink, Mike Kellie offered to take her home, perhaps not realising it involved a trip to Northamptonshire. Though he stayed a couple of days, at Trevor's behest, all that Kellie remembers was this all-pervading sense of sadness and, as he drove him back to London, Trevor expressing his growing concern at Sandy's drinking. No mention was made of Sandy's pregnancy, though she would have been almost halfway through her term. Nor does John Perry remember any signs or mention of her condition, advanced as it was.

That Sandy was blatantly disregarding every word of advice about reducing her intake of substances in her pregnant state has been affirmed by just about all her close friends. Having asked Linda Thompson if she thought cocaine was bad for the baby, she nevertheless continued acquiring it from both her coke-dealing friend, and a close friend of hers whom he was also supplying (both of whom belived that they were supplying Sandy exclusively). However badly the drugs affected the physiology of her forming foetus, they were certainly seriously debilitating Sandy. The only reference to '4/4 Drugs' in her later notebooks, written in a crazed, capital-letter pen-stabbing style, came with a responsibility-denying question to cap it:

"You bring the deadening of the senses
The saddening [lacklustre] of the eyes
The meaningless of the tenses
The amateur of the sighs.
But why choose me?"

Townshend remembers, at this time, that "when she visited the studios she often arrived drunk, but she had the capacity to sober up suddenly. Maybe she was doing cocaine ... Keith Moon always carried it." Sandy and Keith were by now old hands at matching each other's excesses. Neither would live to see their thirty-second birthdays.

Sandy's new-found capacity to drink and drink, and still be standing – the classic trait of a cokehead – was no longer threatening only her well-being. In early July, with an album to promote and a career to revive, she found out the baby she had so long desired was on the verge of arriving, two months premature. Rushed to a hospital in Oxford that specialised in premature births, it was decided that the safest way to introduce the baby to the world was a Caesarian. On July 12, 1977, Alexandra Elene MacLean Lucas gave birth to Georgia Rose Lucas at the John Radcliffe Hospital. Whilst her baby daughter was immediately placed in an incubator, the doctors found Sandy equally in need of serious medical care.

Philippa Clare: When Georgia was born, Sandy was pacing up and down. The baby was premature, and she was in withdrawals and Trevor was doing the alcoholic partner number, defending the alcoholic, "Oh well, she has a few glasses of wine." ... These doctors didn't know. Trevor [finally] decided to tell them [the truth:] Smack, coke, dope, serious drinking: pernod, absinthe – that was what she did when she was pregnant. Once the doctors had that information, they could start taking care of business. But it gives you an idea of how bad Sandy was because there she is, pregnant, with a baby she *really* wanted, and yet she was doing all this self-abuse stuff ... She was in such a state – no booze, no drugs, no nothing, her body's in complete shock [with] heavy, heavy withdrawals.

Only now were the physical and psychological scars of Sandy's addictive passage through child-birth manifest for all to see. Linda Thompson travelled down to Oxford almost as soon as Georgia was born, to find that "even when she'd just had this baby, she was thinking, 'I've had a Caesarian,' she was more thinking of her[self]. It was part of her illness." Trevor must have been equally stunned at the scope of her withdrawal symptoms, and appalled at the way she had endangered the life of his first-born. He may even have begun to realise the depths to which his wife had sunk, though without factoring in his own absenteeism.

Bambi Ballard: Sandy would ring me from the hospital and say she hadn't seen Trevor for three days. The baby was premature, and she was in the hospital for three weeks, and Trevor was hardly there, and she was ringing everybody up 'cause she was lonely ... My reading of that – having heard on the circuit that there was another woman – was that Trevor was taking advantage of Sandy being immobilised.

If Trevor still hoped that having a daughter could turn Sandy around, he soon became overly possessive about Georgia, which may itself have been a factor in Sandy's failure to bond with her child. As Miranda Ward says, "there was the whole thing of the baby staying in hospital and her being discharged, and there must have been a hell of a guilt trip laid on her by Trevor. I think that Sandy couldn't cope." Meanwhile, Trevor had gone out and bought a pedigree Airedale puppy in order that Watson, in Miranda's words, "had a baby to play with, so that he wouldn't be jealous of the baby. So what happens, Watson gets jealous of both."

Despite millennia of mothering instincts in her genes and years of longing in her loins, Sandy was simply not ready to have a child. Discharged from hospital herself, she was obliged to make the daily thirty-five mile round trip to John Radcliffe to breast-feed Georgia, who remained on a respirator for a number of weeks. Finally, Georgia was ready to come home, providing Sandy with somebody as needy and demanding as herself, a twenty-four hours a day headache. Initially, though, Sandy's joy was as boundless as the world at large, prompting one of her last poems, a sincere six-liner of maternal love:

> *"Georgia, though you sleep so soundly now,*
> *When autumn leaves are falling to the ground*
> *You'll reach to catch them with your tiny hands*
> *and gaze in wonderment as only babies can.*
> *How I long to see you wake and smile*
> *My beautiful, most precious child."*

Unfortunately, as Sandy's grasp on this world began to slacken, so did her awareness of her child's needs. All too quickly, she lost the thread that connected her to her offspring. Karl Dallas came to interview her at her home in Byfield, shortly after Georgia came home, and his impression of the new mother was that, "she was very happy ... but she was a bit like a schoolgirl with a new doll, she was so happy having this plaything. It was almost juvenile. She was over the moon about the child but not perhaps in a very mature way." Dealing with the practicalities of life had never been one of Sandy's strong points. As Miranda observes, "If Sandy was writing a song and Watson wanted to go out, he could pee, shit or whatever on the carpet and she wouldn't notice ... It was exactly the same with Georgia. Suddenly, the muse would hit her and everything else went out of the window."

Whatever and wherever that muse was, it was having a hard time breaking through the psychological barriers erected by an increasingly maudlin lady.

The euphoria Karl Dallas witnessed did not last long. Bruce Rowland remembers that second, fleeting "phase of responsibility" when "Sandy had something to focus on, that was bringing her a lot of attention, and the fact that everything was slipping away from her was pushed to the background," but he was also around when "the novelty of the baby wore off." As part of the Banbury band of Fairporters, he saw a great deal of Sandy in the months after the pregnancy and he is in no doubts that a lot of what happened "was to do with [her] post-natal depression; and Trevor trying but not delivering, and not being consistent; and people starting to back off from her ... [But] there was no question it was post-natal depression."

Others are not so sure Sandy's state of mind qualified as clinical post-partum depression, something now known to strike upward of one in ten of all mothers, but all are agreed that, to quote Richard Thompson, "Sandy was having a very hard time being a mother ... she would think the baby had stopped breathing, or was dying instead of teething." That downward spiral was gathering pace.

Philippa Clare: She was very down then. She used to come round to see me a lot, very drunk. I'd arrive home and she'd be sitting on the stairs in floods of tears. ... I think she was disappointed that the baby didn't turn her life around and make everything alright ... Sandy was incredibly depressed, whether it was post-natal or not. The trouble with Sandy is she had so many mood swings, either chemically-influenced or not, I couldn't sit down and say she had post-natal depression. But she was very depressed, which was why the drinking accelerated.

With that sensitivity for which record companies are renowned, Island Records felt that this was a suitably opportune time to inform their finest female singer that they were no longer interested in releasing her records. Thanks largely to the label itself, *Rendezvous* had come out at just the wrong time, as the Sex Pistols' 'God Save The Queen' became the mystery number one that dare not be named, and battlelines were formed. Island found themselves stranded far from this teenage wasteland, as the punk first division were snapped up by the Richard Bransons of this world. Even the Only Ones, courted by Blackwell in person, preferred to attach the CBS label to their vinyl outings. The economics of music-making were also changing, and the Fairport family were out of phase. Fairport had hobbled onto Phonogram, Richard and Linda were about to make the jump to Chrysalis. There was a way back, but it was a time for scaling down operations – meaning all Trevor Lucas-style productions.

> **Dave Pegg:** When Island started up it was a bunch of guys, they were all into the music, they'd do anything for Fairport. They were really good to us, though nobody else in the band would say that. They never ever recouped ... [But] all of a sudden you had to justify the fact that you were spending so much making records, and nobody was buying them. The music industry suddenly became a business, and people like Sandy ... felt really bad about that. It was another insecurity. It was another thing for her to be depressed about.

Chris Blackwell apparently felt bad enough about his decision to make paying off the cottage in Byfield part of Sandy's Island severance package, having been guarantor on the loan in the first place. Linda remembers when she and Richard got the same brush-off, at almost exactly the same time, and that Blackwell in person "came to us at a party and said, 'I love you guys but I'm gonna have to let you go.' And we thought, 'That's fair enough.' But I think it really hit Sandy ... I honestly don't know how aware she was that her voice was going. Trevor always made her feel that she was incredible, that she was special."

If Sandy was genuinely unaware "that her voice was going," the reality was brought home to her in November, when she arranged her own brief tour of the U.K., fronting a six-piece band that comprised three-fifths of Fotheringay, augmented by DM on drums, Phil Palmer and Rob Hendry on guitars, and Pete Wilshire on pedal-steel. It was a quite ambitious gesture, to front a band like this after two years off the road, and the venues on the eleven-date tour were theatres of a sufficient status to represent something of a gamble for promoter Roy Guest. The tour began and ended in the comfortable surrounds of London's Royalty Theatre, the idea being that, come tour's end, the results would be worth capturing on the Island mobile truck – not for Island Records, but for a label as yet unformed, overseen by the first man to have recorded Sandy Denny in the studio, Marcel Rodd of Saga Records.

> **Karl Dallas:** Marcel Rodd was the reason why Sandy's last concert was recorded ... He [had] approached me, [saying], "We were in at the

beginning and we let [folk music] go, and I think that was a mistake. Then it was very easy to find out who we should record. Now I have no idea. So, if we pay you some money, can you mastermind some folk recordings for us?" I said you should reissue the Jackson C. Frank record, and then Sandy was on tour, and I'd gone to Edinburgh to see the opening concert, and it was very impressive. I mean, the band was a great band. It was a bit loose in Edinburgh, and I don't think it got much better, [but] I thought it would. So I said to Marcel, "Let's record Sandy." ... So we hired the Island mobile and [got] John Woods to engineer it, and went to the Royalty Theatre and recorded the whole concert. Somewhere there was a whistle right across all the tracks. John was totally mystified. He didn't hear it when he was monitoring the recording. And Marcel said, "You have saddled me with incompetence, Karl," and that severed our relationship. He refused to pay. How it was all sorted out, I don't know. But she didn't have a deal at the time ... That last recording, she was not well. Trevor moved heaven and earth to stop it ever being released – it's one of the reasons he got Island to buy it. Actually, in retrospect, she's not singing as badly as I remembered ... [but] she shouldn't have done that concert.

Representing her most satisfactory cross-section of material, the sixteen-song sets, all originals save for Dylan's 'Tomorrow Is A Long Time' and Thompson's 'For Shame of Doing Wrong', and a distinctly Fotheringay flavour to the arrangements, made for an audacious series of concerts. But she was pushing herself through some songs she could no longer fully handle, willed on by the disappointing crowds. 'North Star Grassman', 'It'll Take a Long Time', 'Wretched Wilbur' and 'Take Me Away' are audibly drained of drama on the couple of audience tapes extant from the shows preceding that final London concert. By the time Sandy returned to the Royalty, a week after the 'real' tour ended in Bristol, she could no longer control her demons.

Colin Irwin: I saw her beforehand, and she was just pacing up and down, an absolute nervous wreck, shaking, just marching up and down. She was in a terrible state ... There were people around, but we were just [pretending to] ignore her. When I first saw her with Fairport, she seemed totally in control, she was holding the stage, but she'd actually dissolved into this wreck.

What was to be Sandy Denny's final show – save for a brief benefit at her village hall the following April – certainly had its moments, simply because that unerring vocal control had never left her, and the band was as sympathetic to the import of the occasion as any. Opening with a fierce 'Solo', the show was extended, for this night only, to a two-song encore that completed another circle, from the youthful promise of 'Who Knows Where The Time Goes' to the shattering poignancy of 'No More Sad Refrains'.*

After the show, Linda Thompson remembers "going backstage, and [Sandy] just had all these blotches all over her face. She looked fifty. 'Cause she was just hitting it all too hard by then." She was overwhelmed by the turnout of old friends, there to lend their moral support at what they hoped would be the beginning of a second career. When Val Berry ventured to leave, something Sandy said to her suggested that she somehow knew it was unlikely to pan out that way.

Val Berry: I went in the bar and she dropped everything, threw her arms around me, it was all kisses and cuddles and everything, and I said, "So you finally had a baby. How do you feel about it?" She went on and on and on about how happy she was. And then she did the gig, which I didn't like very much, and after the gig I had to go. Sandy was talking to somebody, sitting down at a table, and I tapped her and said, "I gotta go." The next thing, she got hold of my hand really hard, and held it in such a way that I had to get down on my knees, and she just turned and said, "Val, as long as I live, I will never, ever forget you. Your face is imprinted in my memory." And that was the last thing she ever said to me.

Sandy's friends had always been important to her, but the move to Byfield had created an all too real distance between them and her, at a time when many of them were looking for a way to face the onset of responsibility. If an out-on-the-town Sandy would have remained an all too real reminder of the conse-quences of evading those responsibilities, Gerry Conway was one of those who recognised the purchase of Byfield as "the slow disintegration of everything ... she'd hit some kind of slope." The concern many of her closest friends felt for the newly-isolated Sandy had its limits, which one by one Sandy began to test.

---

*The official CD of the show, *Gold Dust*, issued in 1998, bears no resemblance to the actual concert running-order, nor to the original sound of the band.

Linda Thompson: As you get mired in addiction all you can think f is yourself, and the part of you that could lift you up gets drowned in chemicals and stuff … After one too many two o'clock in the morning calls I said to her, "Sandy, don't call me again in the middle of the fucking night. I've got children. I've got to get up at seven in the morning." … Having children is [usually] a wake-up call, but I think it was too advanced. I think I was quite harsh with her. I thought, Pull yourself together. I now know you can't … I just think she felt lost in general. People were discarding her. You couldn't deal with her, she was too difficult … What was witty and charming … for so many years, when she became thirty, it's not cute anymore. It's somehow undignified.

As events continued to conspire against a saddened Sandy in those final months, she found that her closest friends were not necessarily discarding her, but that they had major, life-changing problems of their own to deal with. In Linda's case, "I was living at my mother's. I had left Richard and took the children. I thought, I can't stand this [life on the commune]. I've had enough. So I had my own problems. My father was dying, and according to the commune rules, you just had to forget your parents and I couldn't do that. I went back to live with my mother, and helped nurse him, so I don't think I had time for Sandy's problems. But also she['d] never call up and say Help! She'd call up and go blah blah blah, and you would sorta think, 'She's handling this the way she handles everything.'" Linda was not the only old friend Sandy would call at two in the morning, hoping for someone who might lend an ear. Nor was she the only one who failed to hear the subtext to Sandy's words on the wire.

Pete Townshend: She would not call me at home very often, though there was one call I remember. She was very drunk, and said that she loved me, she needed to see me, then and there. It was in the early hours. My wife woke up, I put my hand over the phone and quickly explained who was on the line. Sandy realised I was with my wife, and it seemed to be a fact that had escaped her up until that moment … I was still trying to work out what to do to start helping her when she died. I had helped others, and I know I could have helped her, but she came into my life too late. She had wanted my scalpel. Instead I'd offered her my dick. I wish I'd been a bit sharper all round.

Bambi Ballard, the person to whom Island had turned at the end of 1976, is another of Sandy's dearest friends who admits to "excruciating guilt about the last couple of years, 'cause I could have helped her and I didn't. She'd ring me up every two or three days, when she was pregnant. When she had her baby I was the first person she called, I think. I meant to go and see her and the baby, and I didn't, 'cause I was going through bad times ... I wasn't there for the last six months, I just wasn't available – 'Sandy we must get together, but not today' – because I knew that, whenever I got together with Sandy, it was three days ... she was all-absorbing." In fact, Bambi's marriage to BBC journalist Robin Denselow was collapsing, and she was understandably wrapped up in her own life-crisis.

Bambi was also one of the two or three friends to whom David Denny had turned, in 1976, hoping to convince them to keep Sandy on the straight and narrow whilst he began a new life in America. Having established a number of contacts during his touring travails with Fairport and Sandy, and with an engineering background, he had been recruited to lend his expertise to the practicalities of touring for some of America's rockier badasses. The loss of her brother must have affected Sandy deeply.

> **Bambi Ballard:** I hardly knew [David] but he suddenly turned up to see me two or three times [before he] went off to America. And he was talking to me about Sandy. He just rang me and said, "This is David Denny, can I come and see you?" I don't remember saying to him, "Why have you come to see me?" And he was saying, "I'm going away. Can you sort of look out for Sandy?" I said, "Sure. In what way?" And he said, "Y'know, just make sure that she's alright. She likes you. She trusts you." ... He must have felt excessively guilty about leaving Sandy ... I'm sure he went to see Anthea in the same way, probably Philippa [too].

Miranda Ward comes close to dissecting the problem when she says Sandy "painted herself into a corner, low self-esteem, always needing help." When it suddenly became a lot harder to muster sympathy, or even to elicit a friendly hearing, then Sandy began to come apart. Of her friends in London, perhaps only Miranda and Philippa saw *that* Sandy on a regular basis in the last year of her life, hence perhaps the shock to the system when Linda saw how ravaged she had begun to look at that final London show.

On the border of Northamptonshire and Oxfordshire, though, the

Fairport family were almost daily recipients of some piece of local gossip that involved Sandy's capacity for self-destruction. Chris Pegg recalls, "People would call and say, 'There's an orange Beetle with a screaming child inside.' We'd go and try and get Georgia, and Watson wouldn't let us in. It sounds terrible, but she wasn't neglecting Georgia any more than she neglected herself." In the days before Rehab entered common parlance, and with Trevor increasingly AWOL and Georgia merely a helpless passenger, there must have seemed a limited number of options available to the diminishing numbers who cared.

> **Dave Pegg:** We didn't have much contact with Sandy but she would turn up at our house sometimes in the middle of the night, or first thing in the morning, or you'd see her car in a lay-by and she'd be in it, off her face. I mean, I've done that, but when you see it happening on a regular basis, and the village community is like very small, and everybody knew what Sandy's car looked like ... it was an orange Beetle with green mudguards. And we'd hear reports. And we would go out and help Sandy, everybody did whatever they can, but we had our own existence.

So did Sandy have any sense of how imperilled her very existence had become? Linda Thompson thinks that if she did, it never articulated itself, "She never said to me, in all the years I knew her, 'I must get out of this. I've got to stop drinking.'" And yet, one of the handful of items written into a notebook of the time, a lengthy lyric, contains a quite lucid disposition on her perenially low self-esteem, as she berates herself into taking responsibility for her own actions:

"If you see me looking down one day
And you think that it's the end
I just have to realise
That I'm my own best friend.

And when I close my weary eyes
And think that it's the end
And then I realise
That I'm my own best friend.

And I've got a lot of things to do
and a lot of time ahead
It's no use taking sleeping pills
and sloping off to bed
There's another day and another chance
to seek for that sixpence in the pie.
And if I don't find it before I die
I just ain't gonna die. No.

Got me a bottle of wine
I don't want to drink
Get me out of my mind
I don't want to think.
But if I don't make it before I die
I just ain't gonna die.

I['m] in such a terrible state
And my country's just like me.
I can't afford to live in this place
And I can't afford to leave.
My friends all say it's a rotten shame
they just can't understand why
But if I don't make it before I die
I just ain't gonna die.

I've been travelling around the world
There's nowhere I ain't been
Everywhere goes by so fast
I don't know what I've seen
They lead me around on a wild goose chase
For those castles in the sky
But if I don't get there before I die
I just ain't gonna die. No!"

The poignancy of that refrain, in the light of events, is undeniable. That Sandy refused to envision an end to all her dreams, even when she was using drink and sleeping pills to shut out the pain of existence, suggests no obvious death-wish. Nor does another contemporary lyric, directed at an unknown dead friend, perhaps Martin Lamble or even Mama Cass, whose death in July 1974 shook Sandy badly, coming only a matter of days after they had finally met and bonded:

"I don't even think you have gone
I still see you here.
There's a time where I've stayed,
And I'm going to stay till my final year."

If Sandy felt the deaths of others keenly, she also had an empathy for those grieving that suggested someone all too keenly aware of the tenuous grip we have in our tenure here on earth. Gina Glazer remembers hearing about the suicide by eletrocution of her dear friend Paul Clayton, in April 1966, when Sandy was barely twenty, and how, "she was wonderful with me that night, she walked me around and came home with me, made sure I was okay. I was in such a state of shock ... Sometimes that age thing sort of reversed and she'd be more the mommy – the caretaker." And, however hell-bent her path seems now, Sandy genuinely does not seem to have had any presentiment of her own death in those last few months. In fact, she displayed a remarkable capacity for surviving near-death experiences.

Bruce Rowland: Sandy was pretty lonely, making cries for help in an incredibly ostentatious manner all the time. It got to the point where people wouldn't answer the phone in case it was Sandy, "The car's in the ditch." Trevor's Beetle. I pulled it out twice – second time, the baby was in the back, in a carry-cot loose on the seat. She'd put it in the ditch about two hundred yards from where she lived. God knows how! I was never absolutely certain whether she'd driven the car into the ditch for somebody to come out and rescue her. We had a mutual friend, the gardener Steve Walker. He did not suffer fools gladly. I was at Swarb's when she did this and Swarb said, "Oh fuck her, I'm not going out. Tell her to call the AA." What I was worried about was the local bobbie, because she was definitely pissed. She'd been in Cropedy the middle part of the evening and she was getting it on then. I tried to pull it out, and I couldn't. So I called Walker, who had a Land-Rover, at four o'clock in the morning – this [being] a guy who's up at six – and he was not best pleased. To his credit he did [it]. But he pulled it out [just as] she walked out, and he cursed her into the ground. [she] dissolved into tears. [But] she had a need for that sort of thing.

If the village as a whole was seriously concerned about the situation, fearing for the safety of the child as much as the increasingly irresponsible parent, Trevor had somehow shut himself off from the reality of the situation. As Bruce Rowland puts it, "Trevor used to have responsibility attacks. He'd clear off to London for two or three days and then come back and be the doting husband." But part of the problem, as Dave Pegg expresses it, is that "Trevor was such an up guy all the time. Complete opposite of Sandy. It took a lot for her to be genuinely happy ... And you can't find out why ... somebody like Sandy Denny wasn't happy – she [just] became so sad. It all went wrong, and she never came back from that low. That was it. There was nothing anybody could do to pull her out of it. But everybody thought Georgia was in grave danger."

Just how real that danger was became clear the last week in March, when Sandy took Georgia to visit her grandparents at their holiday cottage in Cornwall. Because of the tensions that stemmed from Trevor and Neil's Mutual Dislike Society, Neil and Edna had not seen as much of Sandy and Georgia as they would have liked, even though the birth of a grand-daughter had for a long time been a hope that dare not speak its name. And yet, whatever state of denial Trevor was in about Sandy's drinking, it was as nothing to her parents, blinded by a sense of propriety that had all but consumed their finer feelings. When Sandy fell down the stairs at their cottage, presumably pickled, her mother simply refused to take her down to Casualty to have her x-rayed, more fearful of the damage to her own reputation than her daughter's skull.

Philippa Clare: Sandy was complaining of very bad headaches and her doctor gave her Dystelgesic, which are very heavy painkillers. If you mix them with alcohol they can give you brain haemorrhages ... She [had gone] down to Cornwall to her parents, and she fell down the stairs onto the York paving-stone, and Sandy went, "I really need help, Mum," and her mother actually said, "I'm not having you seen drunk." ... So when Sandy came back she was going, I've got terrible headaches ... But it wasn't taken that seriously. She was mentioning it, but she wasn't making a big drama about it.

Miranda also expressed the view that *if* Sandy "was with Neil and Edna, and she was pissed, they wouldn't have taken her to Casualty because they were unable to accept [her problem] ... They didn't like the fact that she drank. I think Neil went to his grave thinking [she had] the odd glass of sherry or gin and tonic, or a glass of wine with the meal." Such a remarkably close proximation to the actual incident suggests that she has somehow forgotten Sandy filling in the details over that weekend, three weeks later, when Edna's daughter, whilst staying at Miranda's, suffered a fatal brain haemorrhage.

That the fall Sandy had taken at her parents' house was serious was evidenced by the bloody great cut she was sporting on her scalp both at the benefit concert she gave on April 1, 1978 – when she gave her finale performance to a hundred and fifty local souls at Byfield village hall – and at Dave Swarbrick's birthday party, just four days later, where she again made light of the fall.

Dave Swarbrick: I do remember her having a bad cut on her head, somewhere up [on top of her head], and she pointed it out to me. But she was drunk at the time. It was the fifth of April, my birthday. She took my hand and rubbed it across the top, and said, "Look at that." But that was all she said. Didn't seem that bad. I never knew how she got it. There was a party at the local pub, she turned up there and she'd been barred from the pub, and they wouldn't let her in, so I took her home. I left my own party, took her back. Trevor came along later. She was drunk when she turned up at the party, and I guess I'd had a few too, by then. We went back to my place, sat down, chatted, then Trevor came along, picked her up, took her back. She was a bit upset.

If Edna showed scant regard for her daughter's well-being, it seems surprising that Trevor also failed to take further action on seeing the cut on Sandy's return from her parents, at least not any attendant to his wife. The question that cannot now be answered is whether Georgia was in Sandy's arms when she fell down the stairs in Cornwall. Trevor began to suspect as much – unless there was a separate fall at Byfield, to which he was witness, something no-one has been able to confirm. But Miranda, in whose flat Sandy would be found unconscious, feels great bitterness towards Trevor because she understandably feels that "this was a tragedy severely compounded by Trevor. Trevor, as a responsible adult, should have said, 'Oh and by the way, she had a rather bad fall, but I think she's okay. She's having the odd headache.'"

Whichever scenario pushed him to take action, Trevor finally became convinced that Georgia's life was in mortal peril, and that his wife, as an unregenerate alcoholic, was a danger to herself and her daughter. The onset of responsibility came hard on Trevor, who had little idea of whom he might turn to for help. His friends were Sandy's friends, and vice-versa. He sounded out some of Sandy's best friends, like Linda Thompson, to whom he confided, on one occasion, "'I've been in London all day, I came home, and the baby hadn't been fed. What am I gonna do?' I said, I don't know what you're gonna do." But he kept his decision to leave Sandy from Linda, who insists she "wouldn't have told Sandy anyway, but maybe he thought I would." He decided instead to confide in Philippa.

Philippa Clare: Trevor rang me up from Byfield. Trevor was very rarely in tears, and he was in tears. He went, "I don't know what to do. I can't cope. She's dropped the baby down the stairs. She's driven [the car] into a hedge. I'm gonna take the kid to Australia because I want my parents to see their grandchild, and I'm *gonna* say to Sandy, I'm just going there for a few weeks, give you a bit of space, and then I'll come back. But you've really got to shape up." Trevor was freaking for the safety of the kid. Trevor could see her getting worse.

Philippa remains alone in believing that Trevor translated, "I'm *gonna* say to Sandy..." into, "I did say to Sandy." She asserts that, "Sandy knew. Before he left." The evidence is against her. Bambi Ballard insists, "She certainly didn't know that Trevor was leaving. And I did. Trevor had intimated at some point over the phone ... He said, I've reached the end of the line, [that] sort of thing."

Bruce Rowland seems to have been the only other person who definitely knew that Trevor was leaving, prior to any calls from the airport (of which there were a couple), and that he intended to take Georgia with him.

Bruce Rowland: [Trevor] was a complete bastard – with a conscience. He had good energy to spare, and you can't make any judgement as to why not enough of it was going into his marriage. But he phoned me up one night, and I think he must have got wind of the incident where Georgia was in the car, or similar events. Trevor had to come to terms with the fact that he couldn't have it both ways. He couldn't go off and leave [Sandy] on her own, without making some kind of provision, and by that time everybody was getting short of cash to cover a succession of people to keep her together. He phoned me up and said, "Look, I'm thinking of taking the baby." I didn't know quite what he meant by that. And I said, "And what?" He said, "Going back to Australia." I said, "Without Sandy?" He said, "Yes." My first thought was he wasn't brave enough to do it. And he said, "What do you think?" I said, "If you do that, you're really gonna hear for it, but if you do do it, you do it with my blessing, for whatever that's worth." ... So he did it. He skipped ... It was five days [later] because he hadn't got the money to go, and his father sent him the money, and that's how long it took to get it organized ... He phoned me when he got to Melbourne and said, "Just keep an eye on things." ... The next thing I had to do was call him in Melbourne and tell him Sandy was on a life support.

No-one seems to agree about whether Trevor planned to come back when Sandy shaped up, hoping but hardly expecting that she would, or had simply had enough and wanted out. However, he only purchased a one-way ticket and when the time came to play face the consequences, he would have to borrow a further return fare off of his father. That Sandy had alienated a man to whom, in Jerry Donahue's words, "she was the greatest thing ever," suggested just how greatly she had tried the patience of those who loved her. However cowardly Trevor's method, few could argue with the decision.

Dave Swarbrick: Trevor was concerned. He'd have to be. We were all concerned ... Trevor did the same thing to me that he did to Miranda. He phoned me up on the morning. There honestly didn't seem a lot of choice at that time.

Sandy's state of mind that final weekend remains a source of contention. Neil Denny said, shortly before his death, "I'm sure that she was drugged, because she never attempted to communicate with her mother, and that was unthinkable." Bambi Ballard, who says she "spoke to her two days before she died [sic]," thinks that Sandy's state of denial now extended to her husband's whereabouts, "She didn't know he'd gone [for good]. She didn't say, he's left me. She assumed he was coming back. She was quite relaxed about it. So Trevor had done the most cowardly thing. When she died, I thought, 'Thank

God she never knew that Trevor wasn't coming back.'" Linda Thompson also thinks that whatever "cocktail of things" Sandy was taking, they made her less than wholly aware of what had gone down – that her husband had left her, flown to the other side of the world, and taken her only child with him.

Linda Thompson: I spoke to Sandy when she was staying [at Miranda's] that weekend, when Trevor had gone, and she sounded mad. Just mad. Doo-lalley ... She was a bit out of it, whether through shock or whatever ... By that time it's perfectly possible that she didn't really know [Trevor had gone], that she was so far gone that it didn't really register.

The only person who can really give an accurate indication as to her state of mind that final weekend is Miranda Ward, the old friend entrusted to look after her by Trevor, from a Heathrow terminal telephone kiosk, and the last person to see her alive in any meaningful sense. Miranda began to make some shorthand diary notes at some point on the Sunday or Monday, which gives her reminiscences an added air of authenticity. However, she also asserts that, contrary to all evidence, the 31-year-old Sandy was not a chronic alcoholic. Given that there was only a third of a decanter of Sandy's favoured tipple, gin, in the house, Miranda asserts that, "if she'd been an alcoholic she'd have started on the whisky or the brandy or the vodka or the tequila. She never did that. [When] the gin was finished, she'd go and have a cup of tea." In truth, any alcoholic as advanced as Sandy would never have entrusted their lines of supply to a third party. She must have arrived in Barnes with a stand-by cache of her own, which had run out by Monday morning, prompting her to drain the decanter of gin.

Sandy doubtless also brought her usual supply of pills, having asked Miranda not to be mad at her for taking two Valiums prior to her arrival at Byfield. Sandy's Valium supply had run out by the end of the weekend, when she was forced to turn to Miranda's own bathroom cabinet for painkillers and Diazepam (though only after Miranda had okayed it with her trusted doctor, with whom she arranged a Monday afternoon appointment for Sandy, who was presumably hoping to restore her own prescription supplies).

That all-important diary provides both a snapshot version of those last few days and a first-hand account of her charge's mood swings. On the Friday evening, Miranda's commonplace book states that they sat up talking and "Sandy [was] very good; talked about [the] psychology [of drinking] and long-term [prospects]. Also where Trevor was." Miranda recalls that Sandy was determined not to plead with her husband to take her back, and talked positively about the future, whilst facing up to the fact that even her best friend thought Georgia was better off with Trevor. Sandy also asked Miranda not to phone Trevor's sister, Marion, in case she was unaware of her brother's disappearing act. She also seemed to finally accept that Miranda had no real idea where Trevor had taken their daughter. According to Miranda's notes, they had a sherry at six and a large brandy and soda at nine, before Sandy went to bed. Unable to sleep, she came back down and they talked some more.

By Saturday night, though, Sandy was no longer exuding positivity. Indeed, the diary says, "Sandy very down. We talked for a while. She attempted to cook a meal – went to bed." The entry for Sunday also mentions in passing that they had discussed the possibility of going down to Casualty on Saturday night. Evidently, Sandy had brought up the headaches, and, though Miranda does not remember it, she presumably related the circumstances of the fall at her parents. Miranda now says, "Sandy told me ... about the fall ... but it didn't register it had been as severe. I mean, we did talk about going up to the hospital, and also she had run out of Diazepam, and I was going to take her down to [my] doctor." The persistent headaches had now become quite bad, such that on Sunday morning Sandy awoke Miranda, asking for some paracetamol, after which she returned to bed.

By the time she awoke again, Sandy felt better, prompting another "long talk, much more positive." Sandy again asked about Miranda's doctor, and whether he might be able to suggest anything for these headaches. That afternoon, whilst out purchasing some necessary supplies, Miranda went round to see her doctor, who was also something of a family friend, and spoke to him about Sandy's headaches. He advised her to bring Sandy to the surgery the following afternoon, rather than taking her down to Casualty.

On Sunday evening, Miranda had another long talk with Sandy that addressed not only the disappearance of Trevor but her drinking problem. Sandy was finally prepared to admit to someone, for the very first time, that "once she started [drinking] she found it very difficult to stop." Miranda's note in her diary reads, "She was hopeful about Doctor, wanted to try, I said I could only help her to help herself. She agreed and said she wanted to try." It seemed that the shock of Trevor's departure had started Sandy thinking along lines that might yet have saved her – if only she could find a way to get shot of these damn headaches! At some point during the evening, David Denny called,

Miranda having left a message for him in Texas the previous day. They had a long talk before Sandy sloped off to bed, at which point Miranda called David back, feeling "very low and inadequate."

All of Miranda's endeavours had failed to yield up a husband. Philippa Clare had called Sunday morning and suggested Australia, "but claimed no proof." Trevor's sister phoned later, to say that she had called Australia and they didn't know Trevor's whereabouts. For a man who had supposedly advised Sandy of where he was going, Trevor was putting up a mighty smokescreen of misinformation. From this point on, the shorthand in Miranda's commonplace book becomes increasingly terse, as if every word requires some extraordinary effort, beginning with another wake-up call from a Sandy bouncing off the walls:

"6.00 am
Sandy woke me. Wanted Painocil – v. bad headache had woken her.
School – I was v. late. Somehow couldn't leave but did.
Couldn't call as I didn't want to wake her.
Ma came over [to my classroom].
Jon had found S[andy] unconscious in hall.
Ambulance on its way.
Went straight to Mrs. M. [headteacher]
Having called Jon to call Dr. G[eorge] B[rown]
Mrs M kind, time off if nec., no pay but her discretion to give support.
Got home. Jon there.
Police arrived 5 mins later. Gave details.
PC David Davies took me to Hosp[ital].
Frightened."

What exactly happened the morning of April 17, 1978, has never been satisfactorily resolved, in part because the parties concerned went to great pains to cover up the fact that Trevor had left his wife and fled all the way to Australia. Though Trevor was called to give evidence at the inquest into Sandy's death, despite being on the opposite side of the world at the time she collapsed, the coroner agreed in advance not to call Miranda, the last person to see her *compos mentis*, sharing a general concern that the tabloids might have a field day if some of the more salacious details came out, and convinced on the basis of a police report that there were no suspicious circumstances. Sandy was alone when she died. It is unlikely that Miranda's presence would have made any difference to the outcome, unless Sandy's draining a third of a decanter of gin that morning in some way precipitated that all-too-final black-out.

The story that was made to fit the facts, and then given at the inquest and to the press, was that Sandy Denny died of a mid-brain trauma, the direct result of a fall at Miranda Ward's flat. This soon became the Authorised Version. In fact, there was no way that Sandy – who was found slumped across the toilet door, on Miranda's landing, at the foot of a set of stairs – could have fallen down the winding stairway. Miranda's books would certainly have broken her fall, as the man who found her comatosed body confirms.

Jon Cole: Those upper stairs were wickedly narrow, and the piles of books on each stair made navigation perilous; but I don't remember seeing books disturbed by a fall. On the other hand, the loo door was closed, and she had fallen across it. It looked to me that she must have collapsed or fallen either coming down the last steps of the stairs or having emerged from the loo, closed the door, and *immediately* [collapsed], when setting off for the living room or heading up the stairs.

The most logical scenario is that Sandy had been suffering from internal bleeding for some weeks, after the serious fall earlier at her parents' – hence the headaches – and she had finally blacked out from an untreated subdural hematoma. Her life had been slowly but surely ticking away ever since her mother refused to escort her to Casualty for an X-ray that might have saved her life.

Miranda Ward: The one thing that I cannot express how much it hurts is to keep reading 'died as a result of falling down stairs whilst staying with a friend.' She didn't fall down the stairs ... [though] outside the toilet sounds so bloody decrepit ... There's no way she could have fallen down the stairs 'cause there were too many obstacles, it was an obstacle course in itself ... Because something was hidden, everyone thought it was something dire. If I'd had my statement read out [at the inquest], or I had been called to the stand, Trevor would have been charged with perjury ... [And] I could just see the tabloid headings, TRAGIC DEATH OF SINGER DESERTED BY HUSBAND AND CHILD.

Miranda spent most of Monday evening phoning round friends and family, informing them that Sandy was in a coma. At this point there still seemed to be hope, and a point to summoning the recalcitrant husband from Melbourne and the distraught brother from L.A. By the time David and Trevor arrived, though, on the Wednesday evening and Friday morning respectively, Sandy had been transferred from Queen Mary's Hospital in Roehampton to the Atkinson-Morley, which specialised in brain injuries, and where on Wednesday evening a surgeon had unsuccessfully operated on the singer.

Linda Thompson had come over to Miranda's on the Wednesday afternoon, having responded to her initial phone-call by snapping, "Oh, what's Sandy done now?" Informed she was in a coma, she suddenly sensed that her best friend was not long for this world. The pair of them traipsed over to Queen Mary's, and then the Atkinson-Morley. Linda still recalls how "she looked better than she had in years. She looked fantastic. All the lines had gone from her face. Her complexion was clear. She was wrapped in silver foil. I sat and talked to her, the way you do with people in a coma."

The hardest moment, though, was yet to come. Neil Denny would take to his grave the image of the moment, "when the surgeon came in and said Sandy would die and there was no way [out] – David said, 'Was there any way we could pay for treatment?' But there was nothing [that could be done]. Poor old David just dissolved – he couldn't stand it." NHS formalities required the next of kin's consent to switch off the life-support machine. It was finally agreed that this would be done at eight o'clock on the evening of Friday the 21st. Sandy, though, spared Trevor that one last guilt-trip, for which he was ill-prepared. She died peacefully in her sleep, just ten minutes before they were due to pull the plug, barely thirty-one years of age, with a lifetime of songs not yet sung. For Trevor, there was little solace in her lyrics and poems, many unfinished, in her notebooks, most of which still resonated through all the avenues she'd travelled, searching for the truth at the heart of her songs – the art of forgiveness begins within thyself:

"I beg that some who said they loved me before
May search their hearts to find not love – but more
A feeling we must learn to harbour often
Sometimes, though we are wronged, we have the grace to soften,
All is well when all again becomes a whole,
Forgive the erring character who's blemished none but [their] own soul."

– an undated ms.

SAND + Georgia
Jan '78 ?

Epilogue:
FLOWERS OF THE FOREST

"It would have seemed weird to try and help Sandy, 'cause she had a very clear picture of where she was going. Like Nick [Drake], she didn't expect to make old bones."

Linda Thompson

The first intimation your biographer had that something had stilled that voice, the voice I knew from 'Who Knows Where The Time Goes' and little else, came that Friday evening in April 1978, at 10 p.m., when John Peel began his nightly Radio One show not with the clarion call of the latest wannabe three chord wonders, as had become his wont in the past eighteen months, but with three consecutive, uninterrupted recordings of that clear, crystal voice, at its Fairport and Fotheringay peaks. Afterwards, Peel simply announced the death of his old friend Sandy Denny before beginning the show proper.

Colin Irwin was in the *Melody Maker* office on the Friday afternoon, when Philippa Clare called and said that Sandy Denny had fallen down the stairs and was in a coma. When she phoned on the Monday to tell him that Sandy had died, Irwin and then-editor Ray Coleman took the snap decision to make it that week's cover story, as much a tribute to Sandy's personal hold upon the magazine's old guard journos as for its newsworthiness. It may not have seemed like the end of an era, but it certainly felt like someone was drawing a line beneath a whole genre of possibilities. As Maddy Prior says, "It was like some reference point was gone, and you could never achieve certain things because of that." Maddy was just one of a number of Sandy's musician friends prompted to write veiled epitaphs-in-song to their favourite songstress.

The funeral, the following Thursday, took place with "the wind whipp[ing] across Putney Vale cemetery, blowing the noise of the nearby dual carriageway away in gusts of sudden silence, as a gathering of family and friends gathered to say goodbye to Sandy Denny, shivering in the cold." So Karl Dallas wrote later in a *Melody Maker* tribute. What most everyone who attended remembers was that lone piper who, after the vicar had read Sandy's favourite psalm – the 23rd ['The Lord is my shepherd, I shall not want'] – played an ancient air commemorating the fallen at Flodden Field. As that desolate refrain from 'The

Flowres of the Forreste' – "the flowers of the forest are a' wede away" – rang in all the mourners' mind, it finally brought home that this sense of loss could never be made good.

If everyone had been keeping their feelings in check until that point, as Miranda remembers, "the piper did everybody in." The piper's refrain seemed to leave some very open wounds visible. Karl Dallas remembers that, "Richard [Thompson] was wonderful, he comforted everyone, but ... some of the things he said were a bit hard to take. He kept on saying, 'We only had her on loan.'" Among the things Richard felt compelled to say was in response to something voiced by a grieving Dave Cousins, but was an undercurrent in many a mourner's thoughts, "What a terrible thing to happen. All this music that she should have written." Richard turned to him and replied, "No, she wasn't destined to write any more music, she was destined to die when she died."

Though Linda considers this an example of, "Richard being ludicrously insensitive ... I know he didn't mean it," Thompson does not remember there being any "hostility in the exchange with Dave Cousins ... I do feel that life had gotten to be too much for Sandy to bear. Accident or not, I don't know how she would have continued beyond that point." He expanded on this belief, to Pam Winters, "Somehow she just couldn't handle the world anymore. I just thought that in a sense, that was it, creatively, and in terms of her life – that it wasn't the wrong time, that that was the way it was going to happen and there was nothing you could do about it ... There wasn't some great body of music that was going to come in the next twenty years."

If Richard's exchange with Dave Cousins was without rancour, there were a fair few recriminations passing from mouth to mouth on the day. The most serious was between Edna Denny and Trevor, who was understandably beside himself with remorse. Neil Denny later said, "My wife asked if we could look after the child, and Trevor was very drunk," but refused to elucidate on what was said. A third party, though, later heard from Trevor that he turned on Sandy's parents and told them that he wasn't going to allow them to do to Georgia what they had managed to do to her mother. Though there had never been any love lost between Trevor and Neil, this verbal volley, on top of whatever Miranda may have said to Sandy's parents about Trevor's act of desertion whilst they were staying at her flat, seems to have definitively alienated Trevor's one remaining ally in the Denny family, Sandy's brother, David.

Philippa Clare: The parents were convinced it was Trevor's fault. Whatever Miranda said, she even managed to turn David Denny against Trevor, who was a great friend of Trev's, to the point when he went to the house, and David slammed the door in his face. That really did him in. The parents wouldn't see him. When we arrived at the funeral, they just turned their backs.

Not that Miranda herself was spared the family barbs. As insensitivity reigned, Edna's one consoling thought to Sandy's dear friend was, "You'll have other close friends, but I've lost my only daughter. You'll get over this, but I'll live with this pain for the rest of my life." As it is, if such pain can be measured in hours and minutes, Miranda's was to prove the greater. Edna would be dead herself within a couple of years, ostensibly from cancer but as much the result of a broken heart, having outlived both her children (David would die in a driving accident in Colorado barely a year after his beloved sister). The nervous breakdown Miranda suffered upon Sandy's death was only the beginning of a twenty-year stint of grieving for her best friend that merged the past and present in a number of disarming ways. The death of her ex-lover Lowell George in June 1979, from a heroin-induced heart attack, in Arlington, Virginia, only compounded her grief. Only now has the healing begun.

For Trevor, there was never any question of rebuilding his life in Byfield. Even when he fell in love with the daughter of Philippa's upstairs neighbours, Elizabeth Hurtt, part of his own healing process in the weeks after the funeral, he continued to plan his return to Australia. However, before he could take his new love to the land of his forefathers, and hopefully begin to live a life at least partially removed from Sandy's spectral shadow, Trevor needed to decide whether to memorialise his wife and love of his life in stone. It was only now, during discussions with Philippa, that he learnt of an incident from the days when Sandy used to frequent the Troubadour, when life itself was up for grabs and the living was free, if not always easy.

Philippa Clare: I said to Trevor, "I remember going past the Troubadour [to] the Old Brompton cemetery, being there very late one night, Sandy and I were wandering through. She was pissed as a parrot, something had upset her, so we were going for a walk, and I always remember her looking at this old gravestone, going, "Well, William [Whoever], we don't know who the fuck he was, but there he is, he's got this stone in the ground. Isn't that great?"

The inscription Trevor chose for Sandy's headstone was simple enough:

The Lady
Alexandra Elene MacLean Lucas
(Sandy Denny)
6.1.47 – 21.4.78

If he was in the mood to forgive, though not forget, such largesse did not extend to Sandy's parents. Through his solicitor, he informed them that he would not be dealing with them directly, only through his legal counsel. Edna would only see her granddaughter one more time before she died; and what news continued to reach Neil in the eighteen years that remained of his solitary existence usually came through Elizabeth Hurtt's London-based parents.

Trevor and Elizabeth settled in Australia, where Georgia grew up alongside a half-brother Clancy. Even this line, though, could not escape further tragedy and, in February 1989, barely a week after an Australian journalist had called to interview him about his late wife for a retrospective piece in an Australian music magazine, Trevor was found by his daughter Georgia, dead from a heart-attack, just forty-five years old. And still, the line endures, albeit on the other side of the world. Georgia herself, Sandy's "beautiful, most precious child," now has twin daughters of her own. Sadly, neither has taken the name of MacLean.

It would take a further two decades before some merging of the public and private Sandy was achieved in print. Jim Irvin's commendable, richly-detailed piece in *Mojo* in June 1998 took the top layer off the private Sandy, all the while celebrating her work. Reconciling the two, though, still bedevils those who knew her best. Just about everyone I interviewed for this book, when asked what they most remembered about Sandy, came up with similar replies.

Richard Thompson: I tend to forget the traumas and tragedies, and I just hear her laughing the most infectiously funny, unique Sandy laugh. I think most people who knew her would share the same memory.

Ashley Hutchings: The abiding memory I have of Sandy is onstage, getting tangled up in her leads, fumbling her song introduction, giggling and then breaking out into singing and suddenly it's a totally different being there onstage.

Dave Swarbrick: She had a laugh that would just come out of nowhere. And there was nothing much ladylike about it ... And she was sharp as a razorblade. If she wanted to get you, she could.

That such a laugh could emerge out of such deep-rooted insecurities remains one of those inponderables. As Linda Fitzgerald-Moore observed, "When you listen to her voice you think, God, what did she have to be insecure about?" That Sandy became progressively more unhappy as she dealt with even the lower rungs of fame she reserved for herself is something many have commented on. John Renbourn, for whom Sandy will always be that young girl on the folk scene, recalls how he has "heard it said that she was hard to deal with, that she was loud, and that she drank too much. That's not how I remember her at all. I remember her as warm and generous, and with a lovely infectious personality."

Sandy's husband came to believe that the problem may have been that "she was incredibly sensitive ... especially in regard to being a woman in rock & roll – and not one of the really glamorous women at that. The industry in those days ... was an almost entirely chauvinist enviroment ... And men are fortunate in that they just don't come under that sort of pressure, they don't have to deal with that kind of bullshit. But she did, and it depressed her."

Her background and personal history suggests that Sandy's depressive cycles stemmed from something far more entrenched. It is there in her work for all to hear, from the very off, an empathy with all the generations of 'knitters in the sun' who articulated their sorrows in song.

Danny Thompson: She had that same quality as Richard. When she wrote a song, you thought it was an old folk classic. The person you're going out with, larking about with, [then] goes off and writes one of these great songs. You can lie about your image, but you can't lie about your music, [not] if you're sincere about it. [JI]

If, as Shane Danielson asserts, "[Sandy] at her best is at once mournful and inspiring – not quite surrendering to her latent pessimism, [rather] infused by it, drawing strength from it," the songs ultimately only document attempts to fill a chasm. Even when she felt good about them, she remained chronically insecure about performing them. It is no coincidence that her stage-fright visibly worsened as she began to fill her shows with songs from her own soul. Dave Pegg believes that, "She just didn't know how good she was, really. She never thought she sang well, and she never thought much of her songs. We all loved them. She'd go, 'Oh, you all love Joni Mitchell. She's much better than me.' We'd go, 'No, Sandy. You're as good as her.' But [there was] this dreadful insecurity – about everything."

As it is, however much Sandy's quest for perfection may have been responsible for a musical legacy richer and more varied than any contemporary female songster, her recorded output remains curiously unsatisfactory on a number of levels. As Richard Thompson wrote, in a brief tribute to Sandy in the *Flypaper* fanzine, "I'm not sure just how much of the real Sandy went onto record. I don't think she was always at her best in the studio, and I'm not sure that her various producers and arrangers really did the best job for her – and I would number myself among this culpable crew." John Wood shares Richard's view, that, "she so seldom fulfilled her potential. Every record I worked on with her has great moments, but a lot of dips and troughs ... [Yet] she was unique because she was such a great writer as well as a great singer."

The posthumous releases, whose number reflect an enduring appeal, have included a lavish four-album set that, for the vinyl era, was a remarkable gesture on Joe Boyd's (and Island's behalf), and continues to reward repeated listenings (certain caveats excepted); a superb single-CD of Sandy's (largely solo) BBC sessions that show the effortless command of phrasing and pitch in that mid-twenties voice; an import-only collection that combines demos and a glimpse at an alternate final album; and a rejigged version of her final performance on a concert stage, that illustrates how even her diminishing light could sometimes outshine all comers. Each has divulged some of Sandy's still unfathomed depths. And the solo albums and her Fairport and Fotheringay albums await imminent remastering (with the propect of bonus tracks), that may yet achieve the critical resurgence Sandy's work so richly deserves.

Of those who knew her music best, it perhaps devolves to Richard Thompson, the other pillar around which the English folk-rock sound was built and bolstered, to remind us of the Sandy who wrote a concise canon of songs compelling enough to survive all the vagaries of fashion posterity tends to bestow on the medium:

> "She never showed off for the sake of it, it was all to the service of the song. I've not heard a singer since with that much of a gift ... She could incline to the obscure in her writing – personal or literary references which are not easy to decipher, and are hard to pin down emotionally ... and for that reason is sometimes not engaging for the listener. But ... some of my all time faves are Sandy songs – some of the best songs written since the war."

Ultimately, it is still by her songs that ye shall know her, and by that voice infused by a inner strength, "whose beauty remains/even when the bloom goes." Listen, listen.

Acknowledgements

This weighty tome began in less than satisfactory circumstances. I was originally asked to give my opinion on a typescript of a Sandy Denny biography commissioned by a friend of mine for his small publishing-house, Helter Skelter. The work in question, by one Pam Winters, had much of the raw material for a biography, but was clearly not the finished article he had hoped for. I suggested he approached Ms. Winters with a view to turning over her numerous transcripts and raw research material to someone who might yet rewrite the ms. into something that might reach a general reading audience. Ms. Winters, for her own reasons, chose to decline, leaving me with the option of taking up the reins. Ever since I wrote a little monograph on Sandy, back in 1988, I had wanted to do a biography and finally the time seemed right.

I took soundings to see if the various weary souls who had offered their thoughts to Ms. Winters, in the belief that this would result in THE biography, would again expose themselves to a biographer's whim. The response was overwhelmingly affirmative, something I believe to be a tribute to Sandy, and Sandy alone. Though I quickly disregarded Ms. Winters' perspective as a possible template for my own, her endeavours left at my disposal an outline of possible willing cohorts and I was gradually able to work my way through all the same major players, with perhaps two notable exceptions, childhood chum Winnie Whittaker, who eluded me, and engineer John Wood, who spurned my advances. I'd like to think I also rustled up a few souls of my own, including Philippa Clare, who had refused to talk to Ms. Winters, a refreshingly forthright Pete Townshend and an aged Judith Pieppe.

So, may I thank each and every one of those first-hand sources: Bambi Ballard, Val Berry, Joe Boyd, Steve Brickell, Philippa Clare, Jon Cole, Gerry Conway, Gill Cooke, Karl Dallas, Jerry Donahue, Linda Fitzgerald-Moore, Geena Glazer, Ashley Hutchings, Colin Irwin, Bert Jansch, Mike Kellie, Peter Kennedy, Richard Lewis, Jacqui McShee, Dave Pegg, John Perry, Linda Peters, Judith Pieppe, Maddy Prior, John Renbourn, Bruce Rowland, David Sandison, Al Stewart, Dave Swarbrick, Richard Thompson, Pete Townshend, Miranda Ward and Heather Wood. If Philippa Clare, Miranda Ward and David Sandison took an especially active interest in this project, entrusting precious sets of tapes and photos to this biographer, I'd like to say every single one of the souls named above responded with great patience to all my enquiries.

On a handful of occasions – and I mean a handful – I felt the quotes Ms. Winters obtained were superior to mine and, with the preemptive publication of her ms. on the ol' www: I had a license to use the quotes best expressed in her interviews (it's called fair usage). The readers will find these marked [PW]. Jim Irvin of *Mojo*, whose 1998 piece on Sandy remains essential reading for any concerned party, kindly turned over to me a transcript of his interview with John Wood, along with similar transcripts for Danny Thompson and the late Neil Denny (his quotes are marked [JI]); whilst Colin Davies, of *Hokey Pokey* fanzine fame, who was a constant source of practical advice, suggested avenues, phone numbers, memorabilia and photos, unquestioningly turned over transcripts of his own series of interviews with Pat Donaldson, Sandy's father Neil, college classmate David Laskey, and Linda Thompson (his quotes are marked [CD]). Finally, the ever generous Patrick Humphries refrained from berating me for hanging onto transcripts of interviews he

254

did with Simon Nicol, Dave Pegg and Ashley Hutchings – for his 1980 Fairport history, *Meet On The Ledge* – for over a decade, and gave me carte blanche to quote from them as well as his Richard Thompson biography, published by Virgin in 1996 (such quotes are marked [PH].

I'd also like to thank those who proved as generous with research resources as the above were with their personal (re) collections. Colin Harper and Neville Judd were ever willing to provide input and, in Colin's case, to even allow me a pre-publication perusal of his own mighty bio of Bert Jansch, due from Bloomsbury. David Thomas also came up with a number of names and numbers, via Colin Davies, for which mucho gratias. Ed Haber confirmed details of a number of American performances. Donna Frantz dug out her own interview with Sandy from December 1974 for KLRB. Malcolm Taylor at Cecil Sharp House was his ever helpful self; and Jon Storey did all that he could to gather together all the visual material. Thanks also to Mod Lang's Paul Bradshaw for his visual input, ditto Linda Fitzgerald-Moore. Especial thanks also go out to Universal's Bill Levenson in New York, and Jane Hitchin and her staff in London, for all their help accessing the studio records that enabled me to piece together a reasonably exact chronology of Sandy's studio activities. My editor, Sean Body, displayed remarkable forbearance throughout. And finally, but most importantly, my undying thanks to Elizabeth Hurtt-Lucas, for making Sandy's personal papers available to me, to Shane Youl for interceding with Liz on my behalf, and to Elizabeth's parents, Pam and Harry, for allowing me the environment and opportunity to notate to my heart's content. I hope that you all feel the end-product repays such acts of faith.

Clinton Heylin

The publishers would like to give special thanks to: Miranda Ward for the index, and for much more besides, Donna Frantz, Robert Greenfield, Kingsley Abbott and especially Colin Davies, for help far beyond the call of duty.

PICTURE CREDITS

Plate section

Neil Denny, Edna Denny, Sandy aged 5, Sandy and David on a family holiday, Sandy and David at Worple Road and Sandy in Trafalgar Square, and later Sandy and David, courtesy of Neil Denny, with thanks to Colin Davies.

Early Sandy promo, Fairport Convention in concert, Sandy and Trevor at Cambridge Folk Festival and Sandy live in the 70s, courtesy of Phillippa Clare.

Sandy in Denver and wedding photos, courtesy of Miranda Ward.

Sandy A&M promo shot courtesy of Linda Fitzgerald-Moore.

Final photo courtesy of Keith Morris.

Other illustrations

Photographs in Chapter 1, courtesy of Neil Denny, with thanks to Colin Davies.

All Sandy Denny's drawings, doodles and hand-written extracts are copyright the Sandy Denny estate and are reproduced by kind permission.

Sandy Denny's letter to Miranda Ward is reprinted with kind permission of Miranda Ward.

Every effort has been made to contact the copyright holders of photographs used in this book, but one or two were unreachable. We would be grateful if the photographers concerned would contact us.

Bibliography

Published information about Sandy Denny and her music remains all too limited, but the below should provide a good starting point:

Davies, Colin [ed.] – *Hokey Pokey* fanzine, various issues [1989–92].
Heylin, Clinton – *Sad Refrains: The Recordings of Sandy Denny* [pp, 1988].
Humphries, Patrick – *Meet On The Ledge* [Eel Pie, 1982 – reissued Virgin, 1997].
Humphries, Patrick – *Richard Thompson: Strange Affair* [Virgin, 1996].
Irvin, Jim – 'Angel of Avalon': *Mojo* June 1998.
Kenney, Martyn – *Unscrapbooking: Another History of Fairport Convention* [pp, 1988].

I have drawn on as many interviews with Sandy Denny as I have been able to locate. The published ones are as follows, in some approximation of chronological order by publication:

28/1/67 – Karl Dallas, *Melody Maker*.
23/9/67 – Karl Dallas, *Melody Maker*.
27/7/68 – Tony Wilson, *Melody Maker*.
16/9/69 – Nick Logan, *New Musical Express*.
17/1/70 – Penny Valentine, *Disc & Music Echo*.
14/2/70 – ???, *Music Now*.
3/70 – Karl Dallas, *Melody Maker*.
20/6/70 – ???, *Disc & Music Echo*.
12/9/70 – David Hughes, *Disc & Music Echo*.
19/9/70 – Michael Watts, *Melody Maker*.
24/10/70 – Jerry Gilbert, *Sounds*.
21/11/70 – Karl Dallas, *Melody Maker*.
9/1/71 – ???, *Melody Maker*.
16/1/71 – Jerry Gilbert, *Sounds*.
20/2/71 – Anne Nightingale, *Petticoat*.
15/5/71 – Ray Coleman, *Melody Maker*.
3/7/71 – Jerry Gilbert, *Sounds*.
10/9/71 – Robin Denselow, *The Guardian*.
10/71 – Rosalind Russell, *Disc & Music Echo*.
1/72 – Steve Peacock, *Sounds*.
15/1/72 – Tony Stewart, *New Musical Express*.
15/4/72 – Tony Stewart, *New Musical Express*.
4/72 – Steve Peacock, *Sounds*.
29/4/72 – ???, *Melody Maker*.
6/5/72 – Karl Dallas, *Melody Maker*.
2/9/72 – Karl Dallas, *Melody Maker*.
23/9/72 – Steve Peacock, *Sounds*.
7/10/72 – Tony Stewart, *New Musical Express*.
7/10/72 – Rosalind Russell, *Disc & Music Echo*.
2/73 – Gordon Coxhill, *Music Scene*.
31/3/73 – Steve Peacock, *Sounds*.
17/4/73 – Myron Bretholz, *Georgetown Voice*.
9/73 – Austin John Marshall, *New Musical Express*.
8/9/73 – Jerry Gilbert, *Sounds*.
15/9/73 – Karl Dallas, *Melody Maker*.
3/74 – Karl Dallas, *Melody Maker*.
20/4/74 – Tony Stewart, *New Musical Express*.
21/6/75 – Angus MacKinnon, *Sounds*.
5/3/77 – Patrick Humphries [pub'd April 1988, *Hokey Pokey*].
16/7/77 – ???, *Melody Maker*.
12/11/77 – Colin Irwin, *Melody Maker*.

Discography

All songs by Sandy Denny unless credited otherwise

ALBUMS

[Please note: All songs listed in italics have been previously released.]

Alex Campbell and Friends (Saga) {1967}. Down In the Mines {trad}*. Freight Train {trad}*. The False Bride {trad}. Dick Derby {trad}*. You Never Wanted Me {Frank}. Been on the Road So Long {Campbell}*. This Train {trad}. Tell Old Bill {trad}*. Freedom {trad}*. *[Note: Asterisked songs feature Sandy Denny. on backing vocals. The remaining tracks feature Sandy Denny on lead vocals.]*

Sandy and Johnny – Sandy Denny and Johnny Silvo (Saga) {1967}. Milk and Honey {Frank}. The Last Thing on My Mind {Paxton}. 3'10 to Yuma {Dunning/Washington}. Make Me A Pallet On Your Floor {trad}. Pretty Polly {trad}. Been on the Road So Long (Sandy Denny version) {Campbell}.

What We Did On Our Holidays – Fairport Convention (Island) {1969}. Fotheringay. Mr. Lacey {Hutchings}. Book Song {Matthews/Thompson}. "The Lord Is In This Place...How Dreadful Is This Place" {trad}. No Man's Land {Thompson}. I'll Keep It With Mine {Dylan}. Eastern Rain {Mitchell}. Nottamun Town {trad}. Tale In Hard Time {Thompson}. She Moves Through The Fair {Colum/Hughes/ trad.}. Meet On The Ledge {Thompson}. End Of A Holiday {Nicol}. *Produced by Joe Boyd.*

Unhalfbricking – Fairport Convention (Island) {1969}. Genesis Hall {Thompson}. Si Tu Dois Partir {Dylan}. Autopsy. A Sailor's Life {trad}. Cajun Woman {Thompson}. Who Knows Where The Time Goes. Percy's Song {Dylan}. Million Dollar Bash {Dylan}. *Produced by Joe Boyd, Simon Nicol, and Fairport Convention.*

Liege and Lief – Fairport Convention (Island) {1970}. Come All Ye {Denny/Hutchings}. Reynardine {trad}. Matty Groves {trad}. Farewell, Farewell {Thompson}. The Deserter {trad}. Medley: The Lark in the Morning/Rakish Paddy/Foxhunter's Jig/Toss the Feathers {trad}. Tam Lin {trad}. Crazy Man Michael {Thompson/Swarbrick}. *Produced by Joe Boyd.*

Fotheringay – Fotheringay (Island) {1970}. Nothing More. The Sea. The Ballad of Ned Kelly {Lucas}. Winter Winds. Peace in the End {Denny/Lucas}. The Way I Feel {Lightfoot}. The Pond And The

257

Stream. Too Much Of Nothing {Dylan}. Banks Of The Nile {trad}. *Produced by Joe Boyd.*

***Sandy Denny* – Sandy Denny (Saga) {1970}.** This Train {trad}. 3'10 To Yuma {Dunning/Washington}. Pretty Polly {trad}. You Never Wanted Me Babe {Frank}. Milk And Honey {Frank}. The Last Thing On My Mind {Tom Paxton}. Make Me A Pallet On Your Floor {trad}. The False Bride {trad}. Been On The Road So Long (Sandy Denny version) {A.Campbell}. *[Note: Compilation of songs recorded at the sessions for* Alex Campbell And Friends *and* Sandy And Johnny.*]*

***The North Star Grassman & The Ravens* – Sandy Denny (Island) {1971}.** Late November. Blackwaterside {trad}. The Sea Captain. Down in the Flood {Dylan}. John the Gun. Next Time Around. The Optimist. Let's Jump the Broomstick {Robins}. Wretched Wilbur. The North Star Grassman & the Ravens. Crazy Lady Blues. *Produced by Sandy Denny, Richard Thompson, and John Wood.*

***Rock On* – The Bunch (Island) {1972}.** That'll Be the Day {Holly/ Petty/Allison}. Don't Be Cruel {Blackwell/Presley}[backing vocals]. The Locomotion {Goffin/King} [backing vocals]. My Girl the Month Of May {Di Mucci} [backing vocals]. Love's Made A Fool Of You {Holly/Montgomery}. Willie and the Hand Jive {Otis}. When

Will I Be Loved {Everly} [duet with Linda Thompson]. Nadine {Berry} [backing vocals]. Sweet Little Rock 'N' Roller {Berry} [backing vocals]. Learning the Game {Holly}. *Produced by Trevor Lucas.*

***Pass of Arms* E.P. – Sandy Denny (Island) {1972}.** Here In Silence/ Man of Iron.

***Swedish Fly Girls* – Various Artists (Juno) {1972}.** Water Mother {Henry/O'Connell}. What Will I Do With Tomorrow? {Henry/ O'Connell}. Are The Judges Sane? {Henry/O'Connell}. I Need You {Henry/O'Connell}.

***Sandy* – Sandy Denny (Island) {1972}.** It'll Take A Long Time. Sweet Rosemary. For Nobody To Hear. Tomorrow Is A Long Time {Dylan}. Quiet Joys Of Brotherhood {R.Farina/trad}. Listen, Listen. The Lady. Bushes And Briars. It Suits Me Well. The Music Weaver. *Produced by Trevor Lucas.*

***The History Of Fairport Convention* – Fairport Convention (Island) {1972}.** Meet On The Ledge {Thompson}. Fotheringay. Mr. Lacey {Hutchings}. Book Song {Matthews/ Thompson}. A Sailor's Life {trad}. Si Tu Dois Partir {Dylan}. Who Knows Where The Time Goes?. Matty Groves {trad}. Crazy Man Michael {Thompson/ Swarbrick}. Medley: The Lark In The Morning/Rakish Paddy/ Foxhunter's Jig/Toss The Feathers {trad}.

All Our Own Work – **Sandy Denny & The Strawbs** (**Hallmark**) {**1973**}. On My Way {Cousins}. Who Knows Where The Time Goes?. Tell Me What You See In Me {Cousins}. Always On My Mind {Hooper}. Stay Awhile With Me {Cousins}. Wild Strawberries {Cousins/Hooper} (instrumental) . All I Need Is You {Cousins}. How Everyone But Sam Was A Hypocrite {Cousins}. Sail Away To The Sea {Cousins}. Sweetling {Hooper}. Nothing Else Will Do {Cousins}. And You Need Me {Cousins}. *Recorded and produced by Karl-Emil Knudsen and Gustav Winkler in 1967.*

Like An Old Fashioned Waltz – **Sandy Denny** (**Island**) {**1974**}. Solo. Like An Old Fashioned Waltz. Whispering Grass {Fisher/Fisher}. Friends. Carnival. Dark The Night. At The End Of The Day. Until The Real Thing Comes Along {Cahn/Chaplin/ Freeman}. No End. *Produced by Trevor Lucas and John Wood.*

Live Convention – **Fairport Convention** (**Island**) {**1974**}. Matty Groves {trad}. Rosie {Swarbrick}. Fiddlestix {trad}. John The Gun. Something You Got {Kenner}. Sloth {Thompson/Swarbrick}. Dirty Linen {trad}. Down In The Flood {Dylan}. Sir B. McKenzie {trad}.

Rising For The Moon – **Fairport Convention** (**Island**) {**1975**}. Rising For The Moon. Restless {Lucas/Roach}. White Dress. Let It Go {Denny/Swarbrick/Pegg}. Stranger To Himself. What Is True. Iron Lion {Lucas}. Dawn {Denny/Donahue}. After Halloween. Night Time Girl {Swarbrick/Pegg}. One More Chance. *Produced by Glyn Johns.*

Guitar, Vocal – **Richard Thompson** (**Island**) {**1976**}. Throwaway Street Puzzle {Thompson/Hutchings} [b-side to 'Meet On The Ledge']. Mr. Lacey {Hutchings} [Stuart Henry Show, 2/12/68]. Ballad Of Easy Rider {McGuinn/Dylan} [*Liege & Lief* outtake].

Rendezvous – **Sandy Denny** (**Island**) {**1977**}. I Wish I Was A Fool For You (For Shame of Doing Wrong) {Thompson}. Gold Dust. Candle In The Wind {John/Taupin}. Take Me Away. One Way Donkey Ride. I'm A Dreamer. All Our Days. Silver Threads And Golden Needles {Rhodes/Reynolds}. No More Sad Refrains. *Produced by Trevor Lucas.*

The Original Sandy Denny – **Sandy Denny** (**Mooncrest**) {**1978**}. This Train {trad}. 3'10 To Yuma {Dunning/Washington}. Pretty Polly {trad}. You Never Wanted Me {Frank}. Milk And Honey {Frank}. My Ramblin' Boy {Paxton}. The Last Thing On My Mind {Paxton}. Make Me A Pallet On Your Floor {trad}. The False Bride {trad}. Been On The Road So Long {Campbell} [backing vocals version].

**Who Knows Where The Time Goes?
– Sandy Denny (Island/Hannibal)**
{**1986**}. The Lady [Royalty Theatre
27/11/77]. Listen, Listen. Next Time
Around. Farewell, Farewell
{Thompson}. The Music Weaver
[demo, 1972]. Tomorrow Is A Long
Time {Dylan}. The Quiet Joys Of
Brotherhood {Farina/trad} [*Liege & Lief*
outtake]. The Pond And The Stream.
One Way Donkey Ride. Take Away The
Load (Sandy's Song) [demo, 1976]. One
More Chance. Bruton Town {trad}
[BBC *In Concert* 16/3/72].
Blackwaterside {trad}. Tam Lin {trad}.
The Banks Of The Nile {trad}. Sail
Away To The Sea {Dave Cousins}. You
Never Wanted Me {Frank} [*Top Gear*
28/5/68]. Sweet Rosemary [demo,
1972]. Now And Then [demo, 1968].
Autopsy. It'll Take A Long Time. Two
Weeks Last Summer {Cousins}
[Fotheringay studio outtake]. Late
November [alternate mix]. Gypsy Davey
(unreleased) [Fotheringay studio
outtake]. Winter Winds. Nothing More
[Rotterdam 1970 w/Fotheringay].
Memphis, Tennessee {Berry}
[Rotterdam 1970 w/Fotheringay].
Walking The Floor Over You {Tubb}
[studio outtake 71/73]. When Will I Be
Loved {Everly}. Whispering Grass
{Fisher/Fisher}. Friends. Solo
[Troubador, L.A. 2/74]. After
Halloween [demo, 1972]. For Shame Of
Doing Wrong [alternate take]
{Thompson}. Stranger To Himself. I'm
A Dreamer. John The Gun. Knockin'

On Heaven's Door {Dylan} [Troubador,
L.A. 2/74]. By The Time It Gets Dark
[demo, 1976]. What Is True? [demo,
1974]. The Sea. Full Moon [*Rendezvous*
outtake]. Who Knows Where The Time
Goes? [Troubador, L.A. 2/74]. *Compiled
and produced by Joe Boyd & Trevor Lucas.*

CDs

The Original Sandy Denny [see album for details] (Mooncrest)

What We Did On Our Holidays [see album for details] (Island)

Unhalfbricking [see album for details] (Island)

Liege & Lief [see album for details] (Island)

Fotheringay [see album for details – includes two bonus tracks: Gypsy Davey. Two Weeks Last Summer.] (Hannibal)

North Star Grassman & the Ravens [see album for details] (Island)

Sandy [see album for details] (Island)

History of Fairport Convention [see album for details] (Island)

Like An Old Fashioned Waltz [see album for details] (Carthage)

Fairport Live [see album for details] (Island)

Rising For The Moon [see album for details] (Island)

Guitar/Vocal [see album for details] (Hannibal)

Rendezvous [see album for details – includes bonus track: Full Moon.] (Hannibal)

Who Knows Where The Time Goes? [see album for details] (Rykodisc)

The Best Of Sandy Denny – **Sandy Denny (Island) {1987}**. *Listen, Listen. The Lady. One Way Donkey Ride. It'll Take A Long Time. Farewell, Farewell {Thompson}. Tam Lin {trad}. The Pond And The Stream. Late November (El Pea ver.). Solo. The Sea. The Banks Of The Nile {trad}. Next Time Around. For Shame Of Doing Wrong {Thompson}. Stranger To Himself. I'm A Dreamer. Who Knows Where The Time Goes?. Compiled and produced by Joe Boyd & Trevor Lucas.*

Heyday – **Fairport Convention (Hannibal) {1987}**. Close The Door Lightly When You Go {Andersen} [Top Gear 28/5/68]. I Don't Know Where I Stand {Mitchell} [Top Gear 28/5/68]. Some Sweet Day {Bryant} [Top Gear 28/5/68]. Reno Nevada {Farina} [David Symonds Show 27/12/68]. Suzanne {Cohen} [Top Gear 26/8/68]. If It Feels Good {Thompson/Hutchings} [Top Gear 26/8/68]. I Still Miss Someone {Cash/Cash} [David Symonds Show 27/12/68]. Bird On A Wire {Cohen} [Stuart Henry Show 2/12/68]. Gone, Gone, Gone {Everly/Everly} [Top Gear 26/8/68]. Tried So Hard {Gene Clark} [David Symonds Show 27/12/68]. Shattering Live Experience {Nicol} [David Symonds Show 4/2/69]. Percy's Song {Dylan} [Top Gear 18/3/69]. *[Note: This is the official release, which differs slightly from Ashley Hutchings' earlier version.]*

Circle Dance – **Various Artists (Hokey Pokey) {1990}**. The King & Queen of England.

Sandy Denny & The Strawbs – **Sandy Denny & The Strawbs (Hannibal) {1991}**. *Nothing Else Will Do*

{Cousins}. Who Knows Where The Time Goes?*. How Everyone But Sam Was A Hypocrite {Cousins}. Sail Away To The Sea {Cousins}. And You Need Me {Cousins}*. Poor Jimmy Wilson {Cousins}. *All I Need Is You {Cousins}*. Tell Me What You See In Me {Cousins}*.* I've Been My Own Worst Friend {Cousins}. *On My Way {Cousins}.* Two Weeks Last Summer {Cousins}. *Always On My Mind {Cousins}. Stay Awhile With Me {Cousins}*. [Note: The songs asterisked have overdubs not present on the original 1973 Hallmark album.]*

Watching The Dark – Richard Thompson (Rykodisc) {1993}. *Genesis Hall.* A Sailor's Life {trad} [Unhalfbricking alternate take].

Folk Routes – Various Artists (Island) {1994}. *Matty Groves. It Suits Me Well. She Moves Through The Fair. Man of Iron. My Girl in the Month of May.*

The Attic Tracks 1972–1984 – Sandy Denny, Trevor Lucas (Raven) {1995}. Moments {Bryn Haworth} [studio outtake 5/77]. Ecoute, Ecoute [French version of Listen, Listen]. One More Chance [demo, 1974]. Rising For The Moon [demo, 1974]. Tears {Trevor Lucas} [b-side to 'White Dess']. Easy To Slip {Lowell George/F. Martin} [*Rendezvous* outtake]. Losing Game {Carr-Weaver} [*Rendezvous* outtake]. Still Waters Run Deep [b-side to 'Candle in the Wind']. *The King And Queen Of England [demo, 1976].* No End [demo,

1973]. Gold Dust [Royalty Theatre 27/11/77]. Stranger To Himself [Royalty Theatre 27/11/77]. Who Knows Where The Time Goes [Royalty Theatre 27/11/77]. *[Note: The songs from the Royalty Theatre are the pre-overdub versions, and therefore do not correspond with the versions on* Gold Dust.]

The BBC Sessions 1971–1973 – Sandy Denny (Strange Fruit) {1997}. Northstar Grassman [BBC In Concert 16/3/72]. Sweet Rosemary [BBC In Concert 16/3/72]. The Lady [BBC In Concert 16/3/72]. Next Time Around [BBC In Concert 16/3/72]. Blackwaterside {trad} [BBC In Concert 16/3/72]. John the Gun [BBC In Concert 16/3/72]. Late November [Sounds of the Seventies 24/8/71]. The Optimist [Sounds of the Seventies 24/8/71]. Crazy Lady Blues [Sounds of the Seventies 24/8/71]. The Lowlands of Holland [Sounds of the Seventies 24/8/71]. It Suits Me Well [Sounds of the Seventies 25/10/72]. Bushes and Briars [Sounds of the Seventies 25/10/72]. The Music Weaver [Sounds of the Seventies 25/10/72]. It'll Take a Long Time [Sounds of the Seventies 25/10/72]. Who Knows Where the Time Goes [Sounds of the Seventies 11/9/73]. Until the Real Thing Comes Along {Cahn/Chaplin/Freeman} [Sounds of the Seventies 14/11/73]. Whispering Grass {Fisher/Fisher} [Sounds of the Seventies 14/11/73]. Like an Old Fashioned Waltz [Sounds of the Seventies 11/9/73]. Dark the Night [Sounds of the Seventies 14/11/73]. Solo [Sounds of the Seventies 14/11/73]. *[Note: This collection of previously unreleased live recordings was deleted from the Strange Fruit catalog after only 3,000 copies were released. The 5 tracks from August 1971 are taken from an off-air copy.]*

"Gold Dust" Live at the Royalty – Sandy Denny (Island) {1998}. I Wish I Was a Fool for You (For Shame of Doing Wrong) {Thompson}. Stranger To Himself. I'm a Dreamer. Take Me Away. Nothing More. The Sea. The Lady. Gold Dust. Solo. John the Gun. It'll Take a Long Time {Dylan}. Wretched Wilbur. Tomorrow Is a Long Time. The North Star Grassman. One More Chance. No More Sad Refrains. Who Knows Where The Time Goes. *[Note: Documents Sandy's last major concert, at the Royalty Theatre, London, on 27 November 1977. The tracks are not in the original order performed, and remixes have added guitar by Jerry Donahue and backing vocals by Simon Nicol and Chris Leslie – none of whom were part of the original backing band. Original concert order is as follows: Solo/ North Star Grassman/ Nothing More/ Gold Dust/ I'm A Dreamer/ John the Gun/ The Sea/ It'll Take A Long Time/ Tomorrow is A Long Time/ The Lady/ Wretched Wilbur/ For Shame of Doing Wrong/ Stranger To Himself/ Take Me Away/ One More Chance/ Who Knows Where The Time Goes/ No More Sad Refrains.]*

Listen, Listen: An Introduction to Sandy Denny (Island) {1999}. Late November. Blackwaterside. Next Time Around. Wretched Wilbur. The North Star Grassman & The Ravens. It'll Take A Long Time. Listen, Listen. The Lady. The Music Weaver. Solo. Like An Old Fashioned Waltz. Dark The Night. No End. One Way Donkey Ride. I'm A Dreamer. All Our Days. No More Sad Refrains. *[Note: All tracks have been remastered anew.]*

'AUTHORIZED' BOOTLEG CASSETTES

Heyday – Fairport Convention (Hutchings cassette version) {1976}.

Gone, Gone, Gone [Top Gear 26/8/68]. You Never Wanted Me [Top Gear 28/5/68]. Some Sweet Day [Top Gear 28/5/68]. Bird On A Wire [Stuart Henry 2/12/68]. I Still Miss Someone [David Symonds 27/12/68]. You're Gonna Need My Help [Symonds on Sunday 4/2/69]. *Suzanne [Top Gear 26/8/68]. Reno Nevada [David Symonds 27/12/68]. I Don't Know Where I Stand [Top Gear 28/5/68]. Close The Door Lightly When You Go [Top Gear 28/5/68]. Shattering Live Experience [Symonds on Sunday 4/2/69]. If It Feels Good [Top Gear 26/8/68]. Tried So Hard [David Symonds 27/12/68].* Meet On The Ledge [Stuart Henry 2/12/68]. *[Note: This cassette was privately circulated by Ashley Hutchings and could be purchased at Fairport Convention gigs.]*

The Airing Cupboard Tapes. That'll
Be The Day [Kingston Poly 12/72]. *Who Knows Where The Time Goes.* It'll Take A Long Time. [L.A. Troubador 2/74].

Doom & Gloom From The Tomb Vol. 1. Eastern Rain [Top Gear 26/8/68]. Book Song [David Symonds 27/12/68].

Doom & Gloom From The Tomb Vol. 2. Autopsy [Top Gear 18/3/69]. Who Knows Where The Time Goes [Symonds on Sunday 4/2/69].

The Attic Trax Vol. 1. Moments. All Our Days (choral version) [Rendezvous outtake]. *Still Waters Run Deep. King & Queen of England. No End. Easy To Slip. Losing Game.* Full Moon (Swarb solo) [Rendezvous outtake]. All Our Days (orchestral intro.) [*Rendezvous* outtake]. *Here In Silence. Man of Iron.*

The Attic Tracks Vol. 3. Blues Run The Game [demo, 1966]. Milk & Honey [demo, 1966]. Soho [demo, 1966]. In Memory (The Tender Years) [demo, 1966]. It Ain't Me Babe [demo, 1966]. East Virginia [demo, 1966]. Geordie [demo, 1966]. Fotheringay [demo, 1967]. A Little Bit of Rain [demo, 1967]. Go Your Own Way My Love [demo, 1968]. Hold On To Me Babe [Cellar Full of Folk 6/3/67]. Green Grow The Laurels ['The Johnny Silvo Folk Four', BBC World Service 7/11/66]. The Boatman ['The Johnny Silvo Folk Four', BBC World Service 7/11/66]. *Who Knows Where The Time Goes [undubbed Strawbs version]. Solo. North Star Grassman. Gold Dust. The Sea. Tomorrow Is A Long Time. Stranger To Himself. For Shame of Doing Wrong. One More Chance. Who Knows Where The Time Goes [pre-overdub versions from the Royalty Theatre 27/11/77].*

The Attic Tracks Vol. 4. I Love My True Love [demo, 1967?]. Let No Man Steal Your Thyme [demo, 1967?]. Carnival [demo, 1967?]. Makes Me Think of You [demo, 1972]. *Ecoute,*

Ecoute. One More Chance. Rising For The Moon. Until The Real Thing Comes Along. Whispering Grass. Dark The Night. Solo. Like An Old Fashioned Waltz. At The End of the Day [studio version minus overdubs].

'AUTHORIZED' BOOTLEG CDS

From Past Archives – **Fairport Convention {1992}.** Nottamun Town [Top Gear 28/5/68]. Meet On The Ledge [Stuart Henry 2/12/68]. You're Gonna Need My Help [Symonds on Sunday 4/2/69]. Sir Patrick Spens [Top Gear 23/9/69]. Tam Lin [Top Gear 23/9/69]. Reynardine [Top Gear 23/9/69]. She Moves Through The Fair [Troubador, L.A. 2/74]. Like An Old Fashioned Waltz [Troubador, L.A. 2/74]. Rising For The Moon [Top Gear 16/7/74]. Down In The Flood {Dylan} [Top Gear 16/7/74]. No More Sad Refrains [Royal Albert Hall, London 10/6/75]. *[Note: 'Fairport'-approved copy of the original bootleg CD.]*

***The Guvenor Vol. 1* {1994}.** *You're Gonna Need My Help [Symonds on Sunday 4/2/69].* Dear Landlord [Unhalfbricking outtake].

***The Guvenor Vol. 2* {1995}.** *You Never Wanted Me* [Top Gear 28/5/68]. Sir Patrick Spens [*Liege & Lief* outtake].

***The Guvenor Vol. 3* {1995}.** Night in the City. Marcie [David Symonds Show 18/6/68].

***The Guvenor Vol. 4* {1996}.** Fotheringay [Top Gear 26/8/68].

[Note: These four Ashley Hutchings retrospective collections were later issued as a set.]

'UNAUTHORIZED' BOOTLEG CDS

Dark The Night (**Nixed 006**). *Green Grow The Laurels. Fhir A Bhata. Blues Run The Game. Milk and Honey. Soho. The Tender Years. It Ain't Me Babe. East Virginia. Geordie. Until The Real Thing Comes Along. Whispering Grass. Dark The Night. Solo. It Suits Me Well. The Music Weaver. Bushes & Briars. It'll Take a Long, Long Time. Man of Iron. Here In Silence. [Note: A combination of home demos, BBC sessions and rare single tracks.]*

One Last Sad Refrain – The Final Concert (**NIX 002**). *Solo. The North Star Grassman & The Ravens. Nothing More. Gold Dust. The Sea. Tomorrow Is A Long Time. The Lady. Wretched Wilbur. Stranger To Himself. For Shame of Doing Wrong. One More Chance. Who Knows Where The Time Goes. Water Mother. What Will I Do With Tomorrow?. Are The Judges Sane?. I Need You. [Note: The pre-overdub Royalty Theatre '77 tape plus the Swedish Fly Girls soundtrack.]*

Sandy at the BBC (**Nightlife N–071**). Autopsy [Top Gear 18/3/69]. Fotheringay [Symonds on Sunday 4/2/69]. Cajun Woman [Top Gear 18/3/69]. Sandy Denny interview [Top Gear 18/3/69]. Si Tu Dois Partir [Top Gear 18/3/69]. The Way I Feel [Top Gear 13/4/70]. Interview ['Fotheringay', BBC 2/4/70]. The Sea ['Fotheringay', BBC 2/4/70]. Eppy Moray [Folk On One 12/11/70].

Lowlands of Holland [Folk On One 12/11/70]. Interview/Gyspy Davey [Folk On One 12/11/70]. Wild Mountain Thyme [Sounds of the Seventies 15/11/70]. John The Gunn [Sounds of the Seventies 15/11/70]. Bold Jack Donahue [Sounds of the Seventies 15/11/70]. *Dark The Night [Sounds of the Seventies 14/11/73]. Whispering Grass [Sounds of the Seventies 14/11/73]. Solo [Sounds of the Seventies 14/11/73]. [Note: CD also features two songs by the 1970 Fairport Convention. From previously unknown BBC transcription discs.]*

Wild Mountain Thyme (**Handmade Productions**). Too Much of Nothing [Beat Club, 1970]. *The Way I Feel*. Interview*. The Sea*. Eppy Moray*. Lowlands of Holland*. Interview/Gypsy Davey*. Wild Mountain Thyme*. John The Gunn*. Bold Jack Donahue*.* Ballad of Ned Kelly [Top Gear 13/4/70]. Intro/Banks of The Nile [Top Gear 13/4/70]. *Late November [from boxed-set]. Nothing More [from boxed-set]. Memphis Tennessee [from boxed-set].* Silver Threads & Golden Needles [Sounds of the Seventies 5/5/70]. *Asterisked tracks copied from* **Sandy at the BBC.**

Poems from Alexandra (**Goldtone GT-004**). *Eppy Moray. Gypsy Davey. Bold Jack Donahue. Lowlands of Holland. Ballad of Ned Kelly. Banks of the Nile. Too Much of Nothing. John The Gun. Silver Threads & Golden Needles. The Way I Feel. Nothing More. The Sea. Two Weeks Last Summer*

DISCOGRAPHY

[from boxed-set]. Gypsy Davey [from boxed-set]. Late November [from boxed-set]. [Note: All songs save last three from misc. 1970 BBC radio sessions. Vastly inferior to the two titles above.]

From Past Archives (Scorpio 92-FC-12-01). *Nottamun Town (BBC, 28/5/68) {trad}. Meet On The Ledge (BBC, 12/68) {Thompson}. You're Gonna Need My Help (BBC, 6/1/69) {Muddy Waters}. Sir Patrick Spens (BBC, 23/9/69) {trad}. Tam Lin (BBC, 23/9/69) {trad}. Reynardine (BBC, 23/9/69) {trad}. She Moves Through The Fair (live-Troubador, LA, 2-74). Like An Old Fashioned Waltz (live-Troubador,LA, 2-74). Rising For The Moon (BBC, 16/7/74). Down In The Flood (BBC, 16/7/74) {Dylan}. No More Sad Refrains (live – Royal Albert Hall, 10/6/75). [Note: Five further tracks from the Full House line-up are included on this title. Later copied by Fairport themselves.]*

A Chronicle of Sorts 1967–1969 (Nixed Records NIX 003). *Marcie [David Symonds 18/6/68]. Night in the City [David Symonds 18/6/68]. You Never Wanted Me [Top Gear 28/5/68]. Eastern Rain [Top Gear 26/8/68]. Fotheringay [Top Gear 26/8/68]. Book Song [David Symonds 27/12/68]. Dear Landlord [Unhalfbricking outtake].* Si Tu Dois Partir [Top Gear 18/3/69]. Cajun Woman [Top Gear 18/3/69]. *Autopsy [Top Gear 18/3/69].* The Lady is a Tramp [Top Gear 23/9/69]. Light My Fire [Top Gear 9/12/68]. *[Note: The first ten tracks on CD*

predate Sandy joining Fairport Convention.]
Doom & Gloom (Silver Rarities SIRA 147/8). *Eastern Rain. Book Song. Autopsy. Who Knows Where The Time Goes. [Note: A copy of the fan-club only cassettes.]*

Sandy's Lament (Head). Rising For The Moon. Solo. Dirty Linen. One More Chance. Sloth. It'll Take A Long Time. Matty Groves. Who Knows Where The Time Goes. Like An Old Fashioned Waltz. Down in the Flood. John the Gun *[Note: All tracks allegedly from Denver 5/74 but evidently from one of the U.S. fall shows; quality horrific – to be avoided at all costs.]*

Borrowed Thyme (SDCD 03). Setting of the Sun. Box Full of Treasure. They Don't Seem To Know You. *Soho. Fotheringay.* She Moves Through The Fair. The Time Has Come. Seven Virgins. *A Little Bit of Rain. Go Your Own Way My Love.* Cradle Song. Blue Tattoo. The Quiet Land of Erin. *I Love My True Love. Let No Man Steal Your Thyme. Carnival. Who Knows Where The Time Goes* [home demos 1967–68]. This Train. Make Me A Pallet On Your Floor. Last Thing On My Mind. You Never Wanted Me [BBC World Service June 1967]. *Hold On To Me Babe.* Blues Run The Game [BBC World Service 6/3/67]. Been On The Road So Long [My Kind of Folk 26/6/68].

Updated, Annotated Discography to Sandy Denny CD Releases 2000–2010.

THE ALBUMS:

Every one of Sandy's original albums, even her pre-Fairport recordings, has been reissued on CD with bonus material since the original 2000 edition of this book. Also released has been a bastardized so-called second Fotheringay album (at least one track of which is actually from the Fairport Convention *Nine* sessions!). The Saga sessions CD, the one title compiled by me, the recent Sandy and the Strawbs CD and the Fotheringay 2 CD are all fully track-listed below. Otherwise, only bonus material is given below:

{Where The Time Goes} (2005)

1. Who Knows Where The Time Goes (solo) 2. This Train 3. 3.10 To Yuma 4. Pretty Polly 5. You Never Wanted Me 6. Milk And Honey 7. My Ramblin' Boy 8. Last Thing On My Mind 9. Make Me A Pallet On The Floor 10. False Bride 11. Been On The Road So Long 12. Two Weeks Last Summer – Denny, Sandy & The Strawbs 13. 3 10 To Yuma 14. Pretty Polly 15. Milk And Honey 16. Last Thing On My Mind 17. Make Me A Pallet On The Floor 18. Been On The Road So Long (with Alex Campbell).

{All Our Own Work} (2010)

1. On Our Way 2. Who Knows Where The Time Goes 3. Tell Me What You See In Me 4. Always On My Mind 5. Stay Awhile With Me 6. Wild Strawberries 7. All I Need Is You Babe 8. How Everyone But Sam Was A Hypocrite 9. Sail Away To The Sea 10. Sweetling 11. Nothing Else Will Do Babe 12. And You Need Me 13. Two Weeks Last Summer 14. Nothing Else Will Do Babe (Sandy vocal) 15. And You Need Me 16. Two Weeks Last Summer 17. Nothing Else Will Do Babe (Sandy lead vocal) 18. Tell Me What You See In Me 19. Who Knows Where The Time Goes (w/strings) 20. Stay Awhile With Me 21. Strawberry Picking 22. Pieces of 79 and 15 23. The Falling Leaves 24. Indian Summer.

{What We Did On Our Holidays} (2003)

Bonus tracks: 13. Throwaway Street Puzzle 14. You're Gonna Need My Help (BBC) 15. Some Sweet Day.

{Heyday} (2002)

Bonus tracks: 13. You Never Wanted Me 14. Nottamun Town 15. Fotheringay 16. Si Tu Dois Partir 17. Cajun Woman 18. Autopsy 19. Reynardine 20. Tam Lin.

{Unhalfbricking} (2003)

Bonus Tracks: 9. Dear Landlord 10. Ballad of Easy Rider (*Liege & Lief* outtake).

{Liege & Lief} (2002)
Bonus Tracks: 9. Sir Patrick Spens 10.
Quiet Joys of Brotherhood.

**Note: A 2007 'Deluxe' 2-CD set also
includes 'Ballad of Easy Rider' (see
Unhalfbricking remaster), BBC
versions of 'Tam Lin', 'Medley',
'Reynardine' and 'Sir Patrick
Spens' (see *Heyday* remaster), yet
another alternate take of 'Quiet
Joys of Brotherhood' and the BBC
session versions of 'The Lady Is A
Tramp' and 'Fly Me To The Moon'.
A right royal rip-off, and no way to
treat such an important LP. They
don't even bother to source a good
'off air' copy of the Danish TV
performance to provide a little
more value for money.**

{Fotheringay} (2004)
Bonus Tracks: 10. Two Weeks Last
Summer 11. Nothing More 12. Banks of
the Nile 13. Memphis Tennessee [all
bonus tracks live from Rotterdam 1970].

{Fotheringay 2} (2008)
1. John the Gunn 2. Eppie Moray 3.
Wild Mountain Thyme 4. Knights On
The Road 5. Late November 6. Restless
7. Gypsy Davey 8. I Don't Believe You
9. Silver Threads & Golden Needles 10.
Bold Jack Donahue 11. Two Weeks Last
Summer.

**{The North Star Grassman and The
Ravens}** (2005)
Bonus Tracks: 12. Late November (*El
Pea* version) 13. Walking The Floor Over
You 14. Losing Game 15. Next Time
Around.

{The Bunch} (2003)
Bonus Tracks: 14. Twenty Flight Rock
15. High School Confidential 16. La
Bamba.

{Sandy} (2005)
Bonus Tracks: 11. Here In Silence 12.
Man of Iron 13. Sweet Rosemary (demo)
14. Ecoute Ecoute 15. It'll Take A Long
Time (live 1974 w/Fairport Convention).

{Like An Old Fashioned Waltz}
(2005)
Bonus Tracks: 10. At The End of The
Day (w/out strings) 11. King & Queen of
England (demo) 12. Like An Old
Fashioned Waltz (live 1974 w/Fairport
Convention) 13. No End (solo).

{Fairport Live} (2005)
Bonus Tracks: 14. That'll Be The Day.
[The other bonus tracks do not feature
Sandy].

{Rising For The Moon} (2005)
Bonus Tracks: 12. Tears (b-side) 13.
Rising For The Moon (demo) 14.
Stranger To Himself (demo) 15. One
More Chance (demo).

{Rendezvous} (2005)
Bonus Tracks: 10. Still Waters Run
Deep 11. Full Moon 12. I'm A Dreamer
(demo) 13. Easy To Slip 14. Moments.

THE ENDLESS BOXED-SETS:

Though there have been three
substantial (one gargantuan)
boxed-sets of Sandy's work in the
past decade, one from the David
Suff Fledgling stable, the other two
from the Sue Armstrong Universal
stable (presided over by the
eminently unqualified 'super fan'
Andrew Batt), in every case these
outlandishly expensive products
have provided more gruel than
hearty fare. As such, all three are
better sampled before purchased.
The (subsequent) single CD 'Best of
the BBC Recordings' and the fifth
CD of demos in Suff's *Boxful of
Treasures* are the only really
essential volumes from what would,
at list price, be a £250 investment!

{A Boxful of Treasures} (2004)
A real hodge-podge and badly
sequenced, t'boot. Slim pickings for
the price.

5-CD set with the following 'unreleased'
material new to official CD:

Disc 1: 2. She Moves Through the Fair
(home recording) 3. Boxful of Treasure
(home recording) 4. They Don't Seem to
Know You (home recording) 5. Go Your
Way My Love (home recording) 6.
Geordie (home recording) 13. Autopsy
(demo).

Disc 2: 12. Silver Threads and Golden
Needles (Fotheringay 1st LP outtake).

Disc 3: 2. Next Time Around (alternate take without strings) 9. Sweet Rosemary (demo) 11. The Lady (demo) 18. Walking the Floor Over You.

Disc 4: 3. At the End of the Day (alternate take without strings) 6. Fairport Convention – John the Gun (live) 7. Fairport Convention – She Moves Through the Fair (live) 8. One More Chance (demo) 13. By the Time It Gets Dark 15. Losing Game.

Disc 5: 1. One Way Donkey Ride (demo) 2. I'm a Dreamer (demo) 3. Take Me Away (demo) 4. Rising For the Moon (demo) 5. Still Waters Run Deep (demo) 6. All Our Days (demo) 7. No More Sad Refrains (demo) 8. By the Time It Gets Dark (demo) 9. The Music Weaver (demo) 10. What Is True? (demo) 11. Stranger to Himself (demo) 12. Take Away the Load (demo) 13. By the Time It Gets Dark (alternate take) 14. Full Moon (home recording).

{Sandy Denny Live At The BBC} (2007)
Beware! Disc 4 has been largely sourced from existing commercial bootleg CDs (and not this fabulous private archive of a certain Mr. Batt!), and consists of poor, generational 'off-air' copies of BBC broadcasts. Disc 3 is a ten-minute DVD of Sandy's one surviving BBC TV appearance:

Disc 1: 1. Fhir ir Bhata 2. Green Grow The Laurels 3. Hold On To Me Babe 4. Blues Run The Game 5. Late November 6. The Optimist 7. Crazy Lady Blues 8. The Lowlands of Holland 9. It Suits Me Well 10. The Music Weaver 11. Bushes And Briars 12. It'll Take A Long Time 13. Solo 14. Like An Old-Fashioned Waltz 15. Who Knows Where The Time Goes? 16. Until The Real Thing Comes Along 17. Whispering Grass 18. Dark Of The Night 19. Solo.

Disc 2: 1. Northstar Grassman And The Ravens 2. Sweet Rosemary 3. The Lady 4. Bruton town 5. Next Time Around 6. Blackwaterside 7. John The Gun 8. The Lady 9. Bushes And Briars 10. It Suits Me Well 11. Blackwaterside 12. The Music Weaver 13. The Sea Captain 14. John The Gun 15. Interview With Sandy Denny.

Disc 3: [DVD] 1. The North Star Grassman And The Ravens 2. Crazy Lady Blues 3. Late November – all tracks One In Ten, BBC-2, 15 Sept. 1971.

Disc 4: 1. This Train 2. Make Me A Pallet On Your Floor 3. The Last Thing On My Mind 4. You Never Wanted Me 5. Been On The Road So Long 6. The Quiet Land Of Erin 7. The Nightingale (duet with Mick Groves) 8. Black Water Side (Richard Thompson guitar) 9. North Star Grassman & The Ravens 10. The Lady 11. It'll Take A Long Time.

{Sandy Denny} (2010)
An eight CD set of Sandy rarities

disguised as, and priced at that of, a 19-CD set, the first eleven CDs of which duplicate the recent Universal remastered CDs, making for a truly shameful rip-off. Universal should be ashamed! The remaining CDs do feature a great deal of unreleased material, though disappointingly much of it has been sourced from bootleg sources. Track listings of discs 12 to 19 as follows:

Disc 12: 1. Blues Run The Game 2. Milk and Honey 3. Soho 4. It Ain't Me Babe 5. East Virginia 6. Geordie 7. In Memory (The Tender Years) 8. I Love My True Love 9. Let No Man Steal Your Thyme 10. Ethusel 11. Carnival 12. Setting Of The Sun 13. Boxful Of Treasures 14. They Don't Seem to Know You 15. Gerrard Street 16. Fotheringay 17. She Moves Through The Fair 18. The Time Has Come 19. Seven Virgins 20. A Little Bit Of Rain 21. Go Your Own Way My Love 22. Cradle Song 23. Blue Tattoo 24. The Quiet Land of Erin 25. Who Knows Where The Time Goes.

Disc 13: 1. Who Knows Where The Time Goes 2. Motherless Children 3. Milk And Honey – Fairport Convention 4. Been On The Road So Long – Fairport Convention 5. The Quiet Land Of Erin – Fairport Convention 6. Autopsy 7. Now and Then 8. Fotheringay 9. She Moved Through The Fair 10. Mr. Lacey –

Fairport Convention 11. Throwaway Street Puzzle – Fairport Convention 12. The Ballad Of Easy Rider – Fairport Convention 13. Dear Landlord – Fairport Convention 14. A Sailor's Life – Fairport Convention 15. Sir Patrick Spens – Fairport Convention 16. Quiet Joys Of Brotherhood – Fairport Convention 17. Quiet Joys Of Brotherhood – Fairport Convention.

Disc 14: 1. The Sea – Fotheringay 2 Winter Winds – Fotheringay 3. The Pond and the Stream – Fotheringay 4. The Way I Feel – Fotheringay 5. Banks Of The Nile – Fotheringay 6. Winter Winds – Fotheringay 7. Silver Threads And Golden Needles – Fotheringay 8. The Sea – Fotheringay 9. Two Weeks Last Summer – Fotheringay 10. Nothing More – Fotheringay 11. Banks Of The Nile – Fotheringay 12. Memphis Tennessee – Fotheringay 13. Trouble In Mind – Fotheringay 14. Bruton Town – Fotheringay [all tracks by Fotheringay].

Disc 15: 1. The Sea Captain 2. Next Time Around 3. The Optimist 4. Wretched Wilbur 5. Crazy Lady Blues 6. Lord Bateman 7. Walking The Floor Over You 8. Losing Game 9. Northstar Grassman and the Ravens 10. Crazy Lady Blues 11. Late November 12. If You Saw Thru My Eyes 13. It's A Boy 14. Northstar Grassman and the Ravens 15. Twelfth Of Never 16. Sweet Rosemary 17. The Lady 18. After Halloween.

Disc 16: 1. It'll Take A Long Time 2. Sweet Rosemary 3. For Nobody To Hear 4. Tomorrow Is A Long Time 5. Quiet Joys Of Brotherhood 6. Listen, Listen 7. The Lady 8. Bushes And Briars 9. It Suits Me Well 10. The Music Weaver 11. No End 12. Whispering Grass 13. Until The Real Thing Comes Along 14. Walking The Floor Over You 15. No End.

Disc 17: 1. Down In The Flood – Fairport Convention 2. Solo – Fairport Convention 3. It'll Take A Long Time – Fairport Convention 4. She Moves Through The Fair – Fairport Convention 5. Knocking On Heaven's Door – Fairport Convention 6. Like An Old Fashioned Waltz – Fairport Convention 7. John The Gun – Fairport Convention 8. Crazy Lady Blues – Fairport Convention 9. Who Knows Where The Time Goes – Fairport Convention 10. Matty Groves – Fairport Convention 11. That'll Be The Day – Fairport Convention 12. What Is True? – Fairport Convention 13. Sandy Denny – Interview 1 14. Sandy Denny – Interview 2.

Disc 18: 1. Blackwaterside 2. No More Sad Refrains 3. By The Time It Gets Dark 4. One Way Donkey Ride 5. Losing Game 6. Easy To Slip 7. By The Time It Gets Dark 8. No More Sad Refrains 9. I'm A Dreamer 10. All Our Days 11. By The Time It Gets Dark 12. Still Waters Run Deep 13. Full Moon

14. Candle In The Wind 15. Moments 16. I Wish I Was A Fool For You 17. Gold Dust 18. Still Waters Run Deep 19. Moments.

Disc 19: 1. The King And Queen Of England 2. Rising For The Moon 3. One More Chance 4. The King And Queen of England 5. After Halloween 6. What Is True? 7. Stranger To Himself 8. Take Away The Load 9. By The Time It Gets Dark 10. I'm A Dreamer 11. Full Moon 12. Take Me Away 13. All Our Days 14. No More Sad Refrains 15. Still Waters Run Deep 16. One Way Donkey Ride 17. I'm A Dreamer 18. Full Moon 19. Makes Me Think Of You.

OTHER FAIRPORT CONVENTION RELEASES W/SANDY DENNY CONTENT:

{A Fairport History} (2002)
A 4-CD 'overview' of the entire Fairport history (and post-history), the credits are so unreliable and the source-tapes so poor that little can be trusted to be what it says it is, but the following appear to be new to officialdom:

Disc 2: 4. Mr Lacey (Dutch TV 1968).

Disc 4: 11. Stranger To Himself 12. Sloth. (both live 1975, probably Royal Albert Hall).

{Before The Moon} (2002)
Disc 1: 1. Solo 2. Dirty Linen 3. One More Chance 4. Sloth 5. It'll Take A Long Time 6. Matty Groves 7. Hens March/Medley 8. Down In The Flood.

Disc 2: 1. Solo 2. Dirty Linen 3. Fiddlestix 4. Who Knows Where The Time Goes? 5. Like An Old Fashioned Waltz 6. Hexhamshire Lass 7. Bring 'Em Down 8. Down In The Flood 9. John The Gun 10. Sir B. MacKenzie. [both sets from Ebbetts Field, Colorado 1974].

{Who Knows? 1975} (2005)
1. Rising For The Moon 2. One More Chance 3. Brilliancy Medley 4. Hexhamshire Lass 5. Restless 6. Stranger To Himself 7. Sloth 8. Iron Lion 9. John The Gun 10. Sir B. MacKenzie 11. Lark In The Morning 12. Down In The Flood 13. Who Knows Where The Time Goes? [live 1975].

{Fairport Convention Live At The BBC} (2007)
This 4-CD set contains the following Sandy-era BBC performances not already available on the expanded *Heyday*:

Disc 1: 6. Marcie 7. Night In The City 8. Jack O' Diamonds 12. Eastern Rain 18. Book Song 19. Who Knows Where The Time Goes?

Disc 2: 1. You're Gonna Need My Help 10. Sir Patrick Spens 11. Medley 12. The Lady Is A Tramp.

Disc 3: 11. John The Gun 12. Fiddlestix 13. Rising For The Moon 14. Down In The Flood.

Disc 4: 9. Meet On The Ledge 10. Light My Fire.

Nothing More?

AN INTEMPERATE DISQUISITION ON THE PLUNDERING OF SANDY DENNY'S MUSICAL LEGACY

It was Richard Thompson who in the early nineties used to regularly sing the jocular 'Now That I'm Dead (I'm Finally Making A Living)'. Has there ever been another song that could be more appositely applied to Richard's dear old friend, Sandy than this French, Frith, Kaiser, Thompson track? Did she jump or was she pushed?

In the decade since I wrote my Sandy Denny biography, there has been such an eye-watering, wallet-busting harvest of Denny product that it has worn clean through the bottom of the barrel, and even now Universal are sweeping up the shavings previous compilers considered mere chaff. Leaving aside 'expanded' remasters of all of Sandy's albums, even the Saga and Strawbs collections, there has been the fake *Fotheringay 2*, plus no less than three boxed-sets of four (*Live at the BBC*), five (*A Boxful of Treasures*) and nineteen discs (*Sandy Denny*) respectively.

For all one's natural curiosity about her 'lost' recordings, amply discussed herein, one imagines Sandy herself would have been appalled to see quite so much of her carefully wrought output second (and third and fourth...) guessed. And the fact that a principal beneficiary of her hard work should be the woman who 'stole' her husband, Trevor's third wife, Elizabeth Hurtt-Lucas, I must imagine would only amplify her hurt.

But in this, as in so many other ways, it was Trevor's actions, or inaction (he died intestate), that ultimately allowed the estate to be controlled by someone whose investment in Sandy, as an artist and as a person, was negligible. As a result there has been no indentured hand on the rudder determined to nix material unworthy of her memory; as has been the case with Sandy's contemporary, Nick Drake, whose estate has been overseen with an iron hand by sister Gabrielle.

As such, at a time when demand for her dead brother's work has never been higher, Gabrielle has resolutely resisted releasing any last scrapings from the Universal (or indeed the BBC) vaults, just for the sake of Universal's bottom-line, and her bank account. She alone knows whether anything worthy of Drake's legacy remains in said vaults, but one thing is sure: it won't appear on a 6-CD boxed-set, five-sixths of which have already been previously available.

And if Sandy was not the perfectionist in the studio that Nick was, she was no less technically accomplished as a singer-musician. So not surprisingly there has been a smattering of life-enhancing wheat in amongst the recently-released detritus. But such has been the indiscriminate use of material excavated, and the lack of any discernible aesthetic displayed by recent archival compilers – loosed on the Universal vaults by recently-appointed, self-proclaimed Sandy fan Sue Armstrong – that the discriminating fan has needed not so much an audio sieve to sift through it all as their own fine-tuned bullshit detector.

The trouble really dates back to 1998 when Jerry Donahue and Jerry Boys, the architects behind the official release of Sandy's last official concert at the Royalty Theatre in November 1977, got away with what was a travesty of a release (*Gold Dust: Live At The Royalty*). Rather than releasing this poignant document with all its inherent flaws, surviving musicians had set about redoing their parts, even as the real focal point (Sandy's contribution) stayed frozen in time. As Peter Gabriel once wrote of his own re-worked live performances, 'The generic term of this process is "cheating".'

But that was not all. The integrity of the original occasion was abandoned as soon as they decided to resequence the entire concert applying a logic lost on me. The result was the worst of all possible worlds, neither a snapshot of a moment, nor an album that was so transcendent musically that one forgave the musicians their trespasses (as, say, most rock fans forgive the Stones *their* trespasses on *Get Your Ya-Ya's Out*, perhaps the most 'unlive' classic concert album in rock history).

Having got away with this assault on Sandy's last sad refrain, Donahue was emboldened to begin work on a wholly unhistorical version of the abandoned second Fotheringay album. As he well knew, this could never be a case of 'completing' a nearly finished artifact – as had been the case with, say, Janis Joplin's *Pearl*, one of Sandy's favourites. Work on the original *Fotheringay 2* had been abandoned with less than a side's worth of songs completed to Sandy's (or producer Joe Boyd's) satisfaction. Even if BBC recordings of these songs could or were added into the mix, the sum total needed some more spare parts.

His solution, sadly, was misguided at best. Choosing not to utilize the rehearsal version of 'Bruton Town' that I had already informed him about (and which was ultimately included on the recent 19-CD set, albeit from a truncated MP-3 dub!); nor the backing track of Anne Briggs' 'Go Your Own Way My Love' completed at those second-album sessions, and still worth hearing despite no Sandy vocal (as per *Pearl*'s 'Buried Alive In The Blues'). Nor did he use Sandy's glorious accapella 'Lowlands Of Holland', recorded the same month as the sessions for the BBC, and extant from a BBC transcription disc.

Rather, he took an outtake from the first Fotheringay album (already released on *Boxful of Treasures*), 'Silver Threads & Golden Needles', and placed it alongside a (rejigged) version of Dylan's 'I Don't Believe You' featuring a Trevor Lucas vocal recorded by a different band at a later album session (it's a *Fairport Convention Nine* outtake!).

The result was an(other) album that was neither an indication of what might have been, nor one entitled to stand alongside (or even in the same room as) its illustrious predecessor. In short, it was an expensive indulgence (all the redubbing and remixing apparently ran up studio costs that ran to five figures). And it was compounded by the baffling decision by Univeral to transfer the copyright in the original Fotheringay recordings to the parties responsible for *Fotheringay 2*. Not surprisingly, such stupidity came back to bite Universal on its golden ass.

When the next quasi-systematic attempt to compile a 'representative' boxed-set of part-released, part-unreleased Sandy recordings, the 5-CD *A Boxful of Treasures*, compiled by David Suff, was released in 2004, he was only able to use two tracks from that ill-fated second Fotheringay LP, 'Gypsy Davey' and 'Late November', both previously released (the latter, in Sandy's lifetime, on *El Pea*). And even when a 2007 3-CD/1-DVD boxed-set of Sandy's post-Fairport BBC recordings appeared, intended to supercede the long-deleted single CD, *The BBC Sessions 1971-73*, it was obliged to omit the many Fotheringay sessions – some of the most intriguing of Sandy's work at the BBC – from this lavish set entirely, even though the set was supposed to cover her non-Fairport sessions from 1966 through 1973.

This was hardly the only problem with the BBC set, which was meant to announce Denny advocate Sue Armstrong's tenure at Universal. In some of the most ill-informed sleeve-notes of the entire CD era, Armstrong revealed that the set had been made possible thanks to one Andrew Batt, "a fan of Sandy's who had somehow managed to obtain copies of her BBC recordings that were so rare they were practically unheard of." He had achieved this remarkable coup by purchasing two commercially released bootleg CDs issued by one Rob Johnstone (now the proprietor of the various Chrome Dreams imprints), prior to his two-year incarceration for bootlegging. Both bootlegs had been detailed in the one Sandy Denny biography then available; and in every instance these bootleg CDs were culled from inferior generational cassette dubs of reels that Sandy's father had dubbed for himself.

But no attempt was made, by Batt or Armstrong, to trace these tapes back to their source (although three separate dubs had been made from Neil's master by a Manchester-based Fairport archivist in the early nineties). Indeed, there seemed to be no underlying archival expertise evident in the entire release, just untramelled fandom.

This BBC boxed-set, a bootleg in all but name, was bad enough, but when Batt, a publicist of sorts with no experience as either an archivist or a compiler of boxed-sets, petitioned Armstrong to do a 'definitive' set of 'everything' Sandy-related, she readily agreed. It was a disastrous decision that, three years later, resulted in the monstrous 19-CD *Sandy Denny* boxed-set, surely the most ill-conceived anthology of the CD era. This outlandish release treated the lady like she was some folk-rock equivalent of Miles Davis, when in fact her performances were almost always measured and exact – meaning that surprises in the studio were few and far between.

Leaving aside Batt's unhealthy obsession with releasing almost every note he could find of his favourite diva, such a project – and a retail price just shy of £200 – was bound to incense not just the fans, but a number of Sandy Denny's closest friends. Miranda Ward, formerly on good terms with Batt, lambasted his project on an on-line Sandy mailing list, calling the set a 'rip off', and voicing a sense of betrayal on her friend's behalf to others':

"For the first time I could actually tell myself that I was glad that Sandy was dead. She would have hated this hotch potch of releases for commercial gain. Even the 'Golddust' Live concert CD was in the wrong running order and did not include all the banter that Sandy had with the audience. She used to spend ages sometimes agonising over running orders and these people behind the money making schemes under the guise of encouraging new fans are actually sullying her memory whilst patting themselves on the back for this seemingly endless stream of 'definitive collections'. They have no real concept of Sandy nor any emotional interest in the person she was and have thus failed to hold true to any 'memory' of Sandy Denny, the musician, songwriter, singer and woman."

For all the talk of hours of rarities and unheard nuggets, when the details of the set finally did appear on-line (and Batt did his damnedest to keep the actual contents close to his chest), it was clear that this third 'career overview' in boxed-set form, for all its implicit claims of definitiveness, would contain less than 5-CDs worth of previously unreleased material; i.e. barely 25% of the set would be 'new' to fans, a percentage significantly lower than either the original *Who Knows Where The Time Goes*, or Suff's *A Boxful of Treasures*. To add insult to injury, not only would the recent Fairport remasters serve as the basis for five of the discs, but Donahue's outfake version of the Royalty concert would again be served up in this tainted form; while the *Fotheringay 2* era was largely passed over, with the usual three Boyd mixes made to suffice.

As for the kind of surprises that all such sets demand, it was only at the last minute that the 'Bruton Town' Fotheringay rehearsal was added to the set, and then only when a long-term collector gave Batt a truncated copy, deliberately downgraded, on the strict understanding that he would receive a copy of said set, and due credit. Rather than get a corrected dub of the track, Batt used the copy he was given for reference purposes; thus, in one swell foop, ensuring he lost a second chance of gaining access to a direct dub of Neil Denny's 'demo' reels. Not smart.

Other genuine surprises proved few and far between: an early demo of 'Methuselah'; half a dozen demos for the *Fotheringay* album that includes a devastating 'Banks Of The Nile'; the much fabled solo 'Lord Bateman' from the *North Star* sessions (actually something of a disappointment, being clearly just a guide vocal); the stunning one-off 'Crazy Lady Blues' from the 1974 Troubador shows; an undocumented 1975 TV performance featuring Sandy playing the new 'No More Sad Refrains' and the traditional 'Blackwaterside'. But the exquisite *Rendezvous* demos had already appeared on *A Boxful of Treasures* (albeit again resequenced), and almost every alternate take on the extravagant set was inferior to the one Sandy had preferred – even if Batt included a smattering of string-free mixes from Sandy's first three solo albums.

As for the one opportunity Batt had to give fans a superior, alternate version of an entire album, he squandered it. In his trawl through the Universal vaults – and he was nothing if not industrious – he had found the original, 1976 sequence of her fourth solo album, then called *Gold Dust*. This ten-track forty-six minute album had many subtle differences and a couple of not-so-subtle differences from the album eventually released as *Rendezvous*. With the likes of 'Full Moon' and 'Still Waters Run Deep' in their correct place (and mixes), and no 'Candle In The Wind', it was in every way a superior artefact. But rather than give this version as a stand alone sequence, Batt scattered a smattering of the choicer alternates across two separate CDs, one an expanded version of the album, one a largely random sweeping up of latter-day Sandy demos and outtakes. Few would wade through the endless alternate takes when sequenced so, and with such minimal annotation in a boxed-set booklet given over largely to some personal fetish for pictures of The Lady, not the recording information expected of fans of her *music*.

And now comes the depressing news that Universal have a 'Deluxe' two-CD version of *North Star Grassman & The Ravens* due for release in June, which merely cherry-picks the tracks found on the 19-CD set, to bolster a straight remaster of an album that was last remastered – and perfectly respectably – in 2005. One imagines the other solo albums will follow, as apparently will a 4-CD boxed-set of Fotheringay recordings that will be both BBC tapes and two previously undocumented latter-day concerts, one from Essen that could well have been their penultimate gig. That, at least, may be something to get excited about. But for the rest of Universal's shameless fleecing of fans' bank accounts, it is hard not to agree with The Lady herself, that the time for more such sad refrains has passed.

Chronology of Recordings & Performances

All media, studio and demo sessions are listed in bold

1965
October 27 – Leduce Contemporary Folk Club, Soho, London.
November 10 – Leduce, Soho, London.

1966
??? – **Home demos**: Blues Run The Game. Milk and Honey. Soho. In Memory (The Tender Years). It Ain't Me Babe. East Virginia. Geordie.
??? – **Home demos**: I Love My True Love. Let No Man Steal Your Thyme. Carnival.
??? – Residency at Leduce.
May 13 – Les Cousins, London.
July 15 – Scots Hoose, Cambridge Circus, London.
October 3 – Deane Arms, South Ruislip.
October 21 – Billericay.
October 26 – The Marquee, Soho, London.
October 30 – Ickenham.
October 31 – 'Which' club, Southend-on-Sea.
November 7 – **The Johnny Silvo Folk Four, BBC World Service**: 3.10 To Yuma. The False Bride. The Wild Rover. [Note: A second session was recorded on the same day but details of the songs performed have been lost – no recordings survive of either session].
November 12 – Cardiff.
November 25 – Swindon.
November 26 – Teddington Folk Club.
November 27 – Brentwood.
December 2 – **Cecil Sharp House.**

Session for Folk Song Cellar: Fhir ir Bhata. Green Grow The Laurels.
December 4 – Nag's Head, Battersea, London.
December 8 – Old Ford, Farnborough.
December 11 – Harrow.
December 18 – St. Pancras Town Hall, King's Cross.
December 20 – The Troubadour, London.
December 23 – Aldous House.
December 28 – The Three Horseshoes, Hampstead.

1967
??? – **Home demos**: Instrumental. Setting of the Sun. Boxfull of Treasures. They Don't Seem To Know You. Soho. Fotheringay. She Moves Through The Fair. The Time Has Come. Seven Virgins.
January 1 – The Marquee, London.
January 5 – White Bear, Hounslow.
January 12 – Folk Centre, Hammersmith.
January 13 – Central Hotel, East Ham.
January 18 – Chelsea College, London.
January 22 – Brentwood.
January 28 – Wellingborough.
February 5 – Norwich.
February 9 – Dukes Head, Addlestone.
February 13 – Orpington.
February 14 – The Crown, Twickenham.
February 15 – The Marquee, London.
February 16 – Black Bull, High Road, Barnet.
February 19 – Manchester.
February 21 – **The Strawberry Hill Boys Sing & Play Folk Songs, BBC World Service**: Blues Run The Game. On My Way. Stay Awhile With Me. Pretty Polly. Tell Me What You See In Me. [no

recording known]
February 23 – Hertford.
February 26 – High Wycombe.
March 3 – Brighton.
March 6 – **Cellarful of Folk, BBC Radio**: Hold On To Me Babe. Blues Run The Game.
March 9 – Loughton.
March 13 – Queen Mary College, London.
March 19 – The Troubadour, London.
March 21 – **Cellarful of Folk, BBC Radio**: Milk and Honey. The False Bride. [no recording known]
March 22 – **Eros Records Session** [Alex Campbell & Friends]: The False Bride. You Never Wanted Me. This Train. Milk and Honey. The Last Thing On My Mind. Pretty Polly. My Ramblin' Boy.
March 31 – Les Cousins, London.
April 3 – Wittering.
April 4 – Leicester.
April 5 – Television appearance [presumably on Alex Campbell's show].
April 5 – Great Yarmouth.
April 6 – Lowestoft.
April 7 – Norwich.
April 9 – Hampstead Folk Club.
April 14 – Beaconsfield.
April 16 – Coventry.
April 20 – Airdrie.
April 23 – Paisley.
April 26 – **Eros Records Session** [Sandy & Johnny]: Milk and Honey. The Last Thing On My Mind. 3.10 To Yuma. Make Me A Pallet On Your Floor. Pretty Polly. Been On The Road So Long.
April 28 – Central Hotel, East Ham.
April 30 – Brentwood.
May 3 – Holy Ground, Bayswater.
?May – Thoger Oleson's Visevers Hus, Tivoli, Denmark [two–week residency].
?May – **Danish sessions w/Strawbs**: On My Way. Who Knows Where The Time Goes. Tell Me What You See In Me.

Always On My Mind. Stay Awhile With Me. Wild Strawberries. All I Need Is You. How Everyone But Sam Was A Hypocrite. Sail Away To The Sea. Sweetling. Nothing Else Will Do. And You Need Me. Poor Jimmy Wilson. I've Been My Own Worst Friend. Two Weeks Last Summer.
?May 13 – Digbeth Civic Hall, Birmingham [as part of Folksingers For Freedom in Vietnam].
May 17 – Surbition Assembly Rooms.
May 25 – White Bear, Hounslow.
June 9 – Les Cousins, Soho.
June 18 – Norbury Hotel, Norbury.
?June – **'The Johnny Silvo Folk Four', BBC World Service**: This Train. Make Me A Pallet On The Floor. The Last Thing On My Mind. You Never Wanted Me.
July 16 – The Troubadour, London.
?September – Alex's Tagalong Folk Club, Norwich.
Late September – 'British Week', Brussels, Belgium.
October 6 – Les Cousins, London.
October 13 – The Central Hotel, East Ham.
November 3 – La Bastille, Soho, London.
November 5 – Norbury Hotel, Norbury.
November 12 – Brentwood Folk Club.
November 16 – The Greyhound, Fulham, London.
November 19 – Manchester Sports Guild.
November 22 – Coach and Horses Folk Club, Kew Green.
November 26 – The Horseshoe Tavern, Tottenham Court Road, London.
December 15 – Les Cousins, London.
December 17 – The Horseshoe Tavern, London.

1968
??? – **Home demos**: Little Bit of Rain. Go Your Own Way My Love. Cradle Song. Blue Tattoo. The Quiet Land of Erin.

January 26 – St Pancras Assembly Rooms, King's Cross, London.
February 23 – Central Hotel, East Ham.
February 29 – Black Bull, London.
March 17 – Starting Gate, Wood Green, London.
March 22 – Couriers, Leicester.
April 8 – White Lion, Putney.
April 27 – Clerkenwell Tavern.
April 29 – Phoenix Pub, Cavendish Square.
May 12 – The Horseshoe Tavern, London.
May 20 – Middle Earth, Covent Garden, London. [first show w/ Fairport].
May 25 – 'Anglers', Teddington. [solo]
May 28 – **Top Gear Session, BBC Radio One**: Close The Door Lightly. I Don't Know Where I Stand. Nottamun Town. You Never Wanted Me. Some Sweet Day.
June 2 – Barn Barbecue Dance, Whittlesey, Peterborough.
June 9 – Blaises, London.
June 14 – 'Summer Ball', Sussex University.
June 18 – **David Symonds Show, BBC Radio**: Jack o' Diamonds. Morning Glory. Marcie. Night In The City. [no recording known of first two tracks]
June 26 – **My Kind of Folk, BBC Radio** [solo session]: The Quiet Land of Erin. Been On The Road So Long.
June 28 – Middle Earth, Covent Garden.
July 3 – **Sound Techniques session**: Close The Door Lightly.
July 5 – Railway Institute, York.
July 17 – Country Club, Haverstock Hill.
July 19 – Westminster Central Hall.
July 23 – Fishmonger's Arms, Wood Green, London.
August 9 – 'Bluesville 68', The Manor House, London.
August 11 – Sunbury Pop Festival, Kempton Park.
Summer – The Frollicking Knees, Market

Harborough.
Summer – **?Sound Techniques sessions**: The Lord Is In This Place. No Man's Land. Meet on the Ledge. End of a Holiday
August 24 – Free Concert, Hyde Park, London.
August 24–25 – Middle Earth, Covent Garden, London [48 Hour 'Freak Out'].
August 26 – **Top Gear Session, BBC Radio**: If You Feel Good. Fotheringay. Gone Gone Gone. Eastern Rain. Suzanne.
August 29 – **How It Is, BBC-TV**: Morning Glory.
August 31 – 'First Isle of Wight Festival' Ford Farm, Godshill.
September – Parliament Hill Fields Free Festival.
September 3 – **De Lane Lea session**: Book Song. Throwaway Street Puzzle. Eastern Rain.
September 4 – **De Lane Lea session**: Fotheringay. Tale In Hard Time.
September 5 – **De Lane Lea session**: Tale In Hard Time.
September 11–14 – Dutch Tour. Includes **TV broadcast**: I Still Miss Someone. Bird On A Wire. If You Feel Good. I'll Keep It With Mine. Mr Lacey.
September 18 – The Marquee, London.
September 19 – **Sound Techniques session**: Mr Lacey. I'll Keep It With Mine. Nottamun Town.
September 22 – Country Club, Haverstock Hill, London.
September 25 – The Marquee, London.
September 28 – 'Festival of Contemporary Song', Royal Festival Hall, London: I'll Keep It With Mine. Reno Nevada. Morning Glory. Suzanne.
October 2 – The Marquee, London.
October 8 – Fishmonger's Arms, Wood Green, London.
October 9 – The Marquee, London.
October 11 – **Sound Techniques**

session: She Moved Through The Fair.
October 12 – Manchester University.
October 16 – The Marquee, London.
October 20 – Mothers, Birmingham.
October 23 – The Marquee, London.
October 30 – The Marquee, London.
November 1 – Queen Mary College, London.
November 23 – 'Festival of Contemporary Song', Philharmonic Hall, Liverpool.
November 24 – 'Festival of Contemporary Song', City Hall, Newcastle.
November 25 – **Night Ride, BBC Radio**: Things You Gave Me. Morning Glory. Meet On The Ledge. Bird On A Wire. Mr Lacey. Autopsy. [no recording known]
November 30 – London School of Economics, Aldwych, London.
December 2 – **Stuart Henry Show, BBC Radio**: Reno Nevada. Bird On A Wire. Mr Lacey. Meet On The Ledge.
December 9 – **Top Gear Session, BBC Radio**: Meet On The Ledge. She Moves ThroughThe Fair. Light My Fire. I'll Keep It With Mine. Billy the Orphan Boy's Lonely Xmas.
December 10 – Dacorum College, Hemel Hempstead.
December 12 – 100 Club, London.
December 13 – **How It Is, BBC-TV**: Meet On The Ledge.
December 27 – **David Symonds Show, BBC Radio**: I Still Miss Someone. Tried So Hard. Book Song. Reno Nevada.
December 30 – **Sound Techniques demo session**: Autopsy. Now and Then. [solo]

1969
??? – **Young Tradition Recording Session**: Interlude – The Pembroke Unique Ensemble [backing vocals].
January 3 – Fishmonger's Arms, Wood Green, London.
January 4 – The Roundhouse, Chalk Farm, London.
January 6 – **Radio One Club, BBC Radio**: I Still Miss Someone. Jack o Diamonds. Bird On A Wire. You're Gonna Need My Help. Meet On The Ledge. [no recording known]
January – Southampton University, Southampton.
January – ?Colston Hall, Bristol.
January 16 – **Sound Techniques session**: Percy's Song. Shattering Live Experience.
January 24 – Lanchester Arts Festival, Coventry.
January 29 – Van Dyke's, Plymouth.
February 2 – Country Club, Haverstock Hill.
February 4 – **Symonds on Sunday, BBC Radio**: Shattering Live Experience. Who Knows Where The Time Goes. You're Gonna Need My Help. Fotheringay.
February 15 – Barking College Students Union.
February 18 – Manchester University.
February 26 – Adam & Eve Club, Southampton: A Sailor's Life. Autopsy. She Moved Through The Fair. I'll Keep It With Mine.
February 28 – City Hall, Newcastle.
February – **Sound Techniques session**: A Sailor's Life.
February – **Sound Techniques session**: A Sailor's Life. Si Tu Dois Partir.
February–March – **Sound Techniques sessions**: Genesis Hall. Autopsy. Cajun Woman. Million Dollar Bash. Dear Landlord.
March 7 – Brunel University, Uxbridge.
March 14 – C.D.T., Charing Cross Road, London.
March 15 – Oxford Polytechnic.
March 15 – 'The Middle Earth All-Nighter', Royalty Theatre, Ladbroke Grove.
March 18 – **Top Gear Session, BBC**

Radio: Cajun Woman. Percy's Song. Si Tu Dois Partir. Autopsy.

March 22 – Enfield College.

March 24 – 'Folk Meets Pop', Royal Festival Hall, London.

April 6 – Mother's, Birmingham.

April 8 – **Sound Techniques session**: Who Knows Where The Time Goes.

April 9 – **Sound Techniques session**: Genesis Hall. Who Knows Where The Time Goes.

April 11 – Van Dyke's, Plymouth.

April 19 – London Polytechnic, London.

April 24 – Students' Union, City of London College, Moorgate, London.

April 25 – Sunderland Tech College.

April 27 – Country Club, Haverstock Hill, London.

May 11 – Mother's, Birmingham.

June – The Troubador, Los Angeles [w/ Richard Thompson & Simon Nicol].

August 2 – Les Cousins, London [solo].

August 14 – **Top Of The Pops, BBC-TV**: Si Tu Dois Partir.

September 20 – Van Dyke's, Plymouth.

September 23 – **Top Gear Session, BBC Radio**: Sir Patrick Spens. Medley. Tam Lin. The Lady Is A Tramp. Reynardine.

September 24 – Royal Festival Hall, London: Come All Ye. Reynardine. Sir Patrick Spens. Farewell Farewell. Matty Groves. The Quiet Joys of Brotherhood. Crazy Man Michael. Tam Lin. The Ballad of Easy Rider. What A Friend We Have In Jesus.

October 10 – Fairfield Halls, Croydon.

October 14 – Civic Hall, Dunstable.

October 16 – **Sound Techniques session**: The Deserter. Farewell Farewell.

October 19 – **Sound Techniques session**: Crazy Man Michael. Ballad of Easy Rider.

October 21 – **Sound Techniques session**: Matty Groves. Reynardine.

October 22 – **Sound Techniques session**: Reynardine. Ballad of Easy Rider. Matty Groves.

October 29 – **Sound Techniques session**: Come All Ye. Jigs & Reels. Tam Lin. Quiet Joys of Brotherhood.

November 1 – **Sound Techniques session**: Sir Patrick Spens.

November 2 – Mothers, Birmingham.

November – **Danish TV Broadcast**: The Deserter. Matty Groves. Crazy Man Michael.

December – Les Cousins, London [solo]: The Pond and the Stream. Bruton Town. The One I Love The Best. She Moved Through The Fair. Blues Run The Game. Green Grow The Laurels. Crazy Man Michael. Bird On A Wire. Who Knows Where The Time Goes.

1970

??? – **Stefan Grossman Recording Session**: A Pretty Little Tune [backing vocals].

February – Country Club, Haverstock Hill [solo].

February 18 – **Studio session**: The Way I Feel. Number Seven. The Pond and Stream. Ballad of Ned Kelly.

February 19 – **Studio session**: The Sea. Winter Winds. Ballad of Ned Kelly.

March 16 – Town Hall, Birmingham [first show w/ Fotheringay].

March 18 – De Montfort Hall, Leicester.

March 20 – Free Trade Hall, Manchester.

March 22 – Colston Hall, Bristol.

March 24 – **Sound Techniques session**: Too Much of Nothing. The Way I Feel. Winter Winds. Nothing More. Banks of the Nile.

March 26 – **Sound Techniques session**: Nothing More. Too Much of Nothing.

March 27 – **Sound Techniques session**: Pond and the Stream. Nothing More.

March 30 – Royal Festival Hall, London: The Way I Feel. The Sea. Winter Winds.

The Ballad of Ned Kelly. Banks of the Nile. The Pond and The Stream. Instrumental. Nothing More. Silver Threads & Golden Needles.

April 2 – **'Fotheringay', BBC Radio**: The Way I Feel. Nothing More. The Sea. Ballad of Ned Kelly. Banks of the Nile. Too Much of Nothing.

April 7 – **Sound Techniques session**: Banks of the Nile. Silver Threads & Golden Needles.

April 13 – **Top Gear Session, BBC Radio**: Banks of the Nile. Ballad of Ned Kelly. The Sea. Nothing More. The Way I Feel.

April 14 – **Sound Techniques session**: Peace In The End. Nothing More.

April 23 – The Roundhouse, Chalk Farm, London: The Sea. Ballad of Ned Kelly. Winter Winds. Banks of the Nile. Too Much of Nothing. The Way I Feel. Silver Threads & Golden Needles.

May 5 – **Sounds of the Seventies, BBC Radio**: Silver Threads & Golden Needles. Peace In The End. Too Much of Nothing. Nothing More.

August – Rotterdam Open-Air Festival: Nothing More. Memphis Tennessee. The Way I Feel.

August – **Dutch radio session**:

August 15 – Yorkshire Folk, Blues And Jazz Festival, Krumlin, Halifax.

September 17 – Town Hall, Cheltenham.

September 26 – University of Wales, Aberystwyth.

October 2 – Royal Albert Hall, London.

October 13 – Town Hall, Birmingham.

October 14 – City Hall, Newcastle.

October 15 – The Lyceum, London.

October 16 – Sheffield.

October 17 – Free Trade Hall, Manchester.

October 25 – St Andrews University, Fife.

October 26 – **possible studio session**. [?Two Weeks Last Summer]

October 27 – Brunel University, Uxbridge.

October 29 – Mother's, Birmingham.

November 7 – University College, London.

November 12 – **'Folk On One', BBC Radio**: Eppy Moray. Gypsy Davey. Bold Jack Donahue. Lowlands of Holland. Ballad of Ned Kelly. Banks of the Nile.

November 15 – **Sounds of the Seventies, BBC Radio**: Gypsy Davey. Bold Jack Donahue. John the Gun. Eppy Moray. Wild Mountain Thyme.

November 17 – **Sound Techniques session**: Eppy Moray. Gypsy Davey. 'New Title'.

November 18 – **Sound Techniques session**: Eppy Moray. John the Gun. Gypsy Davey.

December 2 – Town Hall, Oxford.

December 18 – **Sound Techniques session**: 'New Title 1' [prob. Late November]. 'New Title 2' [poss. Two Weeks Last Summer].

December 29 – **possible studio session**.

1971

??? – **Marc Ellington Recording Session**: I'm Leaving (America). Alligator Man. [backing vocals].

??? – **Ian Matthews Recording Session**: Hearts. Never Ending. If You Saw Thro My Eyes [piano, harmonium & vocals].

January 30 – Queen Elizabeth Hall, London [last show w/ Fotheringay].

?February – **Led Zeppelin Recording Session**: The Battle of Evermore.

March 11 – **Sound Techniques session**: Blackwaterside.

March 14 – **Sound Techniques session**: 'New Title'. Moss. EPNS. [prob. rec. date for Let's Jump The Broomstick]

April 6 – **Island Studios session**: Next Time Around. Lord Bateman.

April 7 – **Island Studios session**: The Optimist. Late November.

April 8 – **Island Studios session**: The Optimist.

April 22 – **The Spinners, BBC-TV**: Nightingale. Blackwaterside.

May 1 – **Island Studios session**: Lord Bateman. Next Time Around.

May 2 – **Island Studios session**: Next Time Around. Crazy Lady Blues. Down in the Flood. The Optimist.

May 7 – **Island Studios session**: John the Gun. Walking the Floor Over You.

May 8 – **Island Studios session**: Walking the Floor Over You.

May 30 – **Island Studios session**: North Star Grassman & the Ravens.

July 24 – Lincoln Festival: Late November. North Star Grassman & the Ravens. Down in the Flood. Blackwaterside. The Optimist. Next Time Around. Crazy Lady Blues. John the Gun.

August 24 – **'Sounds of the Seventies', BBC Radio**: North Star Grassman & the Ravens. Crazy Lady Blues. Late November. The Optimist. Lowlands of Holland.

September – **'One In Ten', BBC-TV**: North Star Grassman & the Ravens. Crazy Lady Blues. Late November.

September 10 – Queen Elizabeth Hall, London.

September 15 – Chicago.

September – Los Angeles.

September – Philadelphia.

September – New York.

October 7 – Kent University, Canterbury.

October 8 – North East London Polytechnic.

October 9 – Reading University, Reading.

October 12 – Southampton University, Southampton.

October 15 – Swansea College, Swansea.

October 16 – Institute of Technology, Manchester.

October 19 – Lady Mitchell Hall, Cambridge.

October 21 – Aston University, Birmingham.

October 22 – Brighton College, Falmer, Sussex.

October 24 – Jazz Club, Redcar.

October 25 – St. Andrews University.

October 29 – Trent Polytechnic, Nottingham.

October 30 – University of East Anglia, Norwich.

October 31 – Keele University, Keele.

November 2 – University College Theatre, London.

November 14 – **Island Studios session**: 'Title 1'. 'Title 2'.

November 15 – **Island Studios session**: 'Title 1' [poss. After Halloween].

November 19 – **Island Studios session**: Quiet Joys of Brotherhood.

November 27 – The Rainbow, Finsbury Park, London [guest appearance w/ Fairport].

December 3 – Cecil Sharp House, London [guest appearance w/ Fairport].

December – **The Manor Studio, Oxon**: That'll Be The Day. Don't Be Cruel. The Loco-Motion. My Girl In The Month of May. Love's Made A Fool of You. Willie and the Hand Jive. When Will I Be Loved. Nadine. Sweet Little Rock & Roller. Learning the Game. Peggy Sue Got Married. Think It Over. High School Confidential. It's So Easy. Twenty Flight Rock. Let There Be Drums.

1972

??? – **Soundtrack session**: Water Mother. What Will I Do With Tomorrow?. Are The Judges Sane?. I Need You.

??? – **Tommy with London Symphony Orchestra**: It's A Boy.

??? – **Fairport Convention Recording Session**: Rosie [backing vocals].

January 6 – Island Studios: That'll Be The Day. When Will I Be Loved Nadine.

[overdubs]
January 11 – Island Studios: Love's Made A Fool of You. Crazy Arms. [overdubs]
January 12 – Island Studios: Sweet Little Rock & Roller. My Girl In The Month of May. Locomotion. Learning the Game. [overdubs]
January 12 – **Sound Techniques Richard Thompson session**: Painted Ladies [piano].
Mid-January – **Sound Techniques Richard Thompson session/s**: Angels Took My Racehorse Away. Cold Feet. Twisted. [backing vocals]
January 16 – **Island Studios**: My Girl In The Month of May. When Will I Be Loved?. Willie and The Hand Jive. [overdubs]
February (first week) – The Bitter End, New York [one week residency]: [set one] Next Time Around. North Star Grassman & the Ravens. Late November. Love's Made A Fool Of You. Matty Groves. John the Gun. [set two] The Sea Captain. Bruton Town. Late November. North Star Grassman & the Ravens. Crazy Lady Blues. Learning the Game. Reynard the Fox.
February – The Troubador, Los Angeles [residency]: Bruton Town. Late November. Learning the Game. Love's Made A Fool Of You. The Sea Captain. Blackwaterside. Listen Listen. Maid of Constant Sorrow. North Star Grassman & the Ravens. Who Knows Where The Time Goes.
February – The Main Point, Bryn Mawr, Pa.
March 6–12 – **The Manor Studio, Oxon**: Sweet Rosemary. For Nobody To Hear. The Music Weaver. The Lady. Listen Listen. Go Your Own Way, My Love. The Lady. After Halloween.
March 16 – **'Radio One In Concert', BBC Radio**: North Star Grassman & the Ravens. Sweet Rosemary. Bruton Town.

The Lady. Next Time Around. Blackwaterside. John the Gun.
April 15 – Corn Exchange, Cambridge.
April 22 – Pier Pavilion, Southsea.
April 28 – London School of Economics, Aldwych.
April 30 – **Sound Techniques session**: For Nobody To Hear.
May 3 – **Sound Techniques session**: The Lady. 'Sitting on a Cliff'(?). The Music Weaver. The Lady.
May – **Sound Techniques session**: It Suits Me Well. Listen, Listen.
May 1 – Kinetic Circus, Birmingham.
May 7 – Alexandra Palace, Wood Green, London.
May 10 – City Hall, Newcastle.
May 13 – St Mary's College, Twickenham.
May – Eltham Well-Hall Open Theatre: For Nobody To Hear. Bushes and Briars. Love's Made A Fool Of You. The Music Weaver. Crazy Lady Blues. Sweet Rosemary. Matty Groves. It'll Take A Long Time. The Lady. John the Gun. Down in the Flood. When Will I Be Loved. Rigs of the Times.
May 20 – **Island Studios session**: The Music Weaver. Tomorrow Is A Long Time.
June 13 – **Old Grey Whistle Test, BBC-TV**: It'll Take A Long Time. The Lady.
July 7 – **Island Studios session**: contents unknown.
July 27 – **Island Studios session**: 'twelfth of never bits'.
August 1 – **Island Studios session**: Here In Silence. Man of Iron.
August 26–27 – Essex Agricultural Showground, Chelmsford.
September 6 – Queen Elizabeth Hall, London.
September 14 – Victoria Hall, Stoke.
October 5 – Liverpool Stadium, Liverpool.
October 6 – Cambridge University, Cambridge.
October 7 – Bath University, Bath.

October 11 – Dome, Brighton.
October 12 – **'Folk Voice', Radio
Newcastle**: It'll Take A Long Time.
Sweet Rosemary. It Suits Me Well.
October 12 – City Hall, Newcastle: It'll
Take A Long Time. Bushes and Briars.
Sweet Rosemary. It Suits Me Well. Late
November. Quiet Joys of Brotherhood.
The Sea Captain. The Sea. The Lady.
John the Gun. Late November.
October 14 – York University, York.
October 18 – Manchester University,
Manchester.
October 20 – Leeds University, Leeds.
October 23 – New Theatre, Oxford.
October 25 – **'Sounds of the Seventies',
BBC Radio**: It Suits Me Well. The Music
Weaver. Bushes & Briars. It'll Take A
Long Time.
October 26 – Mile End, Sundown,
London: It'll Take A Long Time. Bushes
and Briars. Sweet Rosemary. It Suits Me
Well. Late November. The Sea Captain.
Tomorrow Is A Long Time. The Lady.
John the Gun. The Sea. The Music
Weaver. Blackwaterside. Who Knows
Where The Time Goes.
October 27 – **'Pebble Mill At One',
BBC-TV**: The Music Weaver.
October 27 – Mason's Hall, Birmingham.
October 28 – Glasgow University,
Glasgow.
November – **Sounds On Sunday, BBC
Radio**: The Lady. Bushes and Briars. It
Suits Me Well. Blackwaterside. The Music
Weaver. The Sea Captain. John the Gun.
December – Kingston Polytechnic,
Kingston [guest appearance w/ Fairport].
December 3 – Walthamstow Assembly
Hall: No End [mobile rec.]

1973
Winter – Enschede, Holland: Late
November. The Music Weaver. It Suits Me
Well. Listen Listen. The Sea Captain. It'll

Take A Long Time. John the Gun.
Blackwaterside.
April 2 – Philharmonic Hall, New York.
April 6 – Massey Hall, Toronto.
April 7 – Elting Gym, State University of
New York, New Paltz, NY.
April 8 – Constitution Hall, Washington,
D.C. [two sets]
April 10 – The Main Point, Bryn Mawr,
Pa.
April 11 – The Main Point, Bryn Mawr,
Pa.
April 12 – Symphony Hall, Boston.
April 13 – Tower Theatre, Upper Darby,
Pa.
April 14 – Farleigh Exposure Coffeehouse,
Rutherford, N.J. [two sets]
April 15 – Capitol Theatre, Passaic, N.J.
[two sets]
April 24 – Ford Auditorium, Detroit, Mi.
April 25 – Granada Theatre, Chicago, Il.
April 27 – Ebbets Field, Denver, Co. [two
sets].
April 28 – Ebbets Field, Denver, Co. [two
sets].
April 29 – Ebbets Field, Denver, Co. [two
sets]: Late November. The Music Weaver.
It Suits Me Well. Bushes and Briars. The
Quiet Joys of Brotherhood. The Sea
Captain. At The End of the Day. John the
Gun.
May 2 – Chico State College, Chico, Ca.
May 4 – Community Theatre, Berkeley,
Ca. [two sets]
May 5–7 – **A&M Studios, Los Angeles**:
No End. The End of the Day. Solo.
Friends.
May 8 – The Troubador, Los Angeles
[two sets].
May 9 – The Troubador, Los Angeles
[two sets].
May 10 – The Troubador, Los Angeles
[two sets].
May 11 – The Troubador, Los Angeles
[two sets].

May 12 – The Troubador, Los Angeles [two sets].

May 13 – The Troubador, Los Angeles [two sets].

June – European tour.

August – Cambridge Folk Festival.

August – **Sound Techniques sessions**: The Carnival. Like An Old Fashioned Waltz. Dark The Night. Whispering Grass. Until The Real Thing Comes Along.

September 3 – Howff, London.

September 11 – **Sounds of the Seventies, BBC Radio**: Solo. Like An Old Fashioned Waltz. Who Knows Where The Time Goes.

October 30 – Howff, London.

November 1 – Dundee University, Dundee [supposedly w/ band].

November 10 – Leeds University, Leeds [ditto].

November 14 – **Sounds of the Seventies, BBC Radio**: Until The Real Thing Comes Along. Dark The Night. Whispering Grass. Solo. Who Knows Where The Time Goes. Like An Old Fashioned Waltz.

November 20 – Town Hall, Hove [ditto].

November 30 – College of Technology, Hatfield [ditto].

November 30 – The Rainbow, Finsbury Park, London [guest appearance w/ Fairport]: That'll Be The Day.

December 8 – College of Education, Brighton [ditto].

1974

??? – **Brian Maxine Recording Session**.

January – Tokyo: Quiet Joys of Brotherhood. John the Gun. Down in the Flood. Solo. It'll Take A Long Time. Something You've Got. Who Knows Where The Time Goes. Matty Groves.

January – shows in New Zealand, presumably Wellington and Christchurch.

January 25 – Festival Hall, Melbourne.

January 26 – Opera House, Sydney.

January 27 – Opera House, Syndey.

January 31– Troubador, Los Angeles: Something You've Got.

February 1 – Troubador, Los Angeles: [early] Like An Old Fashioned Waltz. John the Gun. [late] Down Where The Drunkards Roll. Crazy Lady Blues. Ballad of Ned Kelly. Matty Groves. That'll Be The Day. Six Days On The Road.

February 2 – Troubador, Los Angeles: Matty Groves. Fiddlestix.

February 3 – Troubador, Los Angeles: Who Knows Where The Time Goes. Solo. Knockin' On Heaven's Door. Sir B. MacKenzie. That'll Be The Day.

April 5 – Begin tour of Scandinavia.

April 19 – University of New York, Syracuse, New York.

April 20 – Cornell Folk Festival, Ithaca, New York: Matty Groves. Solo. Rising For The Moon. John the Gun. Quiet Joys of Brotherhood.

May 10 – Sanders Theatre, Cambridge, Mass: Matty Groves. Solo. It'll Take A Long Time. Like An Old Fashioned Waltz. Rising For The Moon. John the Gun. Down in the Flood. Who Knows Where The Time Goes.

May 15–17 – My Father's Place, New York: Matty Groves. Solo. It'll Take A Long Time. Like An Old Fashioned Waltz. Rising For The Moon. John the Gun. Down in the Flood.

May 18 – Lisner Auditorium, Washington: Matty Groves. Solo. Like An Old Fashioned Waltz. Rising For The Moon. John the Gun. Down in the Flood. Who Knows Where The Time Goes.

June 15 – Town Hall, Harlow, Essex: Matty Groves. Solo. It'll Take A Long Time. Rising For The Moon. John the Gun. Down in the Flood. That'll Be The Day.

June 17 – National Stadium, Dublin.
June 21 – Borough Hall, Greenwich:
Matty Groves. Solo. It'll Take A Long
Time. Like An Old Fashioned Waltz.
Rising For The Moon.
June 22 – Birmingham University,
Edgbaston: Solo. Like An Old Fashioned
Waltz. John the Gun. Down in the Flood.
Who Knows Where The Time Goes.
June 23 – De Montfort Hall, Leicester:
Matty Groves. Solo. Rising For The Moon.
June 28 – College of Education, Hereford.
June 29 – Loughborough University,
Loughborough.
June 30 – The Greyhound, Croydon:
Matty Groves. Solo. It'll Take A Long
Time. Rising For The Moon. John the
Gun. Down in the Flood. Who Knows
Where The Time Goes. That'll Be The
Day.
July 7 – 'Pop Proms', Kensington
Olympia, London.
July 16 – **Top Gear Session, BBC
Radio**: Rising For The Moon.
Fiddlesticks. Down in the Flood. John the
Gun.
Summer – **Home demos**: The King &
Queen of England. Rising For The Moon.
One More Chance.
September 24 – **'The Man They Could
Not Hang', BBC-TV**: The Cell Song.
October 10 – Livingston College, New
Brunswick, N.J.
October 11 – Lisner Auditorium,
Washington, D.C.
October 12 – Theil College, Greenvale,
Pa.
October 13 – Trenton War Memorial,
Trenton, N.J.: Walk Awhile. Rising For
The Moon. Solo. Like An Old Fashioned
Waltz. It'll Take A Long Time. Matty
Groves.
October 16 – State University of New
York, Stonybrook, NY.
October 18 – Indiana State University,

Bloomington, Indiana.
October 19 – St John's Arena, Columbus,
Oh.
October 21 – Olympia Theatre, Detroit,
Mi.
October 22 – Auditorium, Cleveland, Oh.
October 23 – Cincinatti Gardens,
Cincinatti, Oh.
October 25 – Carnegie Hall, New York,
NY: Rising For The Moon. Solo. One
More Chance. It'll Take A Long Time.
Down in the Flood. Matty Groves.
October 26 – Carlton University, Ottowa,
Canada.
October 27 – Convocation Hall, Toronto,
Canada.
October 28 – Harvard University,
Cambridge, Mass.
October 29 – Roxy Theatre, Allentown,
Pa.
October 30 – Joint in the Woods,
Parsipany, N.J.
November 1 – Memorial Auditorium, St
Louis, Miss.
November 2 – Ambassador Theatre, St
Louis, Miss.
November 3 – Assembly Center, Univ. of
Illinois, Bloomington, Il.
November 4 – Civic Center, St. Paul,
Minnesota.
November 10 – Winterland, San Francisco,
Ca.
November 14 – Kent University,
Canterbury.
November 15 – Brunel University,
Uxbridge.
November 16 – Leicester University,
Leicester.
November 17 – Aberystwyth University.
November 18 – Brangwyn Hall, Swansea.
November 20 – Lancaster University.
November 21 – Liverpool University,
Liverpool.
November 22 – Salford University, Salford.
November 23 – Leeds University, Leeds.

November 24 – Apollo Theatre, Glasgow.
November 25 – Usher Hall, Edinburgh.
November 26 – Caird Hall, Dundee.
November 27 – Nottingham University, Nottingham.
November 28 – Oxford Polytechnic, Oxford.
November 29 – Bristol University, Bristol.
November 30 – Essex University, Colchester.
December 1 – Theatre Royal, Drury Lane, London.
December 2 – Guildhall, Southampton.
December 4 – University of East Anglia, Norwich.
December 6 – Reading University, Reading.
December 7 – Sheffield University, Sheffield.
December 8 – Fairfield Hall, Croydon.
December – **Olympic Studios sessions**: Rising For The Moon. One More Chance. White Dress. Restless. Dawn. Tears.

1975
??? – **Charlie Drake Recording Session**: You Never Know. [backing vocals].
December 74/January 75 – **Home demos**: What Is True?. Stranger To Himself.
January – Folk Cafe, Amsterdam, Holland: Matty Groves.
January 23 – Turschip, Breda: Down in the Flood. Rising For The Moon. Solo. It'll Take A Long Time. One More Chance. John the Gun. Matty Groves. Who Knows Where The Time Goes.
January – **Van Speyk Show, KRO-TV**: Rising For The Moon. One More Chance. White Dress.
February – **Olympic Studios sessions**: Let It Go. Stranger To Himself. What Is True?. After Halloween. Night Time Girl.
April 5 – Her Majesty's Theatre, Perth

[part of Australian tour].
April 25 – Queen Elizabeth Hall, London [guest of Richard + Linda Thompson]: When Will I Be Loved.
June 10 – Royal Albert Hall, London: Rising For The Moon. Stranger To Himself. Mr Lacey. No More Sad Refrains. Quiet Joys of Brotherhood. Tam Lin. Listen Listen. It'll Take A Long Time. John the Gun. One More Chance. Who Knows Where The Time Goes.
September 23 – LOEW State Theater, New York.
September 24 – Auditorium Theater, Rochester, New York.
September – Beacon Theatre, New York.
September – Academy of Music, Philadelphia: Tam Lin. Rising For The Moon. One More Chance. Stranger To Himself. Down in the Flood. Who Knows Where The Time Goes. Pick Me Up.
September – Chicago. [set one] Rising For The Moon. Tam Lin. One More Chance. Down in the Flood. Pick Me Up. [set two] Rising For The Moon. One More Chance. Stranger To Himself. Down in the Flood. It'll Take A Long Time. Pick Me Up.
October 6 – Cardiff University, Cardiff.
October 7 – Town Hall, Birmingham.
October 8 – Leeds University, Leeds.
October 9 – Bradford University, Bradford.
October 10 – Sheffield University, Sheffield.
October 11 – UMIST, Manchester.
October 12 – Coventry Theatre, Coventry.
October 14 – Lancaster University, Lancaster.
October 15 – Liverpool University, Liverpool.
October 16 – City Hall, Newcastle: Tam Lin. Rising For The Moon. One More Chance. Who Knows Where The Time Goes. Stranger To Himself. John the Gun. Pick Me Up.
October 17 – Apollo, Glasgow.

October 18 – Usher Hall, Edinburgh.
October 20 – Music Hall, Aberdeen.
October 22 – University of East Anglia, Norwich.
October 24 – York University, York.
October 25 – Nottingham University, Nottingham.
October 26 – Theatre Royal, Drury Lane, London.
October 28 – Colston Hall, Bristol.
October 29 – Exeter University, Exeter.
October 30 – Oxford Polytechnic, Oxford.
October 31 – Brunel University, Uxbridge.
November 1 – Leicester University, Leicester.
November 2 – Fairfield Hall, Croydon.
November 3 – Guildhall, Portsmouth.
November – European tour.
December – **Home demos**: Full Moon. Take Me Away. All Our Days. No More Sad Refrains. Still Waters Run Deep.

1976

?March – **Home demos**: Take Away The Load. I'm A Dreamer. By The Time It Gets Dark.
April 23 – **Island Studios session**: One Way Donkey Ride. Losing Game.
April 24 – **Basing Street Studio session**: Take Me Away.
April 25 – **Basing Street Studio session**: I'm A Dreamer. Full Moon. Sad Refrains.
April 27 – **Island Studios session**: By The Time It Gets Dark.
May 1 – **Basing Street Studio session**: For Shame of Doing Wrong.
May 2 – **CBS Studios session**: All Our Days.
June 7 – **Basing Street Studio session**: By The Time It Gets Dark. Gold Dust.
June 9 – **Basing Street Studio session**: Take Me Away. Gold Dust. By The Time It Gets Dark.
June 10 – **Island Studios session**: For

Shame of Doing Wrong. Sad Refrains. Take Me Away.
June 14–15 – **Island Studios session**: Still Waters Run Deep. Silver Threads & Golden Needles.
June 16 – **Island Studios session**: All Our Days [choral version]. Full Moon.
June 17 – **Island Studios session**: Still Waters Run Deep. I'm A Dreamer. One Way Donkey Ride. Silver Threads & Golden Needles. Full Moon.
June 18 – **Island Studios session**: Silver Threads & Golden Needles. One Way Donkey Ride. I'm A Dreamer. For Shame of Doing Wrong. Easy To Slip. Losing Game.

1977

February 24 – **Basing Street session**: Candle In The Wind.
May 20 – **Basing Street session**: Moments.
November 6 – Sound Circus, London.
November 8 – Dome, Brighton.
November 11 – Fairfield Hall, Croydon: Solo. North Star Grassman & the Ravens. I'm A Dreamer. Gold Dust. Nothing More. John the Gun. The Sea. It'll Take A Long Time. Tomorrow Is A Long Time. The Lady. Wretched Wilbur. For Shame of Doing Wrong. Stranger To Himself. One More Chance. Take Me Away. Who Knows Where The Time Goes.
November 13 – Usher Hall, Edinburgh.
November 14 – City Hall, Glasgow.
November 15 – Palace Theatre, Manchester.
November 16 – Town Hall, Birmingham: Solo. North Star Grassman & the Ravens. Nothing More. Gold Dust. I'm A Dreamer. John the Gun. The Sea. It'll Take A Long Time. Tomorrow Is A Long Time. The Lady. Wretched Wilbur. For Shame of Doing Wrong. Stranger To Himself. Take Me Away. One More Chance.

November 17 – New Theatre, Oxford.
November 18 – Capitol Theatre, Cardiff.
November 20 – Colston Hall, Bristol.
November 27 – Sound Circus, London:
Solo. North Star Grassman & the Ravens.
I'm A Dreamer. Gold Dust. Nothing
More. John the Gun. The Sea. It'll Take A
Long Time. Tomorrow Is A Long Time.
The Lady. Wretched Wilbur. For Shame
of Doing Wrong. Stranger To Himself.
One More Chance. Take Me Away. Who
Knows Where The Time Goes. No More
Sad Refrains.

1978
April 1 – Village Hall, Banbury.

Index